IN THE SHADOW OF SATAN

IN THE
SHADOW OF SATAN

⚶

Janusz Subczynski

KELLER PUBLISHING
Marco Island, Florida

ISBN-13: 978-0-9674128-5-6
ISBN-10: 0-9674128-5-4
Library of Congress Control Number: 2005937112

Composed in Warnock Pro at
Hobblebush Books, Brookline, NH
Printed in the United States of America

Published by
KELLER PUBLISHING
590 Fieldstone Dr.
Marco Island, FL 34145

www.KellerPublishing.com
800-631-1952

Dedicated to the memory of my mother

Contents

Illustrations

Preface

WHEN I LIFT my head, I see through the tulle mist of curtains in the glaring midday sunlight a canal in which manatees swim. They create occasional ripples on the water's surface as they draw air into their lungs. I see palm trees, tropical flowers, and at last the azure blue of a distant bay. A warm breeze reaches me through the open patio doors; the songs of birds' spring mating calls complete the simple beauty of the scene.

According to calendars, I am already old. Yet, I don't feel that way. I think to myself, "Why do I write, what is my goal, what are my motives? Why was I, a retired neurosurgeon, inclined to write about this, what I went through?"

Many years ago, when I lived in Warsaw, I saw a play by Ionesco entitled *Chairs* in the Theater of Dramatic Arts. When the curtain rose, there was nothing on the stage except chairs, and only two actors—"old man" and "old woman." They started talking about the past, about people who had played some kind of role in their lives. Tension grew, as the people about whom they were speaking became more and more real, more and more alive—as though filling up the chairs standing on the stage. The main characters turned toward them and asked questions; experiences and memories replied. At a certain moment, it seemed that the empty chairs were actually taken by the people, that they came back to life; something was happening that could not be fully understood.

In the third act, "old man" and "old woman" came to the conclusion that, because they had gone through so much, that it had been so fascinating, they could not leave it to be forgotten, could not allow the wealth of feelings and experiences to perish.

Because they could not reveal everything on their own, they hired a speaker.

They disappeared. In the middle of the stage remained an empty pulpit, to which a black figure approached. The speaker. He turned toward the auditorium, but from his mouth came only incomprehensible, wretched mumbling.

Perhaps the underlying meaning of this play led me to write about my memories, an account of events seen through the eyes of a child, a growing boy, and a young man.

So many things have been written about that period of history. But so many "historians," especially here in the West, alter the way things were in those days.

No, I wasn't stuck in a prison. I didn't go through the martyrdom that is the lot of so many Polish people.

I led a "normal" life in those times, had dreams like everyone else, hopes and disappointments, and joys and sorrows. Like everyone else, I aspired to attain some purpose.

I differ from others, perhaps only in this: that I do what I set out to do.

As a young boy, I once read a story about a white seal. She put it upon herself to get past some skinners, who rounded up two-year-old seals and took them from the beach up past the hill and killed them. The white seal noticed what was going on there and was aware of the horrors. The rest of the seals never made the effort to look beyond the hill.

The case of the white seal is one of the motivating factors in my life. I grew up in a world dominated by the evils of mad ideology and Nazi crime; I was seen as an inferior person. I grew up under the red banners of the genocidal utopia that was Marxism-Leninism, which killed not only the body, but also the spirit. I grew up like all the rest of my generation in an atmosphere of deceit, hypocrisy, evil, and terror. No one had the courage to speak up; no one could, like that little boy in the Andersen fairytale, call out, "but the king is naked!"

I grew up, like thousands, millions, of others, in the shadow of

Satan. Not in his clutches, but in his dismal shadow that shrouded each and every day.

I was one of those who were able to see this Satan and decide that nothing was to be gained from living under his black wings, from being ground through the mills of the regime into shapeless matter that would only fertilize the soil of further mad ideology.

This is not a memoir, though I do write about myself in the first person. It is a report, a written account seen through the eyes of an authentic witness—not just a frightened observer. And finally, it is, in a way, a historical contribution.

The years go by, my generation dies off; history is quite a malleable science. It can be adapted to current needs and falsified, as has been done before.

I hope that these pages may find their way to the hands of young people, so that younger generations growing up in a completely different world might glimpse the past from the perspective of my generation and contemplate their own lives.

Once, I don't know now where, I read the following maxim: "To destroy a nation, you must destroy its past." This is what was done by both German and Russian occupiers. These pages are my attempt to fight Satan, the Satan of deceit, hypocrisy, and crime.

I do not agree with Ionesco, that you cannot share your life experiences with others. You can, but you must take it upon yourself to make it objective.

—*Janusz Subczynski*

IN THE SHADOW OF SATAN

1

Conscious Stirrings

I WAS FEELING GOOD, sleepy. The sun's trembling rays fell through the window curtains, casting the colors of the rainbow on the light blue carpet. The buzzing of a fly was at once bothersome and lulling, coming closer and then moving away. I was feeling sleepy; I was feeling good. I could still feel the warmth of my mother leaning over me, wrapping me in the comforter; I could feel her presence, even though she had already left the room.

Through sleepy eyes, I looked at the white ceiling, at the sunlit window, at the dressing table standing in the corner. I felt enveloped in the bliss that usually comes just before falling asleep. I was feeling good; I was feeling sleepy, safe.

I didn't realize that this first memory, exactly this moment, marked the beginning of my conscious life. I didn't see that a long and stormy future awaited me, that weighty and dramatic moments would come, and that my fate would be interwoven in a tragic knot with the fate of my nation and generation. I didn't know any of that, for I was only beginning my conscious life. I was feeling good, feeling sleepy. The buzzing of the fly became more and more indistinct, my eyes closed, and maybe, I fell asleep.

My mother confirmed to me later that I was two years old at that time.

I then clearly remember our life in Pulawy. I was four years old at the time. I do not remember what happened between my earliest memory and our move to Pulawy.

My world got significantly bigger there. Now, when in moments of silence and loneliness, I close my eyes my thoughts make the long journey to those past days and times. I begin to see a roomy house with a terrace leading out to the yard, a dining room, in which I spent a lot of time in my folding high chair, and finally the forbidden door, which I was not supposed to open, that led to my father's study.

My grandmother, who was usually warm and loving to me, ruled over the kitchen. I remember how my underwear would feel tight when she put me on her knees. The reason was rather uninteresting; my grandmother was very fat, and instead of sitting on her knees, I simply hung there, held in place with a strong hand under my arm.

I remember sitting in the high chair by the dining room table, where I would gulp down my favorite tomato soup with rice, or drink freshly squeezed grape juice from a wine glass. I remember cod liver oil, which I couldn't stand. I also remember my blocks, from which I built fantastic creations. They were colorful with a smooth, sleek surface; there were no inscriptions on them, no suggestions, rendering the possibilities of creation limitless. I also had other blocks, wooden ones with letters and numbers carved into them.

Apparently, at that age, I had already gathered that learning was not always the most pleasant experience, because I definitely preferred the colorful blocks to these, from which I was supposed to gain the foundations of knowledge. I also really liked when my mother's glance moved off of me long enough so I could sneak into my father's study.

It was a large, spacious room, brightly lit through several windows and by several lamps on drafting tables. A desk, piled high with papers, stood in the corner. What intrigued me the most was the large abacus; its characteristic bang still rings in my ears. My father calculated the data gathered from all his measurements on this very abacus, while young engineers, just out of school at Warsaw's Institute of Technology, drew up plans and made geodesy sketches on the tables. All these mysterious things fascinated me.

One of my greatest pleasures was drawing circles with a compass and lines with a drawing pen on their engineering paper. My attempts didn't turn out too well, and soon, my hands and smock were stained with red and black ink. The young engineers liked me and my surreptitious visits to the study, especially when my father wasn't there. I was a break for them from hard and tiring work, a moment to relax and feel carefree.

These excursions to the study usually ended with my mother's intervention, and I would go back to the blocks, to books that she would read to me, and to playing in the yard.

My mother's cousin, Renia, who was then a student at the University of Warsaw, came to visit us. She and my mother were both very young. Renia impressed me with her academic cap. She also liked to sing and was cheerful and lighthearted. We went for walks to the park with my mother. I remember that I felt afraid when we walked by Pulawy's shrine of Sybil. There were low windows in the foundation, and I imagined that, behind their blackness, something dangerous and threatening was lurking. It really bothered me, and I would shudder with terror.

Usually, I didn't have many fears—I just felt sort of unsure when I had to go into a dark room. I would run in quickly and run out even more quickly with an undoubted sense of relief.

Early on, I noticed a thin figure dressed in black with soot-blackened hands and face on the rooftops of homes. Naturally, this figure intrigued me, and I started asking who this person was who climbs up onto the tall chimneys and cleans them. I found out that it was someone who would come to take me away if I didn't behave as I should. From that moment on, I looked at this soot-blackened, often smiling, figure with great respect.

And then came the day. I remember it very well. I was sitting on the potty, with my underwear down, near the open door of the bathroom—so as to feel near to those around me, usually my grandmother. These times spent sitting on the potty were yet another means of adding variety to life. My grandmother went out somewhere, and then, to my horror, the chimney sweep came through the kitchen door. My heart froze. He walked around the kitchen, which I could see clearly from my position, and I saw mostly his black shoes and pants, as I didn't have the courage to lift up my head. But when I finally did look up, I glimpsed a round soot-blackened face and two laughing eyes. The chimney sweep saw my confusion and terror, and it greatly amused him. He said something to me, though what he said I don't remember, as I was terrified and unsure of what would come next. I also couldn't run away because of the compromising position I was in. Fortunately, my grandmother came home, and it turned out that this threatening black character had come for payment for cleaning the chimney. After collecting what he was owed, he left quietly.

I went through many difficult and dangerous times during my childhood, but that incident with the chimney sweep was one of the worst. It took a long time to calm me down and show me that he was just a person like anyone else—that there was nothing threatening me, that there was nothing of which to be afraid. Later whenever I sensed danger, I acted calmly, even sang something heroic under my breath, and then once the situation was resolved, I cried with relief, knowing that the danger had passed.

I didn't endure many sorrows during this period of my life, though I do remember another episode that was a great trial for me. It was a warm and sunny day. I was dressed in a shirt and short pants. The pants were buttoned to the shirt, creating one piece. I had white socks on my feet and white shoes that fastened with a strap. The day was strikingly bright, and I was unusually excited. I was heading out for a walk to the park with my grandmother. When we reached the main walkway, full of women and children, some in carriages and some older ones, running and playing hopscotch, my grandma sat down on one of the benches. I, not knowing anyone, was determined to find something to do. I started by running around the bench on which my grandmother was sitting. And this very first lap around the bench ended in tragedy. A big pile of human excrement was lying behind the bench, probably left there by some homeless person. I stepped into it in such an inopportune way that not only my shoe but also my sock were completely buried in it. I started crying from disgust and aversion. We walked back home, embarrassed and humiliated in the eyes of the other children. The episode ended with a thorough washing.

My father often went off for field work and sometimes didn't come back for a week or two. I was used to this, to being under the wings of my mother and grandmother, and often played in the study.

Once, in the middle of the night, the hum of voices, first in the foyer, then in the dining room, woke me up. I recognized my father's voice; he had just then come home. I jumped out of bed and ran out barefoot in my nightshirt. My father had on riding pants and tall boots; he looked good in this and had becoming legs. The boots reached almost up to my chin. He lifted me up in his arms and kissed me, and I could see the joy in his face. My father's kiss felt scratchy from a short, stubbly mustache; it was already nighttime, and he hadn't shaved. The black shadow of a thick beard fell on his face. I was still in his arms when I noticed that he was looking somewhere else, sort of down and to the right. And there I saw a three-wheeled bike! It had a comfortable leather seat and sharp-edged pedals. I got on it immediately and started riding around the table. The sharp edges of the pedals stung my bare feet, but I was so happy I didn't feel the pain.

I don't know in the end what happened to this bike, but I do remember that the very next day I was already showing it off on the main avenue in the park to the envy of all the other kids who didn't have bikes. Soon after that, my mother took me to a photographer where I was captured in film on my bike, an eternal souvenir. In this photo, which has since begun to brown, you can see a child looking at the camera through extremely naïve eyes. There is no fear in this glance, only something that could be called innocence.

⊪

When I was five years old, my mother brought me to the dentist, Dr. Davidson, to take care of my baby teeth. I never felt any pain or discomfort at her office. As it was a new feeling, a new experience, for me, I remember it very clearly. When we went from the waiting room into her examining room, I felt nervous and afraid as soon as I saw that white chair, the chrome of the drill, and the tools on the little table near the chair. But, Mrs. Davidson quickly quelled my fears.

She was a young woman with big black Semitic eyes in a laughing, pretty round face that was framed by thick, flowing shiny curls. She made a very nice impression dressed in a white coat that was smartly fitted around her waist. And the impression got even nicer when she started speaking—a kind, warm voice, full of understanding for my childish fears, almost maternal. Without hesitating, I sat down in the dentist chair, let the apron be put over me, and politely opened my mouth.

She would tell me what she was going to be doing the entire time—a tooth was sick and had to be taken care of. She nearly talked my head off so that I hardly noticed when she said, "You see, all done. Now, I have to take care of one of your mother's teeth. Maybe you can play with my daughter, Miriam."

I didn't see any particular reason why not, so we went with my mother to a private part of the house. There, we met a girl who was my age, with bouncing, shiny dark curls, tied in a big ribbon and with the same dark eyes as her mother.

I was formally introduced to this young person, and she curtsied politely. We were both quite shy. After a few minutes, Dr. Davidson and my mother went back to the office, leaving us alone.

My shyness didn't wane. Miriam made up her mind first. She went to get her toys and invited me to play with her. We were soon so busy that when my mom came back with Mrs. Davidson, we didn't want to stop playing. All our following visits happened in much the same way.

I didn't know at that time that my mother's and my fate would cross again with the Davidson family in a strange way.

One night, I heard a commotion, saw a light go on in my parents' bedroom, and heard worried voices. I went in there. The light blinded me, but after a moment, I could see my mother in bed, with dark circles under her eyes, trembling with chills. I understood that something very bad was happening. A plump man arrived shortly who I recognized on sight. He was Miriam's father, Dr. Davidson. I was asked to leave the room and stayed with Grandma. After a moment, my father came in. I saw worry, pain, and sorrow on his face; he was talking about something with my grandmother, but I didn't understand what was going on. Finally, my grandmother told me that my mother was sick and that she would go in an ambulance to Warsaw, that Dr. Davidson recommended it and that he would take her.

I don't know how much time went by; I only remember the banging on the doors and their quick opening. Two people with a stretcher walked into my mother's room. I also remember my mother on the stretcher, how she turned her head toward me and locked her eyes with mine until the last moment, and then the bang of the door closing and the hum of the running engine. My father went with my mother in the ambulance. I took the train with my grandmother the next day.

It was winter. Warsaw was buried in snow. On Marszalkowski Street, where my aunt Janka lived with her husband and three sons, piles of blackened snow were lying on the edges of the sidewalk. By the entrance to the gates of the apartment buildings were semicircular stone and cast-iron decorations with a ball at the top and a barrel-like shape beneath, which made me think of some kind of hunched creatures. There was a lot of traffic. I held my grandmother's hand fiercely as countless wet raincoats passed right in front of me.

My aunt's apartment was located high up on the third floor. She greeted me quite kindly, hugged me into her soft chest, and kissed me, asking if I was hungry. She told her boys, one of whom was nearly three years older than I and two younger, that they were to treat me properly. Despite all the genuine care that I sensed, I felt miserable and troubled. I missed my mother, missed her very much, and I understood that something bad was happening, that she was in unspeakable danger. Truthfully, I couldn't even formulate this thought, but rather instinctively felt some threat hanging over our lives like a black cloud.

My dad came by in the evening. He looked terrible, barely took notice of me, talked with my aunt and grandmother, and didn't touch any food.

The next day, he took me to Dr. Krynicki's clinic, to my mother. There was a long corridor that stunk of disinfecting solution, with linoleum on the floor and a few lamps on the ceiling. There were white doors on the right and, through them, a long room with a sink and table on the right side, a high curtained window at the end of the room, and to the right of it a metal bed, in which my mother lay. She recognized me and asked me to come closer. I was afraid to go closer. Looking at the dark circles under her eyes and drawn face, I saw the full threat of an unknown illness. Though I didn't know it then, I felt the presence of death, lurking in the corner of the dreary room.

Instinct kept me away from my mother; I longed to be next to her and at the same time couldn't go near her. It was a horrible feeling, neither able to come closer or distance myself, nor say goodbye.

After this visit, a few days went by, and my aunt was acting more and more loving. I knew that she went to the hospital with my grandmother, and after coming back, she looked at me and started crying, sobbing, "Poor, poor child!" And I understood that I might never see my mother again. I don't know how many days later, my grandmother came back from a trip to the hospital, wrapped her arms around me, and hugged me close. I saw tears of joy flowing from her eyes, "Listen, Grandson! It's a miracle! Ira is going to make it!"

The next day, she took me to the hospital. My mother still looked horrible, but the threat of death that had once lurked in the corner of the private hospital room had disappeared somewhere. This time I wasn't afraid to approach the bed. I felt the warmth of my mother's emaciated hand on my head, and tears flowed from my eyes.

Recovery took a long time. My mother had been in her sixth month of pregnancy when she developed pyelonephritis, complicated by a blockage of the left ureter and an abscess in her kidney.

In those times, not only did no one know of antibiotics, but even the first sulfa drug, prontonsil, was just appearing on the market. Urologist professor Szenkier said that in this situation, in a state of overall sepsis, operating amounted to a death sentence.

Literally, at the last moment, when everyone had already given up hope, my mother spontaneously delivered the dead fetus, allowing the kidney to drain of pus. Her fever subsided, and slowly, very slowly, my mother regained some strength. The next few months are a complete blur in my mind. I see her once again full of life, a little slenderer, only her eyes seemed to become even bigger, more telling, and deeper.

2

Innocent Youth

SOMETIME IN 1937, the government finally paid my father overdue money for the work he had done while he had his own business. My parent's dream was to have their own house. They bought a small lot in a new suburban area of Brzesc, near Niepodleglosci Avenue. Construction on the house began. What a mess it was—there were so many problems and unexpected expenses.

One important moment sticks out in my mind. When the carpenters finished their work, they placed a traditional wreath on the beams of the roof. I also remember Szulc, the painter, who worked with his son and endlessly approached my mother "for a zloty for varnish." Once he got the zloty, he would disappear for a few hours and return quite tipsy. The house was almost finished by then. My mother had picked out wallpaper for the living room and dining room. It was expensive wallpaper, dark sapphire with a silver pattern for the living room, where there were two huge windows and large glass doors leading to the terrace, and beige wallpaper with a gold pattern for the dining room. They bought light blue wallpaper with a very light pattern for my room. After several outings for "varnish," Mr. Szulc ended up completely ruining the wallpaper in the dining room.

It was awful, because the wallpaper was very expensive, and my parents couldn't afford to get more. After sobering up, the maestro saw what he had done and assured us that he would fix everything. And, indeed, he painted over the wallpaper for several days, using many different patterns and colors, and the overall result was quite pleasant and not that much worse than the original.

The house was spacious. The ground floor had a big kitchen with a small room for the maid, a vast dining room, and a living room. There was a large convertible bed covered with a Kosowski throw in the living room, and an identical Kosowski rug lay on the floor. There was also a standing mirror in the room as well as my mother's piano. A painting hung on the wall depicting Napoleon's retreat from Moscow, painted by Jerzy Kossak—supposedly painted for the son by his famous father—as well as a pastel of chrysanthemums in a crystal vase. My father's desk and chair, always covered with some kind of papers, were by the window. This room had double glass doors that connected it with the dining room. There was a dark brown table with tall chairs in the center of the dining room, and a china cabinet that was glass in the middle with high cabinets on either side. A plush couch from my grandmother's estate completed the picture. From the living room, you could go into the room on the left, the light blue one with white tulle curtains, where my bed was; I was still in the phase of sleeping with a side rail. My parents slept in the living room, so in the evening, it transformed into a bedroom. When guests came over, we would open the doors wide between the living room and the dining room, and a great space appeared in which everyone felt comfortable.

Upstairs, there were two smaller rooms that were very cheerful, wallpapered in yellow, and that's where the main bathroom was, too. The property around the house wasn't that big, but it was planted with roses, and there were even a few fruit trees. The property was fenced in, a bit more elegantly in front with stone poles and a decorated gate, and more modestly in the back with a wire fence.

There was a little bit more space by the kitchen entrance to the house—a small yard—at the edge of which stood a garbage can concealed in some bushes. A winding path led from there to the back of the house, where the flowers were like a rainbow and the bushes got even greener.

The house was built from massive logs, and then plastered. It became the source of my father's pride and his greatest accomplishment.

Now, years later, I look at a very faded picture of the house. Moments spent there come back to me, and I see people who made their way through the house. I see my mother clearly, still young, and my father full of energy and strength; I even see myself, a youngster in shorts and stretchy stockings; I see my grandmother with slightly crooked glasses reading yet another novel. I see all this, and I can't believe it has all been gone, covered by the ashes of the passing years. The grief and pain of the storm of war and the atrocities of post-war Soviet occupation increasingly obscured the real picture of those days and life for me, and it becomes more and more foggy, drowning in oblivion.

Our house wasn't built on an abandoned island; we had neighbors on every side. On the yard side, we bordered a villa, whose owner was a thin older lady. She didn't speak any Polish—only Russian. She was a Russian refugee who came after the outbreak of the Bolshevik Revolution. I can't remember if anyone else lived in that house, but I remember her well—shriveled, tall, with nondescript hair, wearing glasses—and a shawl that was almost always wrapped around her shoulders. She didn't have conversations with anyone except my grandmother, who as a woman of Vilno, educated in a Russian high school spoke Russian as well as she spoke Polish. I see them standing by the wire fence, the plump figure of my grandmother and the tall Russian. I never felt like listening to what they were saying, because I didn't really like this lady who never smiled when she was walking in her yard. She made me feel confused and afraid, and I never had the slightest inclination to confront her one on one.

On the garden side, our property touched the larger property of a suburban house that was divided into several apartments. One of my friends, Adam, lived there. He was quite fat, very calm, and well behaved—overall, a well-grounded child. One problem was that his thighs would run into each other and snag his underwear mid-step; he also had quite a prominent belly. His parents worried greatly about his early obesity, so after a pediatric consultation, he was put on a special dietary regimen. Despite this diet, strangely enough, he didn't lose weight, but rather the opposite happened; his face got more and more similar to a full moon that had been lightly greased with shiny oil. More than once, his mother complained in conversations with my mother, "I just don't understand it. Adam eats practically nothing at home. We keep him on a strict diet. I can't look at my poor child anymore; it must be some problem with his digesting tract."

Diplomatically, my mother didn't give an opinion about Adam's strange problem, for she knew the truth. And it looked something like this: in the afternoon, there was a quiet, discrete knocking on the kitchen door. My grandmother opened the door and saw Adam, neatly dressed, carefully combed, full of smiles.

"Hello, ma'am. Excuse me, but I just got so hungry. Would you be so kind as to make me a sandwich? Some kind of roll, or even two, maybe with ham?"

My grandmother, who was herself inclined to obesity and full of understanding for such cravings, immediately did what she could to help the poor child.

"Come here, come here. I'll make you something in a second, and you can't just eat such dry things. Maybe I should make some cocoa?"

To this, Adam replied, "If you would be so kind, but I really don't want to put you to any trouble."

After being fed by my grandmother, Adam walked around to all the neighbors' houses, where he got all the nourishment he needed.

It was Easter, so we had prepared hams, sausages, colorfully decorated eggs, mazurek (Easter cake), and babkas. My mother and grandmother made me a special table for Easter, on which was a small ham, cold cuts, a small babka, and even a specially baked small mazurek. And there were, of course, eggs and a lamb on a bed of green grass.

It all looked so nice, and it was also great, because then the main table wasn't overloaded with food, so you could actually sit comfortably. And then disaster struck!

Adam came over. He took in the situation in one glance, and his almost cannibalistic stare was fixed on my Easter table. He told my mother that he would just like to taste these treats, just a tiny bit, so as to compare them to the ones his mother made. There was no denying such a request. Adam calmly pulled up a chair and got to work. I looked with dismay as my ham, then babka, then kingly mazurek disappeared through his lips—only a few crumbs and pieces of unfinished bread remained. When he finally left, thanks to my mother's charm, I almost broke down. The only thing left to do was clean up and get rid of my Easter table!

From that moment, my relationship with Adam cooled off quite a bit, despite all his good intentions.

On the other side of the house, the southern side, we bordered Mr. Vorbichler's property. He had a large yard, actually an orchard, in which his house was deeply hidden. There was a birdhouse on the left side of the roof. Mr. Vorbichler, a banker, bred special types of pigeons; he was always taking care of them, whistling at them, feeding them—it was his favorite hobby.

I don't remember his wife very well, but I remember she was Russian, who like our other neighbor escaped before the revolution. They had two children, the older one a boy who was already grown up, and a girl who was about fifteen or sixteen years old. They both went to high school in navy-colored uniforms that I envied.

I don't remember how it happened, but a cat appeared at our house, a male—big, white, with a big masculine breast. He followed his own rules. I think that he came to my grandmother, hungry and worn out. Of course she immediately took care of him providing food and milk. He soon became a sort of house-mate, yet not sleeping in the house, but having his own business to tend to in the mids of the night. I see him now in the kitchen, for milk, lapping it up, and then lying down in the corner, purring with happiness. He was a true cat, quite contemplative and a good hunter. The nearest and most amiable prey unfortunately turned out to be Mr. Vorbichler's pigeons. Every few days, a clump of white, bloody feathers were the evidence of our cat's latest crime. Nearly frothing at the mouth, Mr. Vorbichler would appear at our house demanding to speak with my father about immediately killing the cat. My father, who wouldn't hurt a fly, responded evasively, even when threatened with a lawsuit.

But things turned out a bit differently. Mr. Vorbichler preyed upon our cat, setting up a special bait and trap, and he finally caught and killed him. I remember the sad remnants of white fur, dirtied with blood, in the majestic stillness of death. Unfortunately, his body was massacred beyond recognition, with deep gashes everywhere. Rage and hatred found expression in this sadism.

I didn't realize then who Mr. Vorbichler really was. We all knew that he was German, though his Polish was flawless. He was a prominent official at the local bank. In the first few months of the war, when we were in Lublin, already surrounded by the German army, I ran into Mr. Vorbichler again. He had a swastika on his lapel and was full of contempt for my father and me. When he was in the Polish army, he robbed the army treasury; of course, he was a member of the Fifth Column. Then, he became the head of the district in Generalna Gubernia, distinguishing himself with cruelty and baseness. Later he was executed by the Polish Underground Army. His son was part of the Polish Underground and cut off contact from his father completely. His daughter ended up in the Bund Deutsches Madeln, and rumors circulated that she kept herself busy torturing people as a member of the Gestapo. Overwhelmed with grief and a troubled conscience, their mother died in the early years of the occupation. Thus he reaped what he sowed, being destroyed along with the hated Third Reich.

Now, when I look back, after all these years, I understand why Mr. Vorbichler so eagerly bred pigeons and why our cat brought him to such rage. As a German agent, he undoubtedly used those pigeons to send reports, though no one thought of this possibility at the time.

⁂

I became seven years old on the fifth of September and learned that I was going to begin my education at Mrs. Gorska's school. I was very nervous, knowing that I would meet a whole bunch of kids there. I was afraid of meeting strangers and wondered what the teacher would be like. Truthfully, I already knew how to read and write pretty well; the only thing I wasn't sure of was whether my level of knowledge was sufficient. All these fears came together in a pleasant chill, along with the feeling that I was stepping onto an unknown path—something new and fantastic was opening up in my life.

We wandered on foot down a path planted with old trees. It was a typical fall day, filled with faint sunlight. The leaves on the trees were still green, but you could already sense the sadness of fall in the air. I picked up chestnuts on the way, but I ended up having to get rid of them when we got closer to the vast school building with a big fenced-in yard behind it. We went inside. I squeezed my mother's hand, feeling more and more insecure and losing my nerve. We ended up in a room with a hardwood floor and light walls that smelled of disinfecting solution. Several doorways led out of this room. And then I heard a bell and the sound of young voices. One of the doors opened wide and a group of children spilled into the room. I looked in awe, agitated and intimidated. The children got in a circle and began playing under the teacher's watchful eye. I was introduced to her, and to the circle, slightly stunned.

I don't remember well what happened after that. I only know that I was assigned a place at a school desk, and the first lesson of my life began. I remember the first elementary textbook from which we had to read, something about a goose egg that was rolling, a dog named Kruczek, and a cat named Mruczek. The tale was rather involved, and it took a lot out of me. After a while, I got up the nerve and lifted my head. A little girl was sitting at the school desk with me, her sun-tanned face framed by dark curls of hair, with a big ribbon on top of her head, dimpled cheeks, and dark, smiling eyes. I didn't really know how to act. She looked at me from time to time, twisted and turned, doing everything so as to draw attention to herself. Later, when we got to know each other better, I found out that she was Tala Nizienko, a Ukrainian. Her parents lived near us. Her father was an engineer like mine. They had one other daughter besides Tala who was considerably older, about sixteen years old. On the first day of school, I was a bit too busy with my own problems and fears to pay much attention to her.

All of a sudden, I felt a painful jab in my back and turned around. It was a boy with dark hair who was jittery, very restless, and who later became one of my closer friends, Danek Wolczacki. Sitting with him was a boy with short, light red hair, greenish eyes, and a face so freckled it reminded me of a turkey egg. He was Zbyszek Szmurlo, who eventually came over to my house with Danek quite often. They were very rambunctious. My mother didn't care for these visits too much, more than once running out of the house at the sight of those two, saying, "I don't want to see any blood spilt!" My grandmother remained in the battleground to intervene constantly and to make peace between those two restless souls. They were quite different from me. It's not that I was really lacking anything, but my nature was more contemplative than destructive.

I looked around the classroom and counted more than twenty heads. I remember Ksenia with light flaxen hair and porcelain-blue eyes, and I remember the only Jew in the class, a boy with dark hair and a characteristic nose. He wasn't treated well on account of his guttural accent—he spoke "Jewish" at home. He was very different from the other children and for this reason was turned away from our group.

After a few weeks, I felt completely fine in the first grade, even started to get into trouble for talking and squirming during class.

Everyone was dressed in gray smocks that buttoned in the front; the smocks had one bar sewn on the sleeve that signified first grade. When we walked out onto the street in pairs, we wore red berets on our heads with a white triangle on them that represented Mrs. Gorska's school. Mrs. Gorska herself, who was already old and hefty and who was the wife of the czar's colonel, came across as admirable, with a somewhat black and usually slightly crooked wig on her head.

Overall, she was a good person; she didn't teach any subjects, but she tried to gather all the children to her with motherly care. The old czar's colonel could have been Santa Claus, with a bushy gray mustache, a gray lion's mane on his head, and friendly blue eyes.

From the first day, our teacher didn't treat me with much kindness, and I reciprocated the feeling of ill will. She didn't know how to establish a real connection with children, and besides that, she often fell into fits of rage that were not always justified. I ended up in one of those situations with her. I don't remember what I did wrong, but I think I had turned my side to the blackboard, not paying attention to what she was saying. Suddenly I felt a sharp pain in my right ear; I was pulled up out of the school desk by my ear and made to stand in the corner. I always felt that I was justified in my actions, and this time, I really felt innocent and thought I had been treated unfairly. I told my mother what happened, and she went to the school to talk it out with my teacher. I don't know what happened during the course of their conversation, but I do know that from that time on, the teacher left me alone.

Our lessons lasted about half the day, and then we had to do our homework, but it still left a lot of time to play. My most frequent playmate turned out to be Tala. As she was rather lonely at home, because her sister was quite a bit older than she was, she looked for someone to play with her. I could see her, walking down the street; I was hanging on the gate and pushing off with my leg, swinging back and forth. Tala had a confident stride, as though she didn't notice me. But after a moment, she was by the gate.

"Let me try."

"Oh, you can't do it."

"But I'll try."

After a moment, she was already hanging on the gate and swinging. "See, I can do it."

The problem with Tala was that she was a girl, so her interests and understanding of playtime differed from mine. I remember once we found a huge cardboard box. We cut out a window and a makeshift door, and we sat inside it, pretending we were married and this was our house. Tala loved this game, but I quickly got bored with it. I would have rather played ball or even jump rope. Tala was a bilingual child, though I didn't know it. Her Polish was flawless as far as I could tell, but at home she spoke Ukrainian. The first time I found myself there, I felt intimidated, in spite of the fact that I was very warmly welcomed by her mother and father. They offered me some cookies, said something to me that I don't remember. My responses weren't particularly intelligent. I wanted to get out of there as quickly as possible. Tala took me to her room, where she had a ton of dolls, herself resembling one of them, with the only difference being that her eyes were full of life and energy.

Despite her seven years, Tala was undoubtedly a woman; she could be coquettish, her movements were full of charm and already full of intrigue. One time, we spied on her sister kissing a boy.

"See, you should be doing the same thing," she said to me.

"What are you, stupid? What are you thinking?" I replied, and it ended at that.

For many years, I had a photograph of Tala, just as if one of a living doll. Later, it disappeared somewhere. Our fates took different turns, though some distant and unconfirmed information reached me after the war. I don't know what she's doing, or if she's still alive. She was my partner when we danced in school, she was my playmate, and she was also, in the most innocent definition of the word, the first woman in my life.

⫶

I couldn't stand cod liver oil. Everyday, by the pediatrician's recommendation, I had to swallow a full tablespoon of the thick oily liquid that stuck to the lips and throat; it was even difficult to wash it off. I resisted stubbornly when I could, but my mother, believing faithfully in the doctor's orders, was unyielding.

One day, Richard Wiszowaty came to our house; he was the husband of my grandmother's youngest sister. He was then an Uhlan (cavalry) lieutenant of the tenth regiment. In the war with the Bolsheviks of 1920 he was courageous and daring.

With a ring of red hair on a balding head and spectacles sitting on his meaty, bulbous nose, he looked strangely impressive in his officer's uniform, especially when he put on his cap and cape. He didn't have any children, so he immediately took an interest in me. I really liked his company. I too had a sword—though truthfully it was made of sheet metal—and an Uhlan shako helmet. That's how we played together on the floor, much to my mother's pleasure and my grandmother's displeasure.

But there came a moment when I had to take the cursed spoonful of cod liver oil. Sensing an ally in Richard, I resisted it fiercely. Suddenly he smacked his forehead and yelled out, "Listen, I'll make a deal with you. If you drink a spoonful of cod liver oil, I promise to drink an entire small carafe of cherry liqueur."

I didn't have a response to such a decree and swallowed the disgusting stuff, trying to kill the taste with a piece of bread. Shortly after that we had dinner. Richard, an honorable officer, asked for a small carafe of cherry liqueur and, much to my mother and grandmother's disapproval—my father wasn't home then—drank it all. We didn't have to wait long for the effects; his face turned purple, he got even more animated, and became incredibly talkative.

Unfortunately, my mother had said earlier that she would have to go to her seamstress, Sarka, who sewed all her dresses, in the afternoon. Sarka was a thin Jewish woman with a characteristic accent. I think she had four young children. She lived with her husband somewhere just off Trzeciego Maja Street.

The lieutenant, despite having drunk a small carafe of cherry liqueur, hadn't forgotten about my mother's trip to see Sarka and, complaining of the heat, decided it would do him good to go for a walk, keeping my mother and me company. My mother's pleas for him to stay home didn't do any good. He put on his cape and cap, and we went on our way.

Sarka opened the door; the fittings were done in the dining room, and you could see the bedroom with a large bed and fluffy comforter through the doors. Richard, for whom the fresh air was not so much refreshing as it was lulling, spotted Sarka's marriage bed. He got up from his chair and went into the bedroom, and then fell down on the bed—only his officer's boots hung off the side. Soon, you could hear the sound of his snoring. It was hard to imagine the confusion and concern my mother felt, or even mine, but the strangest reaction was actually from Sarka, the woman of the house.

"My God, what an honor for me! An officer in my bed, I will never forget this!"

The fitting was pleasant for both sides, and the question then arose as to how to tear this lieutenant away from the comfortable bed. My mother didn't think twice—grabbing him and pinching until he woke up. We came home, and when Richard sobered up, my grandmother scolded him thoroughly.

He was a strange person—a carouser, a gambler, he could drink a lot—and during the September military campaign, he fought against the Germans as well as the Bolsheviks. He moved his squadron to Romania, fought a battle in France, and then through Dunkirk, reached England. There, a cavalry man, he was trained to be a pilot or a flight technician. I know that he flew in the Spitfire division.

He never came back to Poland; actually, he couldn't, because his past was well known to the NKWD (*Narodnyj Komitet Wnutriennych Diel*, the National Committee of Internal Affairs or the Soviet Security Ministry, which later became the KGB). He died of cancer alone in London. After many years, when I was already in the United States, I came upon the journals of a Polish officer from the time of that famous battle of England. The officer remembered a bet that was made in the officers' club in which one of the officers would shoot a pack of Lucky Strikes off another one's head from a distance of thirty feet using a German Mauzer (a pistol). I knew immediately whose bald head had supported the pack, and I was not mistaken. It had been placed on the head of Richard Wiszowaty!

Besides the time we went for the fittings, I also remember Sarka at Easter time and Passover. She brought my mother some matzo. She knew I liked to munch on it, and for all the time we lived in Brzesc, she never once forgot.

⫷⫸

I was five or six years old—in any case I wasn't yet going to school—when my mother and I went to Mejszagola, the small mainly Jewish town in the province of Vilno. My mother was from Vilno, and the pastor of the parish in Mejszagola was Father Stanislaw Klimm, my grandmother's brother and my mother's uncle. My great-grandmother lived with him. She was over eighty years old.

This visit made a great impression on me. The church was in a cemetery; it was huge, with Baroque altars and statues of saints serenely watching with still pupils. It was surrounded by massive old trees whose shadows fell on moss-covered tombs. A brick wall separated the cemetery and church from the yard by the rectory. In the wall, there was a gate through which the priest and parishioners could go from the rectory to the church.

The rectory was vast, almost drowning in flowers. I remember the mallows outside the front windows and two flower beds surrounded by bricks that had been bleached white. In the back, behind the rectory, there was an orchard, and just off to the side there was a barn.

You walked into the rectory from the front, between the flower beds, though the entrance was actually not used that often. Most people went through the side entrance coming from the church. In the rather dark hallway, you could see doors on both sides and one straight ahead. The first on the right led to a large room with a window opposite the door. Under the window was a high table, covered with a white tablecloth, and on it a large black crucifix, a container of holy water, and a stole. That's the room where baptisms took place. The next room served as an office. Two small rooms one right after the other, flooded with smoke from good tobacco, served as the private sanctuary of Father Klimm. He hid there when he could no longer take the bustle that was so often found in the rectory. Guests would indeed arrive from all over. On Sunday, after attending the long eleven a.m. mass, nearby land-owners would drop by for small talk. There was never a lack of interested folks looking for advice or help from Father Klimm.

MY MOTHER, IRENA SUBCZYNSKI, OF THE
SKORWID-MIKULSKA FAMILY

At the end of the hallway was a large dining room. A little corridor led away from it to the side and toward my great-grandmother's room, which had a window overlooking the orchard.

At first, I was very intimidated; the black Cossack that Father Klimm wore, the bustle of people, strangers—everything contributed to my anxiety. I did know that we were greeted very warmly, and that my mother felt good here, so I got up my courage and started looking around.

My great-grandmother, Ewa, was a thin older woman, with a bun of gray hair tightly fastened at the back of her head. Her eyes were pretty and lively, and despite the huge age difference, you could see a resemblance between her and my mother. She seemed tall to me, even though she was of average height. This impression was created by a long, black dress that almost touched the floor and that had a white ruffle by the neck, as well as puffed sleeves. After dinner, she and my mother went to her room, but I was allowed to play in the orchard. I think it was late spring, because the trees were already covered with light, young leaves. The whitened tree trunks stood out sharply from the deep, full green of the grass. The air was filled with the scents of herbs. The buzzing of bees from a nearby hive completed the serene atmosphere with a sense of calm that can only be found on a warm, still day.

There was a small ladder in the orchard that was used to gather fruit. With quite a bit of difficulty, I dragged the ladder underneath the wide, open window of my great-grandmother's room, and from this position, feeling safe because I could always climb down, I peeked into the room. My mother was sitting on the edge of the bed, and my great-grandmother was in an armchair. The room was very bare. Besides the bed, there was an old-fashioned trunk filled with all her treasures, a crucifix on the wall, and a few toiletries and a rosary lay on a dresser that had a mirror attached. On the wall, there were dried herbs tied in bunches, giving the space a nice, unique fragrance.

When I close my eyes, I see my great-grandmother exactly as she was then, against the background of that old-fashioned room.

Not much is said about love these days, though a lot is said

MY FATHER, MASTER ENGINEER
STANISLAW SUBCZYNSKI
(A PORTRAIT BY THE AUTHOR)

about sex. My great-grandmother's story, told by my grandmother, was very strange and romantic. As a young girl, she began losing her vision quite rapidly so that eventually she only saw shadows. In despair, she went to the statue of Jesus Antokolski in Vilno, where she lived then with her parents. She prayed and prayed there, cried, and then prayed some more. The next day, she noticed that she could see a little bit better. After a month, her vision returned to normal. When I met her as an old lady, she was reading, a lot I might add, without glasses! She was very religious and deeply believed that Christ had heard her prayers.

Because she regained her vision so remarkably, she decided to help others. She went through special training and soon became the right hand and first assistant of the most well-known oculist in Vilno as well as the head nurse of a small eye-care hospital.

A young man from Kurland, von Klimm, found his way to the hospital as a patient; he was descended from one of those German Catholics who, after the Arabs took Jerusalem, had to escape to Malta. When even that was taken, they traveled around Europe until they reached a pleasant northern place on the Baltic where they founded Kurland. They couldn't return to Germany, as the Reformation was in full swing there. They preserved their language, in its medieval form, as they didn't have the means to develop it. They established a unique enclave among the Lithuanian and Polish people that was tightly closed off from others and governed by its own laws.

Then, this von Klimm fell in love with the young head of the hospital—my great grandmother. They got married quickly, unfortunately to the deep resentment of both families. My great-grandfather died at the age of forty from colitis, which was actually just acute appendicitis but not recognized as such then. My great-grandmother put on a black dress and didn't take it off until she died. She raised four children and waited for the moment when she would once again join her husband. She died three years after our visit.

⫶

My great-grandmother was about thirteen or fourteen years old at the outbreak of the January uprising of 1863, so she must have remembered that Polish tragedy well. She was a descendant of the Miakiszewski petty gentry; her family had owned a small piece of property in the province of Vilno. Her uncle, who took part in the uprising found his way to the citadel in Warsaw at the same time as Traugutt and other leaders of the uprising. The Russian henchmen tortured him terribly. He lost his mind, and as a madman and thus no longer a threat, he was released after a while. He walked through fields and forests, talking to himself and shaking his hands. He didn't harm anyone; the local villagers knew him and treated him well.

⫞

As terrible as the uprising was it also had some lighter moments. This anecdote—it came, of course, from my grandmother who was an endless source of information. The Russians caught a peasant who was helping the revolutionaries. Without any due process, they put a rope around his neck and hung him on a tree by the road. And they left him like that. At dawn, some men saw someone hanging and came closer. To their astonishment, they noted that he was still alive. His hands had been tied behind his back, so he couldn't do anything. The noose had been put on carelessly, so thankfully, it stopped at a point on his neck where he could breathe. They cut him down immediately and cut off the ties around his hands.

"How do you feel?" asked the rescuers.

"Well then," responded the almost-hanged man in the most beautiful Vilno accent, "my neck hurts, I'm hungry, and obviously, I didn't get used to being hanged!"

It seems to me that this event gives a certain impression of the nature of Eastern Poles in that time.

⫞

One day I returned a bit early from school. I already heard that there was a riot against the Jews, because they had supposedly killed a Christian child for matzo, and that a crowd was looting stores. That day, there was also a local peasant fair in the town, and a lot of goods were brought in wagons from neighboring villages. Someone started a rumor that a Christian child had been found killed in a ritual sacrifice. After hearing this news, a crowd gathered, grew, and spilled out onto the main commercial street, named Trzeciego Maja. With poles and crowbars, they broke the windows of Jewish stores—and there were a lot of them—beat up some of the owners, and took what they could. By the afternoon, the situation was already under control by the police. My mother, undoubtedly motivated by curiosity, went into the city with me. Trzeciego Maja Street was covered in broken glass and tattered fabrics. Strongly fragrant, little puddles of broken colognes and perfumes appeared by the Taksin perfume shop. I remember devastated Mrs. Taksin, wringing her hands at the scene of destruction.

"What will we do, what will we do? My God, what will we do?" she repeated over and over again.

Other Jewish stores were similarly ruined. The next day, the shops' display windows were boarded up, and the street was dead and dismal.

I was horrified by what I saw, as I couldn't understand hatred that could lead to such violent acts. I couldn't fathom why people I knew and felt sympathy toward, and who had never hurt me,

WITH MY PARENTS IN BRZESC
ON THE BUG RIVER, 1937

suffered. I just couldn't get my mind around it. In the demolished stores and in the thoughtless, brutal destruction, I could see evil, the same evil that I saw when I picked up the tortured remains of our white cat.

A lot was said about the "Riot of Brzesc." And it was usually said by those who didn't know anything about it, who claimed that the pogrom was proof of Polish anti-Semitism, proof of a deep-rooted, "weaned" hatred of Jews. The truth was actually very different. In that eastern city, that was Lithuanian Brzesc, the Jewish population was very large. It had in its hands not only most of the commerce and industry (sawmills, factories), but the population was also very well represented in the rather large group of well-educated intelligentsia (doctors, lawyers, engineers).

No one disrupted their peaceful lives of working and making more for themselves. There was also no discrimination. In those days, the vice mayor of Brzesc was Jewish; I know this first-hand, because he lived close to us, and his son, my peer, often came over to play in our yard.

I also clearly remember the Jews in Brzesc (I'm not talking about the intelligentsia or wealthier buyers), who isolated themselves from the rest of society, and who communicated in Yiddish and preserved traditional dress, wearing yarmulkes and long black cloaks.

This isolation from the rest of society must have caused negative reactions, especially among the primitive and usually illiterate peasants.

What's more, the rumor about the ritual sacrifice of the child, at least in those days, wasn't completely groundless. No one likes to talk about the fact that there existed a Jewish sect that practiced ritual sacrifice. This tradition is very old, and it could be reflected in the planned sacrifice of Isaac to be carried out by Abraham. My grandmother told me that at least one such instance was documented and proven. It took place before the First World War in Vilno. In the late 1930s, the affair of Zdunska Wola was quite well known; it was a matter in which it had been determined that this type of killing had occurred.

In every society, and so also in the Jewish society, there are deviant and mentally ill people. The riot was indeed a thoughtless, brutal blow against those who hadn't caused anyone harm. In those days, I saw for the first time how an agitated and ignorant mob can be led to immeasurable aggression, forgetting about justice and acting out against humanity. Now, having gained the perspective of many years, I see the Riot of Brzesc as a tragedy, not only for Jews, who experienced such destruction and disturbance, but also for Christians whose honor was smeared by the ignorant mob

⫶

The events of Brzesc were not an expression of Polish anti-Semitism, as many Jewish radicals claim today. No, they were the result of a sad tradition based only partly on the reality of racial and cultural isolation, and based mainly on the ignorance of the mob. And that's the truth.

⫶

One day, I came home from school, just as my father came home from work. The pleasant aroma of a soon-to-be-enjoyed dinner drifted from the kitchen. Immediately, I sensed that my father was quite agitated, that he was not thinking about dinner and had gotten some very important information. It turned out that he had received an official letter from the Ministry of Agriculture offering him a position as director of agricultural surveys in Poznan. It was a considerable promotion from the position of a senior inspector, not to mention that a move to such a big and beautiful academic city like Poznan from the eastern hole that was Brzesc in those days was in itself a big advancement. And finally, the salary of a director was considerably higher than the salary of an inspector, and that meant that the standard of living of the household would be much better. The question of my future and still far-off studies was raised during the long discussion my parents had. The main argument against leaving Brzesc was the house—it was our own, and it was comfortable, a place to which we were all accustomed.

The seemingly inextricable knot was unraveled by my grandmother, who after listening to all the arguments concluded, "There is nothing to discuss; you absolutely have to take this position. The house can be rented, and you might even make some money from it."

Some quiet rumors were already circulating then about the strengthening of the German military, but Poland, who had not long ago defeated the Bolsheviks, was strangely confident in her own strength. At least that's how it was where I grew up. News of the macabre Bolshevik terror never reached us, and if anything was said about the German military, the Nazi movement, and Hitler, it was only in joking. And that's why the possibility of a German threat in Poznan was never taken seriously into consideration in making the decision to move. My father and mother agreed with my grandmother's opinion and decided to move to Poznan.

Today, after many years, when I remember that heated debate that took place in the light of the shaded lamp that hung above the dining room table, when I think about what would have happened if that decision had been different, my hair stands on end.

My father handled mainly the consolidation of farmlands, thus from the Bolshevik point of view, he was only good enough for being shot. My mother, grandmother, and I would have ended up in a Soviet concentration camp—that is, if we would have even made it there alive—and we would have died in anguish a long time ago. During these discussions among the adults at the dining room table, there was someone beside me, another who was invisible and who directed our fates. I don't know what to call him—fate, destiny, a guardian angel—or maybe, simply, God.

3

Quiet Before the Storm

OW DIFFERENT LIFE was in the years of my childhood in Brzesc when I compare it to life today! That's not to say it was easier or without its share of problems and tragedies, but it seemed to be truly serene and carefree.

It's strange how an entire society wasn't able to perceive the danger that threatened from the West and from the East. Josef Pilsudski, the leader of the country, did foresee this danger in 1933 and proposed a united attack on Germany to both France and England. The threat was particularly obvious to him just before his death, when he foresaw a Second World War and a fourth partition of Poland. Just before the actual war, Polish intelligence had been informed about military buildup in Germany, yet the nation believed in its own strength, in the strength of Polish weapons, and in the army and its skillful defenses. This belief rested on the not-long-ago experience of war with the Bolsheviks, a war that had been won on the battlefield by a Polish army that had been thrown together quickly in the field, lacking even shoes and weapons. People believed that we now had a well trained army and a naval fleet, ready for combat. The best bomber at the time in Europe was of Polish production called "Moose," not to mention

WITH MY PARENTS' FRIENDS' DAUGHTER
BY CHRISTMAS TREE IN 1937

that our pilots (Bajan, Zwirko, and Wigura) were winning all the international competitions. Why then should we fear a Soviet invasion or the insolent German Nazis?

I remember carefree and pleasant evenings in our house, when my mother was playing duets of the Moonlight Sonata by Beethoven with Doctor Kalwaryjski, she on the piano and he on the violin. He was a neurologist and the stepfather of my buddy, Danek Wolczacki. The captivating sounds of that music remained in my memory always. A lot of people would come over, the Syrewicz's, my father's boss with his wife, the engineers Jermolajew and Jaworski, two radical Ukrainian nationalists who had no trouble then getting educated in Poland and who worked in their field like everyone else. They were quite open with their political views. They liked me a lot; I remember how they would lift me up high, almost to the ceiling, and how they laughed and joked around. I was still small then, so they seemed like giants to me.

I remember yet another of my father's friends, an engineer named Zelenay. He was of Hungarian descent, olive-skinned with dark hair and eyes. He had two sons. The younger one was a few years older than I, and the other was five or six years older. I played with them often, though I was a terrible playmate for them, because I was just too young.

Many years later, during the Occupation, my father found out that Germans had arrested Zelenay and his two sons. Awaiting torture, he supposedly tore a board from the plank-bed, and when the guards walked into the cell, he attacked them furiously. He got his revenge, but then he and his two sons were immediately killed in a round of gunfire.

My parents bought a radio—a Telefunken with a round dial. The reception was good, and you could listen to international stations. This was my first contact with the outside world. Up until then, I couldn't imagine that anything existed outside my country. Fascinated, I would often turn the dial, catching Italian, French, or German stations. These foreign and completely incomprehensible languages fascinated me. I felt instinctively that I needed to know more, that I had to get to the point where I could understand what these distant foreigners were saying.

In first grade, we already had the beginnings of French language study, but for unknown reasons, my teacher left, and my education ended after a year. I remember how we used to sing French children's songs with her and how she would greet us and rebuke us in that language.

Going to the movies was a great entertainment then. I loved films with Shirley Temple. I don't think I missed a single one— my parents made sure of it. My earliest favorite book was *The Adventures of Koziolka Matolka* (literally, "Adventures of Goofy Kid"), and I kept the series of "volumes" in order as they came out, whether I got them as a gift for a holiday or a name day. My name day is on eleventh of November, exactly on Poland's Independence

Day which coincides with America's Veteran's Day, for the same reason. It was on the eleventh hour of the eleventh day of the eleventh month in 1918 that the guns finally fell silent. As a result of the peace treaty wrought by U.S. President Woodrow Wilson, Poland regained its independence.

An old Polish tradition is to have a "name day" separate from one's birthday. It is given when one is Christened. My day was for the Roman god Janus because of my name Janusz. I remember how I would freeze that day, dressed in white stockings and a winter coat with a wool hat on my head, standing in the crowd on Niepodleglosci Avenue awaiting the military parade. I held my father's hand, the crowd was pushing us back and forth. It was very difficult to maintain the position in the front, though my father usually managed it so that I could clearly see the entire celebration. He also told me that the parade was happening especially for me, because it always happened on my name day. Being a skeptic by nature, I had serious doubts that all the military and crowds came out solely because of my name day, especially because no one paid any particular attention to inconspicuous little me and instead pushed as much as possible.

Near Brzesc, there was an old fortress from the czar's time where military units stood. I remember cavalry and Uhlan orchestras riding on beautiful horses with shining coats—the horses seemed to dance to the rhythm of the military music. After the cavalry, equal groups came on foot with a row of standing rifles, and behind them, there were small tanks, and then large ones, with huge bodies that rumbled over the cobblestones. The noise of airplane engines could be heard high above. Everyone was enthusiastic about this demonstration of Polish strength, and people applauded, yelled, and waved red and white flags.

In the evening, when the parade was over and the crowd dispersed into the twilight, the only things remaining on the poorly lit street were horse feces and an occasional tossed bouquet of flowers.

Once my grandmother and I went to Vilno to visit her sisters, who lived there with her husband and children. I really liked this city from which my grandmother came. The first difference that I noticed when I compared it to Brzesc was that the carriages had big inflated tires, not metal rims on which rubber was placed. The city was clean and picturesque. At that time, a cavalry captain, Ryszard Wiszowaty, and his wife, one of my grandmother's sister, lived by Orzeszkowa Square. They had a nice apartment on the third floor. He then worked in the DOW. I think this abbreviation stood for *Dowodztwo Okregu Wojskowego* (Military District Command), but I'm not sure. Orzeszkowa Square bordered the main streets of the city, which was the Avenue of Mickiewicz, a famous Polish poet and patriot. I remember the castle on the hill, a countless number of churches and holy statues, and Ostrobramska Gate with a crowd of praying people. I went to Rossa and to Bernardynski Cemetery, where all the Klimms were buried.

Vilno was a Polish city; you didn't hear Lithuanian spoken on the streets at all. The surrounding villages were also Polish; the entire Vilno province was a Polish enclave. Perhaps because of its particular location, the city was very patriotic.

I remember an incident that happened at cavalry Captain Ryszard's house during our visit to Vilno. He came to the logical conclusion that I had enough strength to wield a heavy cavalry sword. And so he placed a candle on the dining room table, despite the urgent protests of his wife, Aunt Jadza, and then with one lighting-fast stroke, he cut off the tip of the candle.

"Well, now you try."

The protests didn't deter me, and I grabbed the sword, swung it, and struck the very center of the table, cutting a deep ugly scratch into it. I better not say what happened later. The man of the house decided that the best solution was a tactical withdrawal from the fury of both sisters.

A Polish film about Mr. Twardowski was playing in the local movie theater in Brzesc, where I would go with my parents from time to time. The film horrified me from the first moment. Besides the Twardowski gentry, there was a devil to whom Twardowski rather foolishly sold his soul. I don't remember the plot of the movie anymore, but I do remember that devil and the scene in which he carries Twardowski into space, while Twardowski, consumed with despair, begins to say some Hail Marys. The devil can't stand it, and Twardowski falls onto the moon.

After returning from the movie theater, I was awfully afraid. I didn't want to go into any dark room, as I could see this devil everywhere in the dimness. Even in the bathroom, where there was a small window in the back, I imagined the devil peering through it. These fears lasted many months; it wasn't easy to get rid of them. A child at that age has a wild imagination and can create an entire world of imaginary dangers for himself—luckily, a shining light and a mother's care can easily quell the fears.

This encounter with the figure of the devil eventually had its repercussions when I started going to catechism classes in preparation for my first confession and Holy Communion. The catechism teacher and a priest discussed all our sins with us, talking about damnation if you had committed any cardinal sins. I could see souls that already belonged to the devil and could see him carrying my rather pitiful little soul to hellish damnation. Of course, I thought I had a ton of sins, not only those actually committed but also those committed in my mind—in accordance with the catechism, a sin that is contemplated is just about the same as a sin that is committed. Up until I began going to catechism class, my religious practice was limited to saying a nightly prayer for the health of my mother, father, and grandmother. I had been taught about the Virgin Mary, who takes care of everyone, even a little tyke like me. Only once I got to catechism class did I understand that it wasn't child's play, that the road to salvation was long and strenuous, and that my chances as a sinner to reach sublime happiness were not really that great. Finally, after a rather long period of reflection in church, the moment came for my first confession.

Everything was ready for my first Communion. My father's tailor, whose quite appropriate last name was Mantelmacher, had sewn a white woolen suit for me. They were the first long pants I had in my life together with a suit jacket—the short fancy outfit of officers. I felt incredibly elegant in this outfit, though the entire time all I could think about was the quickest way to get it off so as to be comfortable again.

So that's how I found myself with the rest of my class that afternoon at three o'clock, in the dark inner depths of the church, standing in single file for confession. I feverishly went over all my sins in my mind and came to the conclusion that I had also stolen—once I had dug up and baked several potatoes from a stranger's field. I had somewhat of a problem understanding the commandment, "Do not commit adultery." This topic was not clearly explained by our catechism teacher.

Danek Wolczacki, my good friend, was behind me in line waiting to cleanse his soul. He distinguished himself by not being able to stand still for even five minutes. Every once in a while, a cleansed little soul would come out from the confessional after the priest's knock, but the line was long, and the waiting was becoming boring. Finally, Danek couldn't stand it and gave me a punch so as to kill time. I had no choice but to punch him back. We didn't notice that a commotion erupted, because we were rather busy with our own sparring. Suddenly, I felt a strong hand grab me by the ear. Danek found himself in a similar situation, and both of us were shamefully sent out of the church by the confessional priest. We were in a pretty awful predicament.

First Communion was to take place the next morning, and everything was ready, but we sinners weren't good enough to get Communion. After everyone's confessions, we went to the priest; he scolded us thoroughly and said that we should come to confession early in the morning. Stealthily, we got ourselves to the church and after receiving the appropriate penance—I think it was three Hail Marys—we gained reconciliation. I was so worried about this whole situation that I don't even remember the ceremony of receiving first Communion.

That same year, we went on vacation to Mrs. Alymowa's house. She was an older gray-haired lady with a soft pink face and sparkling eyes—she could easily have been the good fairy in a Walt Disney movie. She had something unearthly about her, something ethereal. And in fact, earthly matters didn't concern her much; she had a white scruffy dog named Puszek and a countless number of cats—strays that were a mix of all kinds and breeds to whom she gave shelter. When she set out for a walk on her property at sunset, wrapped in a white shawl with the red rays of fading sunlight brightening her gray hair, a white dog slowly circling in front of her, and dozens of cats behind her, she really gave a fairytale impression. She was the widow of a czar's officer and lived a lonely life with Tekla, who can only be compared to Sienkiewicz's Horpyna[1]—big and bulky with a row of white teeth which were visible when she smiled, vulgar, and unfortunately not willing to share in her lady's love for cats.

When Mrs. Alymowa's glance was somewhere in the distance, or when she herself wasn't nearby, more than one cat got smacked with a broom, and more than one even lost his life. In such a case, there would be a ritual burial involving the entire cat family. I felt sympathy for her dog, Puszek, who despite his healthy canine instincts had to cope with this feline company. Despite her modest needs, Mrs. Alymowa's pension money was not sufficient, so she rented out half her house to vacationers, saving her budget in this way. Her house was surrounded by an old, unkempt, and yet beautiful orchard. Off to the side, a forest stretched out, as well as sandy dunes and birches, under which mushroom caps reddened, and further along there were meadows and hazelnut trees on the Bug River. You could also see smoke billowing from a nearby village.

I spent an entire summer there with my mother and grandmother. My father dropped by when he could. We would go for long walks in the fields and meadows, into the forest and near the river, where you could swim near the sandbar. The water was clean, rapid, and cold, and I could see schools of swimming fish, changing direction together as if on command, throughout the clear waters. The Bug is a dangerous river—the water swirls in currents that beat on the steeper bank. There was a spot there, however,

---

1. Horpyna is a character familiar in Poland in a famous novel by Henryk Sienkjewicz, *With Fire and Sword.*

where you could go in up to your waist without too much risk. Usually I spent most of the mornings on the small beach building castles from the sand and splashing myself with water while my mother was bathing in the sun.

I went for a swim once with my grandmother, mother, Mrs. Alymowa, Tekla, and Natalka, our maid. My grandmother was wearing some old-fashioned swimsuit; my mom's was very modern and she looked good in it. Praying loudly, Mrs. Alymowa stepped into the water up to her knees while wearing her nightgown; Natalka was wearing a tight, button-down work smock. I will never forget the sight of Tekla, who put on a short apron that tied with string at the back. Her whole great big behind was exposed; she didn't pay much heed to my presence or that of the rest of the company.

One day, after my father came, we went for a horse-wagon ride that lasted the entire day; we sat on a bed of straw that had been covered with a colorful kilim. We had a basket of food and drinks. The purpose of this journey was to see the White Lake. I will never forget this part of Polesie. There wasn't a single living soul except for hundreds of hummingbirds singing in the acacia bushes that surrounded the ruins of an old Russian Orthodox cloister. The scent of wildflowers was overpowering in the blazing afternoon sunlight. A flowery meadow gradually sloped down to a lake that was surrounded by a white ring of sand. You could see every detail on the bottom of the clear water. When a light breeze moved the water, reflections of light played on the little shells, on the numerous fish, and on the brownish backs of countless crawfish walking on the smooth bottom. Being at the edge of this lake, it seemed that the other distant world did not exist, that there was no poverty or suffering, and that there was only great silence, drenched in the sweetness of summer and the unspeakable beauty of nature.

Often later, when I was having some troubles or feeling unwell, I would close my eyes and recreate the image of that place. Gradually peace would come back to my soul.

Differences in political opinions were striking in pre-war

Poland, and the events of May and the shift of power to Pilsudski[2] created great controversy in society; it even showed up in our house. My mother came out of the national democratic tradition, while my father was an ardent Pilsudski follower with socialist tendencies.

Usually, such political puzzles didn't lead to disagreements. Of course I didn't understand them at all during our years in Brzesc. Only much later did I recognize their causes. My father was the youngest son in his family, which had a forty hectares estate in the area of Sieradz and a house in Zdunska Wola. They were doing pretty well. I never met my grandparents on my father's side, but I know that my grandmother was of German descent. My mother told me she was very kind, petite, and withered; she suffered through tuberculosis and died from it. My grandfather was a large man with dark, graying hair, black eyebrows, and a despotic nature. Besides my father, they had two other children—the oldest a son and the younger a daughter.

My father was the one who wanted to study. His older brother finished agricultural school and decided to be a farmer. His sister married a musician from the Warsaw Philharmonic. Frankly, she wasn't that pretty. Their marriage quickly ended in separation and then divorce, but a daughter, Zosia, came out of it. I still keep in touch with her today.

My father turned down his portion of the inheritance and gave it to his older brother and sister. After finishing high school and after the war with the Bolsheviks, he went off to Warsaw without a dime in his pocket to register at the Warsaw Institute of Technology.

In his high school years, he belonged to the underground Polish Military Organization created by Pilsudski. He didn't talk much about it, but I was told that he would carry secret papers and documents in his schoolbag risking his entire future. When the time came for war against the Bolsheviks, he reported, as most young people did, to be a volunteer for the army.

---

2. Pilsudski regained power in a military coup in 1926. He had been the savior of the country in the War in 1920 and returned now to power.

He was incorporated into a unit that was then stationed in the old czar's barracks under the Kierbedz Bridge in Warsaw. There, like many others, he fell ill with dysentery. The situation was urgent, because they wanted to complete the front line quickly, so my father's unit was sent into battle after very brief training. My father stayed in the barracks with dozens of others, lacking strength from dehydration and electrolyte imbalance. His unit was almost entirely massacred during the heated battles—the illness saved him from certain death. At that time, Polish forces fought the Bolsheviks first by the Vistula River, then by the Narev river. Eventually, they no longer needed more volunteers, and my father was let go, though he was not in the greatest state, still quite weak and emaciated.

Getting an education at the Warsaw Institute of Technology was not easy for a man without money or a roof over his head. You had to pay tuition, and put food on the table. My father managed to make a living by tutoring, and after a while, he was able to get a place to stay with several other students in the Dziekanka dormitory on Krakowski Przedmiescie Street. After finishing his education, he met my mother, and soon after that, they got married.

This past influenced my father's politics slanting him towards socialism. He had also the highest respect for General Marshal Pilsudski. Difficult years of study had inclined him to adopt socialist ideas of which my mother did not approve. They never had intense discussions about it, but I know that they went to vote separately and, obviously, for different candidates.

I didn't know much about my father's past during my years in Brzesc. Because he often had to leave for many weeks due to the nature of his work, we weren't that close. I was raised under the watchful eyes of my mother and grandmother. It wasn't until the years of the Occupation that I began to understand my father better and grow closer to him.

Once the decision was made to move to Poznan, things happened rather quickly. My parents went first and rented out a nice apartment in a brand-new building at Asnyka square, in the district of Poznan called Jezyce. Soon, my grandmother and I got there as well. Poznan made a huge impression on me. I was struck by the cleanliness of the city, the lack of dirty sewers, which unfortunately still existed in Brzesc, and, of course, the yellow-green streetcars that were completely different from those in Warsaw.

Pre-war Poznan was a beautiful northern European town. In the center, close to the square dominated by a mighty statue of Christ the King, surrounded by the old trees, was Collegium Maius, dating back to the Renaissance. This was a beautiful building used for ages by the university. Near by towered a dreary "Kaiser Wilhelm" castle indicative of German insolence and violence. Countless churches created a charming skyline for the city. Old Market surrounded by medieval buildings, decorated with sculptures and wall paintings, gave proof of riches and abundance of medieval Poland. An old renaissance city hall with a pillory decorated the center of the Old Market. Over the Warta River was Ostrow Tumski, the oldest part of the town. The cathedral there had a base, which was built in a Roman style. On top of the base was Gothic architecture and on the very top Baroque. We often walked to Solacki Park and then further toward the fortress, where the city ended and the fields began.

I was registered at Saint Kazimir's school, which had nice classrooms, a big field, and a lot more space than Mrs. Gorska's little school. I didn't have to walk very far to get to school. On my way I would pass by a zoo that fascinated me terribly. Often, when I was walking in the morning, I would hear the roaring of impatient big cats waiting to be fed. I was then in fourth grade. In the first difficult months, I missed Tala and my other friends. Besides that, I was in some way different from the other children. Their diction was rougher, not melodic like mine, and they would look at me askance, as if looking at an intruder. After a short while, I was able to adjust to the new surroundings and even ended up being the captain of one of two teams of handball. I was quick and agile, and these traits convinced pretty much everyone that it was worth having me on their side.

I had to learn quite a lot as the level of education was high. In the evenings I had to spend usually a few hours on homework. At that time I discovered a great love of reading—historical novels, young people's novels, adventure novels. I remember that when we were still in Brzesc, I read both *The Secret Garden* and *Anne of Green Gables*, and then in Poznan, I got Sienkiewicz's *Trilogy* for my birthday. I couldn't tear myself away from the adventures of Skrzetuski and Zagloba, was fascinated by Kmicic, and could sense the charming manor of Ketling. After the *Trilogy*, I discovered different books, mainly historical ones. For that same birthday, my father bought me a book about dinosaurs; I looked in wonder at these strange reptiles and became fascinated by the natural history of our world. I still attribute all that I know today about the prehistoric world to that particular book.

Living life in terms of fulfilling orders never really appealed to me. A division of the Boy Scouts was organized in my class, beginning with the creation of a team of little boy scouts. I went to the first meeting and listened to how we would be marching together, going on trips, and putting up tents, and quickly came to the conclusion that these meetings would take up too much time that could be better spent otherwise. Besides, I preferred making my own decisions rather than leaving them up to some older boy. I didn't go to the next meeting.

There was a movie theater named the Sun in downtown Poznan. I really liked watching movies for kids my age there. *Snow White and the Seven Dwarfs*, the first feature-length Walt Disney movie, was a real revelation for me. I was thrilled with the vivid colors, loved the seven dwarfs, and later requested my mom play the songs from the film on the piano.

My older cousin, the son of my aunt Janka, came over for Christmas in 1938. He stayed with us for almost a week. We played together and went for walks with my grandmother or mother.

I really enjoyed playing with tin soldiers at that time. I had various divisions, an army service corps, and even artillery. You could buy a small firecracker with a fuse for the tin divisions and set them off with a bang and a burst of flames. One of the cannons was a bit bigger. My cousin got the intriguing idea to put some pellets in it and to light a dozen of the firecrackers, and then see what happened. Of course, I listened to him; we loaded the cannon to the end of the barrel and lit the fuse. There was a pretty strong explosion, and scraps of metal tore the wallpaper in the room. Strangely enough, neither of us got hurt.

At the beginning of the year 1939, we went with my mother to visit my aunt Janka in Warsaw. When we were already sitting in the express Pullman train car at the Poznan train station, an international train from Berlin came onto the same track as our train just before our departure. There was a group of traveling young Germans on board. They were dressed in brown uniforms with red stripes and swastikas on the sleeves. When they saw me gaping at them, they opened the window and began yelling something in a mocking tongue, threatening me with fists, and sticking out their tongues. I couldn't understand this hostility and didn't know what they wanted, but I was really hurt, because I didn't feel that I was in any way at fault. This first encounter with the Hitlerjugend (Hitler youth organization) became a kind of prelude to everything that would soon begin.

⫿

The year 1938 was full of historical events. The danger lurking in the West became more and more apparent after Anschluss (inclusion) of Austria in the Third Reich. German tanks rolled into beautiful Vienna, greeted by a somber crowd. Hitler's rhetoric didn't leave any room for doubt as to his desire for aggression and further invasions. Jozef Beck, the Minister of Foreign Affairs in Poland, proposed a military alliance with Czechoslovakia so as to establish a line of defense against a Nazi attack, but the Czechs declined, counting on the illusion that they could come to an agreement with the Reich. These hopes were totally futile, especially when the Germans soon occupied purely Czech land, called by Germany Sudetenland. Unfortunately, Poland also participated in this disgraceful partition of Czechoslovakia by occupying the Zaolzie region. The more sensible people considered this simply madness, if not, even worse, a national disgrace; the newspapers, however, were filled with celebratory headlines about the recovery of Polish territory and the Polish army that occupied it. There were also photographs of tanks and marching armies.

The feeling within the Polish intelligence network was that we would survive a war with the Germans, even though it would likely be trying and difficult. A possibility was considered that in the first phase the Germans might even occupy Poznan, but no one dreamed a horrifying defeat awaited us. A lot of upheavals had already passed through Polish territory, and the Polish nation had somehow survived them. Now, after twenty years of independence, people believed that the Polish army and industry would endure such a blow and manage to fight it off. You could read about this feeling in the newspapers and hear it on the radio. People were giving donations to reinforce our Navy and Air Force. Still, no one in my immediate surroundings took the danger seriously. The one exception was my grandmother, who clearly saw black clouds gathering on the Polish horizon. In 1939, she sent a huge basket—a trunk full of all the winter clothes of the whole family—to her son Wladek in Lublin. She did this entirely on her own, foreseeing that the whirlwind of the war would force us to leave Poznan. She was convinced that Lublin, located in the center of the country, would be safe.

⁂

One day, during the winter of '38 to'39, an unusual guest came to our house. I remember his visit clearly, as I was incredibly troubled by it and by what he said and proposed to my father.

He was an engineer and one of my father's old friends. He had signed a contract with an English company, Cook, for engineering work in the Middle East. A group of about a dozen Polish engineers was supposed to first do the survey work and then build roads and an electrical network.

Cook happily hired engineers from the Warsaw Institute of Technology, for they had a great reputation in Europe as terrific specialists. The benefits offered by the company were fantastic, including a very high salary, special tents, numerous servants, education for children, and special language courses for the adults. You could go with your whole family, comfortable living was guaranteed. My mother listened to him, and her eyes sparkled.

My mother speaking to my father said, "Listen, Stach, listen, we'll go there. The situation here is getting more and more dangerous, and we'd also get to see a part of the world. Sign the contract, and of course there isn't much risk."

But my father didn't even want to hear about it. In this phase of his life, as the director of agricultural surveys, he felt comfortable and good in his position; it was a fulfillment of his dreams. He not only provided for his family, but was doing a lot of good for the country. My grandmother, who always had a fighting streak in her, also supported leaving for the Middle East. Perhaps it was the experience of the First World War and the loss of her husband in Russia, or maybe the Bolshevik's war that convinced her it was better to avoid yet another war.

I was fascinated by what my father's friend said. He had worked only a short time on that ground where the work was to be done. I don't remember exactly where it was, but he described the climate, the environment, and the people. I really wanted to go there and to see it all for myself, to see this new exotic world. The Middle East was something I knew only from *A Thousand and One Nights*, and that's how I imagined it. I got a somewhat better impression from Sienkiewicz's *Trilogy*, though this impression was both naïve and unclear.

After a long discussion with my stubborn father, our guest left without having achieved anything.

After many, many years, when I was already in the United States, I met an older man who found out that Stach Subczynski's son was in America. This man turned out to be the same engineer. He met with me for a little while, as he was leaving soon. He and his family had escaped the horrors of the war. He was still working and living on a small island in the South Pacific, where besides him and his wife, there were only 360 natives. His children had been educated in the United States. Once a day, he had to conduct

a survey at a specified time, and then he would pass the results on the central radio line. The rest of the day was his. He complained that he felt uncomfortable in a suit and tie; on his island, he wore only shorts and shirts.

My mother never rebuked my father for his decision, not in the difficult moments of the Occupation when our lives hung by a thread, nor later when we had to live under the Soviet regime.

Any fears of the approaching conflict with the Germans weren't strong enough to change vacation plans in what became the memorable year of 1939. I finished fourth grade at public school with good grades. Our financial situation was much better than it had been in Brzesc, so we were able to plan a more luxurious vacation than that at Mrs. Alymowa's house.

Aunt Jadza, the wife of cavalry Captain Wiszowaty and my grandmother's youngest sister, found a pension in the old Karoliszki estate in the province of Vilno. Mrs. Bohuszewicz, the wife of a retired judge, ran it. As my aunt had described, it was a beautiful place, hills, surrounded by forests and fields, and just next to the Wilia River. There were kayaks there that the guests could use at their disposal, and an old, rather phlegmatic mare was found for me to ride. She walked over the fields totally ignoring my commands.

My parents decided to rent a room with full service for the whole summer season of July and August. My mother and I would be there the whole time, and my father would come in the first half of August for vacation. My grandmother initially stayed in Poznan, then went to see her son in Lublin for a few weeks. And so our preparations for vacation began.

A beautiful dress of crinkled silk was sewn for my mother with huge flowers on it, and another, much more simple one, was made that was navy with white polka dots. My mother had a third, inexpensive one made from a cheerful and colorful calico that buttoned in the front. She also had to buy a bathing suit and swim trunks for me, as well as new sandals from Bata (a former big Czech company) and, as a treat, beautiful cream-colored pigskin shoes.

Thus, well-equipped, my mother and I left on the long journey from Poznan to Vilno and then took a bus to Karoliszki. The train trip didn't stay in my memory, but I remember the bus ride very well—the winding roads of the province of Vilno, climbing up the hills, going down into the low valleys, surrounded by vast meadows and thick forests, with hamlets hidden in between them. I looked at all of this and felt happy in the way that you can only be happy at that age, having tons of energy and a poor understanding of the reality. Finally, the bus stopped. Karoliszki, an old country manor, could be seen not too far from the road. There was a wide path leading to the main entrance. Mrs. Bohuszewicz was already waiting there. As she took us to our room, she was asking on the way if we were hungry, what she could make for us, how was our trip, etc.

The manor seemed huge to me at that time. It was a wooden building with a large main room—the dining room of the pension. Vast rooms surrounded it, lit up by large windows and furnished with beds, dressing tables, tables and chairs, and closets. It was warm and sunny. We quickly made ourselves at home and went for a walk after having a light meal. There was certainly enough space to walk around. The nearby forest didn't have much vegetation, mostly pine needles. It was full of mushrooms, from chanterelles to porcinis. The chanterelles were yellowing under the pine trees, the brown caps of boletuses were rarer, but there were still quite a few of them. The smell of resin filled the air. It flowed from the trees as if in long tears, partly hardened but still sticky to the touch. Here and there you could see large swarms of red ants, green large ferns and lower down moss—the kind that was bright green and reminiscent of plush Old World drapes—and the silvery-gray, dry and gently scratching bare underfoot. From the coolness of the forest, you could walk into the blazing sunlight of the meadow, through which a small brook flowed lazily emptying eventually into the larger river—Wilia. The meadows were covered in flowers and herbs.

I remember seeing a crumbling tree stump, where a little lizard was warming herself. I stared at her, though I didn't feel like touching her. Anyhow I am sure she would have run away long before I would make up my mind to do it. She made her home in this tree trunk, and almost every afternoon, she would warm herself in the sun. Partly darkened by wetland trees, the river broke off into a small branch that extended wide and deep, right there near the rotten tree trunk. The edges and bottom were sandy, and the water lay in a smooth slab that was disturbed only by some insects that ran across it, not breaking the surface. Through the mirror of water, you could see countless small fish. The beauty and peace of this place left a permanent imprint on my soul.

I waded through the shallow water frightening the fish, and often I lay down on the fragrant grass looking at the clouds wandering through the sky, admiring how they would move slowly, how they would change shape, how they would dissolve in the summer sun's rays. I felt good, safe.

After breakfast, we would usually go to the beach on the Wilia River. You could walk at least ten steps into the water from the sandy shore before reaching the deep currents. There were also other guests from the pension on the beach. After so many years, I still remember them well. I even remember some of their names. There was Mrs. Truszkowska from Latvia with her daughter, a very attractive teenager who was cheerful and naïve; there was a businessman, born in Georgia who lived in Poland with his mistress— to the shock of all those around him—with full approval from his deceitful mother. Supposedly, he was very wealthy, and his "mistress" was a kind, overwhelmed woman, terrorized equally by him and his moody mother. The older lady never failed to emphasize her two-faced role; she didn't distinguish herself with excessive social awareness or tact. There was also an older man named Kaduszkiewicz, who I remember floating on an automobile tire in the Wilia's rapids. I remember this well, because at one moment, after a rather clumsy move, that rubber wheel jumped out into the air and landed with two skinny legs sticking up through its black ring. It looked really funny, but of course, it wasn't for the unfortunate one himself, who sank underwater. He swam out quickly, grabbed the tire, and got out at a safe place. When he came over to us, he wasn't in the best mood.

There were two kayaks on the beach, and I used one of them almost all the time. A nice couple was also on the beach with a little girl, Marysia, who was somewhat older than me; small breasts were already growing under her bikini top. Very serious, she stayed with her parents, though after a while she built up some courage. I gave her rides in a kayak on the Wilia, though she wouldn't touch an oar and was afraid of the water. I didn't have that particular fear, because I already knew how to swim, though not that well. I knew that I shouldn't go into deep water, and I also discovered that if the kayak tipped over upside down, there was a space underneath in which you could comfortably fit your head and have a lot of extra air. It's also quite bright in there, because the sun's rays reflect off the bottom.

With this knowledge, I took the kayak upstream, then turned it upside down, put my head in that space, and holding on to the sides, swam calmly toward the beach. My mother saw the tipped-over kayak but no sign of her son. She fell into a panic, and through the body of the kayak, I could hear desperate voices and calls. I poked my head out, and when I got back to the shore, I understood what I had done. I was ashamed and embarrassed. My mother, shaken and horrified, didn't even scold me.

On Saturday, Mrs. Bohuszewicz and her army of women were busy with furious preparations, because special guests were going to arrive for the weekend. These people were various: cavalry Captain Wiszowaty came with my aunt Jadza, people from Vilno came for a day or two of rest, and groups of gamblers came who played bridge. Soon after arriving, they sat down on the large veranda by a table, and they left the table only for meals. I remember their faces full of tension and sometimes pale with anxiety. You could easily get tense at this table, as the game was played for big money. At times it wasn't just a couple of hundreds lost, but thousands and hundreds of thousands—these were very rich people for which hazard was the main stimulant in live.

This gaming table fascinated me. I would often sit beside it, not bothering anyone and silently watching the game and the people who were caught up in it. Soon, I understood the rules of the game and noticed the mistakes that were made by the players.

The summer of 1939, at least there in the Vilno province, was unusually beautiful and warm. Because I spent three-fourths of my time by the water in my swimsuit, I soon got a dark, golden-bronze tan. There were a few rainy days, after which the sun seemed even fuller and more intense. Thirsty for the sun and beach after having to devote several days to reading books on the porch, I spent the whole day near the Wilia. At night, when I was getting undressed for bed, my mother fell into a panic:

"Oh my God, what is going on with this child? It's some kind of horrible illness—he is simply black!"

I wasn't black, but indeed I was dark brown. Because intention often turned into action with my mother, we were next day in Vilno seeing a pediatrician. He asked what was wrong with me. I responded that nothing was. Furious, my mother said that it was enough just to take one look at me to know that something wasn't right. When the poor doctor finally understood what the problem was, he began to laugh heartily and calmed down my mother, saying that the changing of skin color was a natural phenomenon. I carried this suntan from Karoliszki on my back through the whole Occupation; it faded a lot but was always there.

⫯

Dinner was the main focus of the day in Karoliszki. After a morning swim and some sun tanning, and then a whole day of running, I was always hungry like a wolf. Dinner was the one time of the day when all the pension's guests would meet. More and more often usual chat related to the events of the day turned into discussion related to the last political news. The increasingly more and more arrogant German territorial demands, the fact that England objected to the mobilization of Polish forces, lukewarm position of the France to a possible, even probable, conflict worried and irritated everybody. Still, these matters didn't overwhelm us; most of the people simply could not believe that danger was so close. Everyone was living for the present moment denying the imminent danger.

⊷

The businessman's mistress often had red eyes, for his mother treated her horribly, even at the common table. The son, however, whose last name was Gazalian, aimed to please his mother in every way possible. One day, he caught some small whitings and triumphantly carried them to the kitchen, demanding that they be fried for his mother. At dinnertime, there was a small dish of fried fish on the table in front of old lady Gazalian. This alone upset everyone around, but it became even more upsetting when the old lady started greedily eating the fish without even offering to share. What happened next could have easily been predicted— she choked on a bone to her son's shock—and to the satisfaction of everyone and the quiet joy of the persecuted young woman. I was amused watching her run from the dining room, choking and coughing.

Among other guests there was also a family with their son about sixteen years old. I remember him very well; tall, lean and lanky, with an Adam's apple that jutted out. Afternoon tea was usually served along with some pieces of cake. There was just about enough of it so that each person could have two pieces; with his huge thin hand, the young man could clear out half the dish in a flash. I looked at his actions in horror, almost choking on my cake so as to eat my portion faster. In the end, the other people complained, and eventually the young man was forced to restrain himself.

One Sunday, a wealthy manufacturer came with his wife and son, who was my age; there would be nothing unusual about this, except for the fact that they came in their own car. The boy showed off in front of me by climbing into and out of the car, turning the steering wheel, honking the horn. In the end, he concluded that I still wasn't that affected or wallowing in jealousy. Of course, I couldn't go near the car or, God forbid, go inside it. Then, he ran up to his room, came back with the keys, and started turning the engine on and off, looking at me triumphantly. Well then, this episode didn't end well for him. Soon his father showed up, took away the keys, and quickly led the young person into the house. After a moment, a loud yell proved that the difference of opinion between the father and son took on a concrete form. I am embarrassed to say it, but that loud cry didn't elicit any sympathy from me.

At the end of July, my uncle Wladek came to visit for a week. He was a young and handsome blonde with fair skin and broad shoulders. That fair skin turned out to be his demise. After a day spent near the Wilia River, he looked a lot like a freshly boiled lobster, with the only difference being that his skin was covered with the blisters of a second-degree burn. Someone suggested that covering his back with an egg white might offer some relief.

The appropriate treatment was brought from the kitchen, and his whole back was thickly covered with the stuff. Nothing special happened at first after this procedure, but once the egg white began to dry and shrink, my uncle began whimpering in pain. There was no alternative other than to remove this dry shell, along with some skin, with the help of a sponge and some lukewarm water.

⁂

In the beginning of August, my father came. We would go for long walks together in the forest and the fields, where there was already new greenery among the rough brushes of freshly cut rye or wheat. Hummingbirds hung in the sky, and figures of the Virgin Mary and saints decorated with dried flowers stood on the green borders and roads with deep track marks. Despite the warmth and stagnant heat, you could already feel the coming of autumn.

The second week of my father's stay was suddenly cut short. He received a telegram that called him back to Poznan. The

Ministry of Agriculture was preparing to evacuate its Poznan branch because of the possibility of war. Important documents had to be taken to the center of the country for safekeeping; those that shouldn't fall into enemy hands had to be destroyed in case Poznan was occupied. The threat of an attack became more and more serious and more and more imminent. Polish government did not agree to a "corridor," which would cut off the northern part of Poland from the rest of the country and especially our pride and joy—the port in Gdynia. Troops were mobilized, though a bit too late. The English government was fully responsible for this, particularly Neville Chamberlain, who up until the last minute prevented any attempts at organizing a defense against a German attack on Poland.

No one in Poland knew that Chamberlain had made an agreement with Hitler, giving him Poland, and that actually, despite a signed agreement for united defense, he was preparing to betray us. Additionally, no one knew that on the twenty-seventh of August, Molotow and Ribbentrop signed an agreement that ratified the fourth partition of Poland. This pact removed any significant obstacle to the Third Reich's attack on Poland, now certain of the position of Soviet Russia.

In the last week of August, it was clear that war was practically unavoidable. My mother shortened our vacation and took me to Warsaw to her sister, my aunt Janka. My grandmother was already there; she had just gotten back from a visit to my uncle Wladek in Lublin.

My aunt Jania was my mother's older sister, a plump blonde with light eyes, a good heart, and a healthy appetite. Her husband was a geodesy engineer from the Warsaw Institute of Technology, Mieczyslaw Malesinski. They had three sons, of whom the oldest was Bohdan. He was two-and-a-half years older than me and the closest to me. The middle son, Wladek, was six months younger than I. The youngest was still quite small; the age difference between us was about six years.

We knew each other well. Besides the time of my mother's illness when I spent several weeks with my aunt, we would often take the holidays together. I can't forget the vacations in Urle near Warsaw, where we, my cousins and I would play together all day long. Our games didn't necessarily reveal a lot of common sense, but we never lacked innovation. We broke apart a wasp nest hanging in a tree with some sticks. I and the two older cousins got a little sick from the stings, but the youngest, Stefan, who couldn't run away as fast as we could, got a high fever and fell really ill. We also tied Stefan to a tree with the real intention of shooting at him with a bow and arrow, just like the Indians did in a book that we had read. Fortunately, my aunt saw what was happening and quickly intervened. The mastermind of all these games was Bohdan, the oldest. We just followed in his footsteps.

My uncle's family had a large corner piece of property with a nice garden in a settlement in Bielany. When I arrived there with my mother, they were busy taping up the windows so as to protect the glass panes in the event of a bombing. Sirens wailed often, preparing people for air raids. There was a talk of making a trench out in the yard to hide from the bombs.

4

And Then the Storm

NCLE MIETEK WAS very skeptical; he didn't believe that the war was so imminent. He thought it was just a scare and that the Germans wanted to bargain from the position of strength, attempting to get as much concession as possible from Poland. The radio, which stood in the dining room, continuously gave information about the political situation, mobilization, and the preparation of defenses in the event of an attack.

The end of August was nice and pleasant. Bohdan and Wladek got new navy-colored uniforms for school; my aunt who was thinking not only of school but also of the possibility of a lack of basic necessities of life started necessary shopping. My grandmother, who had the experience of two wars—the First World War and the war with Bolsheviks — helped her with these preparations.

We didn't hear from my father. My mother was very worried, because she thought, rightly so, that he was in the most danger, not us.

On the first of September, in the year 1939, I woke up early in the morning, got myself dressed quickly and went outside the house where there was a small yard and a flower garden. An alarm sounded with wailing sirens. Uncle Mietek, who was just then taking out the garbage, cursed under his breath: "dammit, they could finally get some sense not to wake people up unnecessarily so early in the morning!" His words of disappointment and disapproval were interrupted by the sudden sounds of explosions. Columns of black smoke were visible all over the city. He and I both knew that war was now a reality.

The first bombardment of Warsaw didn't last long, though the losses were great, in both the destroyed possessions and the loss of life. The German bombers didn't choose a target; they were bombing randomly a defenseless city. The point of their actions was to terrorize the population and provoke panic. The reaction they got was one of rage, desperation, and hatred toward the murderers.

⊪

The last of the preparations to safeguard the house were made that day. I remember that my aunt told the boys to dress in their new uniforms, for it was impossible to determine what might happen at any moment. The first bombardment quickly taught us that no place was safe.

The radio informed about a border crossing made by German tank columns, about terrible weapons, and about fierce battles. Each communication was, in turn, more frightening, talking about the approaching German armies, about the occupation of large territories of the country, about the losses and the beastly German pilots who murdered even shepherds in the fields with machine guns. My mother was horrified, still having heard nothing from my father. German panzer divisions were getting closer and closer with each hour to Poznan. We heard about a very fierce battle that was even closer to us, near Kutno.

In the breaks between communications, Radio Warsaw played the religious song, "Holy Mother, Don't Abandon Us." This song still rings in my ears today; I don't think anything better captured the tragedy of those days or better represented the feelings of millions of Poles than that old, strikingly beautiful, and sad song.

·||·

My uncle was drafted. Thus the women were left to maintain the household with the children. Rumors spread that the Germans were taking older boys so as to denationalize them and reform them into future soldiers of the German Reich. My aunt was horrified by this rumor, because she thought that Bohdan was in real danger.

I don't remember now on which day it was in September that my father suddenly showed up. He was tired, emaciated, and unshaved. Dark stubble created a shadow on his face. We found out that he had come on an evacuation bus along with his whole office; the workers and all the documents were to be evacuated to Przemysl, in the south of Poland. The bus was already on the other side of the Vistula River near Praga. My father left the group in order to pick up my mother and me and together reach the designated destination. There was no time to get ready. My mother and I didn't have any clothes other than summer clothes. I had one sweater, and my mother had a moleskin wrap. We put them on and were ready for the trip. My aunt asked my father to take Bohdan with us, because she was very worried about him. My parents agreed immediately. And then the moment of departure came; it was so hard because no one knew what was to come. We only knew that we were all in danger and that there was a real chance that we would never see each other again. My grandmother hugged me close to her; I felt her warm tears on my face. Jania kissed me tenderly while the younger boys stood in silence. Bohdan didn't move or say a word when it came time to leave his mother.

We left the house quickly and walked toward Praga. I was quite tired from the fast pace and thirsty, but the point was to get across the bridge over the Vistula River as quickly as possible, as the Germans could bomb it at any moment. We finally found ourselves on Grochowska Street, already over the Vistula, on the side of Praga. The street made me think of a real hell, crowded with people escaping to the south. There were so many wagons full of those escaping: people were running away with bundles on their backs or hanging on bicycles. Military wagons heading for the Warsaw periphery brought supplies to the Polish division that was preparing to defend the capital.

I heard sirens and then, right after that, the awful rapidly growing noise of engines. Before I knew what was happening, the noise had turned into an awful screech just above my head. You could see low-flying bombers all over. They dove and then suddenly flew up again.

In the moment that they dove, you could hear the whistle of machine guns and the cries of the people they hit. My father grabbed my mother and Bohdan sharply, and we shielded ourselves from the machine-gun fire behind the main door of a three-story apartment building. After catching our breath, we figured out that we could get to the basement from there. We went down there quickly with a group of other people. It was mostly dark, for there was only one candle burning. My eyes soon got used to the darkness. People sat slumped by the walls on the dirty cement, covered in charcoal dust—women, children, and men, with horror in their eyes. They prayed loudly, begging God and the Virgin Mary for mercy. The blare of attacking bombers' engines and the whistles of falling bombs drowned out their voices. After such a whistle, when it seemed like the bombs would fall directly on our heads, there was a brief moment of silence and then a horrible explosion and shaking. Clouds of dust wafted in that would get stuck in your throat and make it difficult to breathe.

The Germans used special bombs, complete with a whistling sound devise. What they wanted was to terrorize the civilian population, to lead them into such a state of shock and terror that any kind of resistance would be pretty much impossible.

I was scared—sat in the corner curled up in a ball with my eyes closed when I heard that horrible whistle. In that instant, I noticed a young couple—they were in each other's arms—and when you could hear the beginnings of the whistle, they held each other's arms tightly and crouched down lower as the bombs got closer. I was struck by the senselessness of their behavior; they looked like caricatures, funny and wretched. I was overcome by some kind of hysterical desire to laugh, and all of a sudden, I stopped being so afraid. I don't know how long the bombing lasted—it seemed to last for ages—but I think it couldn't have been more than half an hour.

Finally, everything got quiet, and people started looking outside. We also went out. The street looked terrible. I saw a military carriage on large metal wheels, harnessed to two hefty and crazed horses. The figure of a headless soldier sat on the wagon, still holding the reins in his cramped palms. The uniform was spattered with blood. The corpses of people and horses lay in the street. The air carried the horrible smell of exploded bombs. Flames burst from the ruins of destroyed apartment buildings. We ran out quickly and started moving further along Grochowska Street toward the periphery. I don't know if we had even walked a hundred feet when we again heard the hum of engines behind us. Bullets from machine guns littered the streets. Our natural reaction was to shield ourselves behind the first door we saw. We were in danger of imminent death. But my mother started yelling, "No, not here. Let's go back to the other door where we were before—to the other door!"

To this day, I don't know why my father and I listened to her. It was almost insane, because we made the return trip under heavy fire. We finally made it through the door of the same apartment building and into the same basement. The whistles and explosions of bombs were affecting me a little bit less now. I felt numb, without feeling, with dry lips and a dry throat. Finally, there was silence. No one really wanted to move, but when nothing was happening for another moment, we carefully stepped out onto the street. I looked around. In the sea of flames, the apartment building we had been in stood out like a sharp spire amidst fire and ruin. We had hidden in the only undestroyed building. My mother saved all our lives. What had come over her? Somehow she knew and was adamant about which building to seek shelter.

〜

We went further along Grochowska Street. I was exhausted, hungry, and thirsty, yet it was imperative to reach the evacuation bus as quickly as possible. At this point neither I nor my cousin Bohdan were able to walk fast. My father had no choice but to leave us and look for the bus. He quickened his pace so as to join the rest of the group and continue the evacuation to the south. The goal was to reach Przemysl. I don't know how much time went by when the ominous sirens howled again in alarm and bombs fell on Warsaw. This time we didn't escape to look for protection; the bombardment was of other areas, though machine-gun fire littered the small square outside the church where we were waiting on the bench and an old chestnut tree. I remember its particular whistle and the rustle of falling leaves that had been hit by bullets. Nothing happened to us.

My father didn't come back for a long time. The sun was already leaning toward the west when I finally saw his silhouette approaching us quickly. His eyes were full of despair. The bus that was supposed to wait for us had simply driven off and left us alone in the blazing suburbs of Warsaw. There was no possibility of going back to my aunt's house in Bielany. The battle for Warsaw was to begin at any moment. The only thing left was to move south as fast as possible. We joined thousand of people on foot with our bags in the dismal walk of refugees. The traffic was awful—wagons, bicycles with bundles, crowds of frightened and angry people, the occasional passing of the military, crying of the lost children. There was also the suffocating smoke of burning houses and the despicable, difficult to describe smell of exploded bombs. The diagonally falling rays of the slowly setting sun enlightened this danteic scene. The contrast between the hell on the road and the pleasant sunset of an early Polish autumn was jarring; the misery, suffering and waste of human life set against the beauty and vastness of nature.

〜

Well into the evening somewhere on the periphery of the city, we stopped by a small, single-story apartment building with the hope that someone would let us rest there and quench our thirst. We walked into a cramped stairwell. I could hear a woman's voice on the floor saying something to her children. My mother knocked on the door. A middle-aged Jewish woman opened the door. She immediately understood our predicament, and she invited us inside. We fell down on an old plush couch, finding it hard to catch our breath. She got busy in the kitchen. After a few moments, she came back with hot tea and bread. We sat there for about an hour, but darkness was falling quickly, and we had to get away from Warsaw—the battle was supposed to begin at dawn.

I will never forget this woman and her warm heart. I don't know what happened to her and her family. I'm convinced that she died like thousands of others in the concentration camps in the Third Reich's mass exterminations. At this moment, when I write these words, I would like to honor her memory as well as the memory of all those who, in a sea of cruelty, lawlessness, and murder, were able to preserve some dignity and be good to others. And there were a lot of such unknown people in those days of national disaster.

When we again found ourselves on the road, it was completely dark. The houses appeared less and less frequently; you could see only the black strip of forest in the distance on both sides of the road behind the fields. It was there, near the forest, where the Polish army was preparing for battle. I saw armed cannons, soldiers wearing gas masks, and the flash of weapons, and I heard the hum of tanks and wagons. The mass of refugees moved at a snail's pace. We were walking on the side of the road, moving a little bit faster than the wagons and countless cars. They were intermingled with the mob of desperate refugees. It was clear to everyone that, at dawn, that road would turn into a battlefield and that death would be unavoidable. This gave the refugees strength and propelled them forward, despite fatigue, so as to get further away, further from danger.

A wagon rode by next to us; actually, it was more of a platform attached to two massive horses. The wagon was loaded with various kinds of food. It turned out that a butcher's whole family was on it; he had taken all his merchandise and escaped before the German attack. My father pleaded with him to let us ride along. Soon we found ourselves on the back of the wagon with some bundles that smelled of smoked bacon. Fatigue was slowly overwhelming me. The slow rolling of the wagon with its constant stops, the clamor of the crowd of refugees, the flashes of army weapons being prepared near the forest, the navy color of the serene September night—everything began to swim in my head and meld together. I fell asleep.

A sudden pull of the wagon woke me up. We were standing somewhere on the road to Garwolin in a new traffic jam. People were yelling to move forward, but it didn't have much of an effect. A tall wagon with ladder-like sides stood next to us that was filled to the hilt. Without thinking, and not having anything better to do, I found myself staring at the other wagon. At the sight of a stiff hand sticking out, I understood in a flash—the wagon was full of corpses! The corpses were already stiffened and twisted grotesquely; they had been hurriedly thrown onto the wagon and were on their way to a common burial.

So, on that memorable day I had my second face-to-face meeting with death, but fatigue and all that we had endured tempered my reactions of fear and shock. The awful reality became somewhat illusory, like a deep sleep, a nightmare. I would of course wake up in my own bed feeling safe, with everyone I loved around me. I would be looking at the familiar wallpaper on the walls of my room and at the rays of sunlight falling through the window.

I didn't realize that my entire life up until that moment, and with it the life of my nation, had been broken, stepped on, and irrevocably destroyed. I didn't realize that from that moment, I would be living another life, in an atmosphere of constant danger. That I would be living in the shadow of Satan.

At first light, barely visible in the east, we were already pretty far from Warsaw. At my father's suggestion, the butcher had turned into a side country road which was winding through the fields to a nearby village.

There was no question that the battle would begin at any moment, and that we had to find shelter. We stopped near a hut on the outskirts of a village. After a lengthy discussion with the owner and a hefty bribe, we got milk and bread. The butcher had cold cuts, so we could finally satisfy our hunger. Near by the hut had a basement for potatoes, which was really just a pit dug out of the earth, then covered with a lid and some branches. When the first shots of artillery were fired, and the ominous sound of Luftwaffe engines could be heard in the distance, we all sheltered ourselves in there. We spent the entire day there into the night. When dusk fell, the butcher harnessed the now-rested horses again, and we went further on our way. I don't remember how long we rode. There were considerably fewer people on the road. We saw explosions on the horizon; it was the battle near Ryki. In the early morning, we reached the Wieprz River, and our paths diverged, as the butcher decided to go to Brzesc. My father and mother, however, decided to go toward Lublin, where my uncle lived with his wife and son.

And so, just like that, we were alone again. The sun was already high in the sky, and it was warm and calm, complete with the hush of Polish autumn. We bathed in the Wieprz; the water was cool, but what a delight it was to wash off the dirt and feel refreshed. We were hungry. My father went by himself to a nearby hamlet and after a few hours came back with a small wagon with ladder-like sides attached to an old mare, along with a bucket of cream, a sack of apples, and a large loaf of bread. We ate these treats under the open sky. I thought at that moment that bread with clotted cream and then a tart apple were the greatest things people could ever have.

We went further on our way, though we didn't sit on the wagon as the old mare wouldn't have been able to pull it. And so we took turns; as the youngest one, I got to ride the most often on the wagon, though at times I had to walk next to the wagon holding on to a ladder. We made headway like this during the day, then the night, then again the day. The unfortunate old mare started limping, but we found a blacksmith who was able to give her a new horseshoe. Today, I can't even guess how much time that trip took. Walking next to the wagon, I was delirious with fatigue, often almost falling asleep. I read once that soldiers learned how to sleep as they marched. I know now from those experiences that it's true.

We reached Lublin in the middle of the night. The city looked terrible, and not a single light was on because of the possibility of bombardment. The streets were empty, and you could see missing chunks of buildings that had been destroyed by bombs in a lot of places. The most awful smell drifted over from these places—the sweetish odor of decomposing bodies mixed with the scent of exploded bombs. Completely exhausted, we reached Weteranow Street, just near the university, where my uncle lived. After banging on the door for quite some time, some strangers opened the door—they didn't want to let us in and were actually quite hostile. It turned out that my uncle and his family had escaped over the Bug River after the bombing of Lublin, leaving the house empty. The people who were inside had gotten in there illegally and decided to take it over.

We almost had to force our way in, and then all four of us—my mother, father, me, and my cousin Bohdan— collapsed onto the large bed. We were so tired that we didn't even drink or eat anything. The only thing my father did before that was to unhitch the horse and set her free; the wagon stayed on the street. In the morning, the wagon and the horse were both gone.

My uncle's apartment was located on the ground floor of a new building with a stairwell in the center and two apartments—one on the ground floor and one on the first floor. Just next door were identical apartments, built according to the same design, pleasantly located among trees and flowers, with a view of a very overgrown square that separated them from the university buildings. The owner of the building lived on the first floor. Once he had spoken with my father and understood what had happened, he immediately ordered the uninvited guests to leave. And so we were left alone in that apartment without any means of survival. The reserves that my uncle's family had prepared before escaping had already been completely pilfered. I don't remember now what we ate and drank; I only remember that the next day artillery fire started in Lublin. Zigzagged trenches were dug in the forest near the university, and above them a group of Polish soldiers set up field cannon and responded to the Germans' cannon fire. The residents of the nearby buildings sheltered themselves in that trench, because staying in the buildings wasn't safe.

I remember that trench well. While curled up on the very bottom; I saw some bones stuck out of the clay sides. My mother sat next to me. Along with us was a young mother with a small four-year-old girl, shielding the child with her body at every explosion. The girl had beautiful dark hair tied in a big ribbon, and was wearing a light dress and shoes. Lifting my head in between explosions, I glimpsed that she was sitting in a pile of human excrement that someone had left on the bottom of the trench. I will never forget that sight.

German artillery kept shooting at the Polish side. First, you could hear a distant explosion, then the whistle of firing artillery, and finally a deafening blast. The explosions occurred with a certain regularity; the German side obviously had only one cannon and you could predict when the next hit would be. The two sides fired more and more accurately at each other; the last explosions covered us in dirt. My parents decided that it would be safer to go behind the university walls. After the next explosion, we moved quickly and ran as fast as our legs would carry us to the university buildings. We got there in the nick of time; we heard the next explosion just as we crossed through the university building's front doors. On the way, I could see a broken Polish cannon and the bodies of several soldiers in the corner of my eye.

The artillery fire of that part of the city lasted until dawn. There were a lot of people like us in the university rooms. We sat on the floor against the wall, and the dust of plaster choked our lungs after nearby explosions shook the foundations of the entire complex. It was made up of four buildings that formed a square, with a courtyard in the center. Two gates, heavy with iron hinges and locks on two sides of the University complex.

The cannon fire ceased in the late hours of night. We spent the rest of the night on the floor, not knowing what was happening or what would come next. In the morning, at first light, I had to go to the bathroom, so my father went with me to find a place to go. We couldn't find anyplace close by, so we went outside to the yard to look for a bathroom on the other side. We were just about in the middle between the two buildings when the gate opened with an awful blast, probably blown out by a grenade, and I saw German soldiers running straight toward me and my father. I remember the helmets above the horrified eyes of an attacking soldier who didn't know what awaited him. A lot has been written about soldiers going into an attack. That day, on the university grounds in Lublin, I had the opportunity to observe them first-hand. The attacking soldier was full of terror and feverishly clutched his weapon, awaiting shots from all sides. He was also unspeakably dangerous, because his human reactions had been completely thwarted by survival instincts.

My father and I, a little tyke, raised our hands above our heads. The attacking soldiers positioned their machine guns in a flash, pointed them at the inner windows of the buildings, took my father with them, and didn't pay any more attention to me. My father only had time to yell out to me that I should immediately go back to my mother.

There was no battle, no defense. The rest of the Polish army left under the cover of darkness; the only people left were professors, university workers, and people from the surrounding homes. All these people were gathered together. The men were separated, while the women and children were allowed to go home.

There was no response to all the desperate pleas as to what would happen to the men—though people quickly figured out that they had been taken as hostages. The men were surrounded by machine guns and would have certainly been killed if any shots had been fired in the city.

We went home; I was sick with worry and shock. I knew very well what danger threatened my father. My mother tried hard to comfort and take care of us, listening all the while for any shots. My cousin sat silent in shock, especially as he had been torn from his home and away from his family. He was only thirteen years old.

The horrible waiting lasted over twenty-four hours. My father finally returned with thick, black stubble on his face, looking thin—he hadn't been given anything to eat.

5

Occupation

N OW, AFTER MANY years, the period of German Occupation presents itself to me as a series of images, which despite the passing of time, haven't become any less clear.

The gray days of the Occupation run together like a string of Holy Mary's, as similar to one another as the beads of a rosary, but certain situations, certain moments, were branded in my memory as if with a hot iron, never to be rubbed out, never to be forgotten.

Even at this moment, when I close my eyes, I see a crowd of dreary faces, poverty-stricken people, standing near Raclawicki Avenue in Lublin, looking dully at the approaching German divisions. First, countless trucks full of soldiers wearing helmets and gray-green uniforms went by, with bayonets positioned on their rifles, then motorcyclists with thick rubber coats and capes rode by in a long line. Another soldier holding a weapon in his hand sat in the sidecar of each motorcycle. I see tanks full of soldiers that were somehow different, with square edges and black crosses on the side, slowly rolling over the pavement of the street. I see other tanks, frightening and horrific, with long-necked cannons sticking out in the front.

They rode in as the victors, looking at the crowd with contempt.

This image fades away, and another appears. I see my father walking into the house with a sack of flour. We didn't have anything to eat; my father got that sack from the mill—the owner of the mill, a Jew named Slimak, gave it to him. He gave it just to be of some help. I never met him, but I know he was an older man with a large family, wife, kids, and nephews. In the years to come, his family was gradually exterminated, though he was kept alive until the very end; he knew how to run the mill well and understood its mechanics. Supposedly, he survived the war alone, abandoned, without any loved ones.

I remember the middle school behind the Krakowski Gate where my mother signed me up. I don't know why there were no openings in the fifth grade, which is where I belonged; you could only get into the sixth grade. Over the course of two days, my mother went over the lessons of fifth grade with me as best she could, tested me, and then decided that despite the things I had missed, I would manage.

I didn't really have any clothes. My father found some bright blue—almost the color of laundry detergent—thick cloth somewhere. My grandmother made me some pants and something like a windbreaker. I looked quite unique in this outfit, and, of course, the other kids made fun of me at school.

The class was strange. There were boys who were much older than me there, grown up and strong, with big broad shoulders and fists.

I realized quickly that I was in a completely different world from the one of St. Kazimir's private school that I had attended in Poznan. One of the boys with dark curly hair and dark eyes particularly scared me. I remember that his name was Wrobel. He was undoubtedly some kind of sexual deviant, and I didn't even know anything about sex yet! He did what he could to corrupt other children. He would stick pornographic photos in their faces. I remember when he slipped a photo of a penis just next to a woman's vagina in front of me. I didn't understand any of it;

I just had a vague feeling that it was improper and bad. But his efforts didn't stop at photographs. He liked exposing his genitalia; I remember the black hair of his pubic area and a large adult penis hanging down. I also remember that he would attack a smaller fat boy; he would put his hand down his underpants and feel his privates. These types of events scared me terribly. I waited until the time when he would assault me and decided to defend myself to the last minute. I didn't say anything to my mother or father—I just couldn't let myself be defeated. I did think about it desperately, though, and wondered how I could garner some kind of protection. Wrobel was only one of many in that class who had been exposed to the worst that life had to offer. There were also thieves and gangsters, the dregs of society from families living in the Stare Miasto area together with the Jewish working-class.

Full grown and older by at least five or six years, Piekutowski was the biggest and strongest boy, and he was also a thief and bandit. I remember his huge fists and slow, heavy step. He wasn't known for his intelligence; he went to school, because he had to, though he had completely different interests. I came to the sneaky conclusion that if I could win him over, he could be my bodyguard, and then I could somehow survive in that place. I told him that if he would protect me, I would do all his homework for him, every day, so that he wouldn't have any more problems at school. He agreed happily and from that moment on I was left alone. That Wrobel did try to get to me, but once he came in contact with Piekutowski's rugged fists, he decided it wasn't worth bothering me.

The son of the local psychiatrist, Dr. Kossowski, was also in our class; he was about two or three years older than me. He studied Greek mythology intensely, but not because of its historical uniqueness or importance. There were a lot of statues of naked bodies in the book—those of the women particularly excited him. He would spend hours drawing those naked bodies in various positions, while making all the appropriate comments. Once, when for some reason he wanted to insult me—which he often did with others, as he was very strong—he started saying something to me, beginning with the words, "You son of a bitch." I didn't understand a lot then, but I did know that he had just offended my mother. With all my strength, I slapped him across the face. My whole hand smacked his face, all the fingers included, and he became speechless with rage, then grabbed me by the chest, turned me upside down, and started bashing me as hard as he could. I heard something crack and felt a sharp pain—it turned out that he had broken my sternum. My mother tried to intervene by talking to his father, but it didn't do much good. He did leave me alone after that incident, and I walked around in pain for a good six months.

One day, my mother showed up during a lesson. My teacher looked confused and surprised. We walked out of the school quickly—I didn't know what was going on, but I came face-to-face with the awful reality of that day very soon.

At the beginning of the Occupation, the Christian population was given booklets of personal identification called Ausweiss; they were gray with an image of a German eagle on them which to us looked like a crow. These booklets, as far as I can remember, were written in both German and Polish. The Jewish population got similar ones, but theirs were yellow with the Star of David on them. During the first few weeks, directives from the German commander, threatening the death penalty for almost everything, appeared all over on the round announcement poles. There were anti-Jewish flyers affixed everywhere. One of them showed the caricature of a Jew who was feeding a rat into a meat grinder with an angry look on his face. Oddly enough, after many years, I saw this same flyer in the Holocaust Museum in Detroit. One glance at it took me back immediately to those days.

The Jewish population lived mostly in the area around Lubartowski Street, which was close to my school and the Krakowski Gate.

That memorable day, when I left school with my mother, we ended up in the middle of a commotion created by a cordon of Germans, both the police and the Gestapo. Huge canvas-covered trucks stood there. The Jewish people were being brutally

1941 IN THE MEADOWS OF LUBLIN.
MY GAUNT PHYSIQUE IS EVIDENCE OF
THE POVERTY FORCED UPON POLAND.

pushed into these trucks. I saw people being beaten across their backs with the butts of rifles, heard winces and cries, saw terrified children, and mothers with shock in their eyes. Here and there, human corpses lay in grotesque positions, so still, like dirty gray bundles that had been thrown all over the place.

We were horrified. We walked through that hell with the gray Ausweiss that my mother held tightly in her hand. One scene I will never forget. It wasn't the death and brutality, or even the pain and suffering that made the most horrifying impression on me. I was horrified most by a different scene, one that occurred when we were already out of the tumult. A few German soldiers were chasing a dozen or so Jewish girls. They were laughing and joking. The girls, with dark horror in their eyes, wore short dresses and skirts and tried hard to warm up to the soldiers, tried hard to be sexy. That human degradation, that desperate fight for survival, which forced them to deny all their human feelings and dignity, was the most horrifying sight to me.

A lot is said and written about the suffering of the Jewish population in the dark days of the German Occupation. It is good that it is written, for it is written truthfully—I myself was a witness to it. It is odd, however, that not many people know about the discrimination against the Christian population, and that their losses were equal to those of the Jewish population.

During the first months of the Occupation, when the formal authority of Lublin was still in the hands of an army commander, the Gestapo arrived. They surrounded the entire area near Raclawicki Avenue and the university called Wienawa, and then proceeded to divide families into separate groups of women, men, and children. The horrified people didn't know what was going on, but they knew that they might never see their loved ones again. We were living not too far from Wienawa then, and rumors were spreading that our area could be next. My mother sewed something like a backpack out of a sack and stuffed it with my warmest clothes and some bread. We waited for long hours in terror. I have to stress that this terrorist action organized by Gestapo was against the Christian and not Jewish population. A Wehrmacht commander stopped this action, threatening the chief of Gestapo with a gun.

Over the next few years, murder and terror among non-Jewish populations grew more and more. Each day, yellow lists hung on the announcement poles bearing the names of people who, the previous day, had been "sentenced to death" and executed. The lists were very long, with tens and sometimes even hundreds of names. Horrified women stood in front of them, and every once in a while, one of them would cry out in despair.

We spent the first months of the Occupation together with my uncle's family in his home at Weteranow Street. It was near the university, and the only thing separating us from it was a small forest—a park that was called the "monkey grove" for whatever reason. There were quite a few of us in this house—my parents and grandmother, Uncle Wladyslaw and his wife Natalia, their young son Andrzej, a four-year-old angel with light-blonde curls and blue eyes. And there was also his nanny, Karolina, who soon returned to her family in the country.

But, our living together didn't last long. A Gestapo official showed up one day and ordered us to leave the house immediately—it had been designated living quarters for the officers of the Gestapo.

The furniture was divided as best it could be. My father found a nearby third-floor apartment on Piechoty Street. My uncle's family moved into a similar small apartment all the way over on Gliniana Street. From our new apartment you could see vast meadows, where cows were still at pasture. To the left, the long, gray stone wall of the Lipowa cemetery dragged on and on, above which the tops of old trees were gently moving in the wind. If you stuck your head out the window and looked to the right, you could see the yards of nearby homes that stood in a row by Weteranow Street.

Soon thereafter, new tenants moved into the abandoned apartment houses; they were noisy, wearing their uniforms unbuttoned at the neck and drinking beer with women in the yards. There were also children there, and once in a while, you could hear a cry when a father punished his offspring by hitting him on the face.

Looking at these women, children, and laughing men, who were basking in the warm sun, it was hard to imagine that they were, well, murderers and executioners. From morning until night, they were busy torturing and murdering people. After a long day's work, they came home for some well-deserved rest, laughing and being loud. No one even thought of going near those homes.

There were many sites of execution, such as the castle, in which thousands of people died; the Gestapo building, gray and large on Chopin Street, inspiring terror in the heart of every Pole; and finally, the awful Majdanek camp, where in the black smoke of the common crematorium, Christians and Jews died in agony.

Though I was only about twelve years old, I knew very well what was going on. I heard horrible tales of torture—drowning in tubs so as to get information, being tied up under the elbows and knees and then hung on a stick so as to make it easier to beat the genital area, breaking bones, drilling teeth and putting sugar underneath special fillings to cause long, unendurable pain.

I looked in horror at the gray, cold walls of the Gestapo building that stood ominously silent. Then I looked in fear past the walls of apartment buildings to the massive castle on the hill behind the city which was converted by Germans into a horrible torture and extermination facility.

From those days, one event particularly sticks out in my mind and heart. It was already late afternoon, and the Gestapo officials had come home after a day's "work." And there, in front of their houses on Weteranow Street, an older woman showed up crazy with despair, crying out, "You murderers, why did you kill my child, why? May God curse you, murderers!"

The yelling didn't last long. From one of the houses, two young, twenty-something Gestapo officials came out; they went up to her laughing, saying something insulting. Not paying any attention to her cries, one of them suddenly pushed her strongly. She fell. And then calmly, not in any hurry, they began to kick her with their shiny boots. An awful cry filled the air that slowly turned into a wail and then began to quiet down.

They made sure the woman was dead, and then returned to their homes, laughing and talking. I heard that woman's cries and wails, and other people saw the whole thing and told us about it.

Shortly after Lublin was captured, the commander of the city gave strict orders that everyone was to go back to work. My uncle was a geodesy engineer like my father; both were schooled at the Warsaw Institute of Technology. Before the war, he had taken the position of director of planning and surveying of the city of Lublin. My uncle went back to his office, where a few other engineers worked under his supervision. I remember all of them; they were young and full of energy—Janowski, who was thin and small, Sadownik, who was stocky with a white, round face, and Plominski, who was taller than everyone and had dark hair and black eyes. I can see them all right now, despite the many years that have passed since those days.

It soon became clear that pursuing higher education wasn't possible. During the first months of the Occupation, many university professors and people of science and culture were killed. My father was in terrible danger because as the director of agricultural surveys of the province of Poznan, he had been instrumental in the reincorporation of land recovered by Poland from Germany after World War One. Of course, if that had been found out, he would have been killed immediately. The fact that we were in Lublin and away from Poznan saved my father to a certain extent. He understood his predicament very well and didn't admit to having a diploma or even having lived in Poznan. He was hired as an assistant to the accountant of the *Ehenerungsamt*, the division of food supplies that was created by a German occupier. My father knew German pretty well, and that helped him. He made a pittance there, but we did somehow survive that horrible period of our lives, living mostly off the produce from our garden.

The first months of the Occupation, the defeat of those September days, the deceitful attack of Soviet Russia on Poland—all this came as a shock. The entire life of a free country that had been lifting itself from terrible years of crisis was eliminated. Nothing remained. The name of the country was erased from the map of Europe, and part of Poland was incorporated into the Third Reich. The rest became a parody of a country in the form of the *Generalna Gubernia* (German Protectorate). The whole eastern part of Poland was left in the murdering hands of Soviet imperialists.

As if that weren't enough, the news that reached us from the rest of the world became more and more horrifying. We realized we were abandoned by the French and English. A "strange war," was conducted when more than one hundred French and English divisions did nothing, opposed by only four German divisions. They waited so that the Third Reich could dismember Poland. They hoped that would enable them to make a peace treaty with the Reich. However the German tank divisions easily went around the Maginot line and seized Belgium, Holland, and then France itself. Greece fell, Romania was in German hands. Hungary was working with the Reich going into battle together.

Only England defended itself. From secret communications, we knew that Germany had lost the "battle over England." The news also reached us that Polish pilots were fighting against the Germans on foreign territory. Increasingly darker clouds hung over Poland, and increasingly more hopelessness, despair, and doubt crept into our souls.

And yet, from the first days of the Occupation, despite increasing terror, a quiet, stubborn resistance awoke and spread, that was later paid for in blood and suffering. The desire to fight, if not even for freedom but for human dignity, for the soul of the nation, became a driving force that made endurance easier.

Resistance took on various forms. It was not unified and was poorly organized, but it existed, grew stronger, and didn't fall. One of its forms was secret schooling. The German Reich had decided to reform Poles into slaves with no wills of their own who would instead serve this "higher" race of men. In the first phase of murdering university professors and killing the creators of the intelligentsia, they tried to destroy the intellectual leaders of the nation. Priests also belonged to this class, for the Catholic Church had close ties to the national freedom movement and was an obstacle to the mad plans of the Nazis.

I was a boy who was growing up quickly in an environment of incredible danger. I understood what was happening and saw my parents' despair at the step-by-step German victories on European fronts. In our house, the spirit of resistance, of not surrendering, never disappeared.

In the education of this new class of slaves, it was forbidden to teach history, Polish literature, and humanities, because these subjects could open your eyes to the world and possibly salvage national traditions and identity.

The punishment for learning such things was a painful death. Not only secret teachers, but also parents and children were punished. Still, such secret education spread very quickly. It was led

by one of the divisions of the Home Army, an underground freedom organization called the *Szare Szeregi—*Gray Formation.

I remember my first textbooks of Polish history, Polish language, and Latin, and I remember the teachers who would come
over on the sly and leave just as stealthily after the lesson. I don't
know their names, but I remember their faces. The first one was a
forty-year-old, slightly balding, dark-haired man in horn-rimmed
glasses. One day, he disappeared, and then another showed up,
a thin, young fellow. I suspect that he was a student in pre-war
Poland. But this one also soon disappeared; I have no idea if he
escaped or was killed.

Like my father, a lot of high school teachers who understood
that they were in danger didn't admit to their occupations, and
they worked instead as the most subservient clerks in various
administrative organizations created by the German occupier,
just so as to survive and see better days, in which everyone still
believed, despite all the horror and hopelessness.

Ms. Kissewetter, a classical scholar and high school teacher,
started working in the same *Ehenerungsamt* (food distribution
office) where my father was an accountant's assistant. I suspect
that her name helped her stay afloat. She was petite, already quite
old, ugly, and didn't draw any attention to herself. She lived with
her mother, who was already over eighty years old, in a tiny apartment somewhere near Okopowa Street and Chopin Street. The
room was cluttered with knickknacks and books. The rarely aired-
out apartment had a particular smell that you can experience
today in old libraries. There were a lot of books—some of them
dated back to the nineteenth century. Was there anything she
didn't have? Historical tomes, Polish literature classics, composition notebooks in Polish, Latin textbooks, Ovid's and Horace's
poetry—all of the prohibited knowledge! I don't remember when
my father got to talk everything over with Ms. Kissewetter—she
was an old Ms.—but soon, I secretly began frequenting her apartment for regular lessons.

So many years have passed since those days, when I was pouring over Cicero's words against Catiline, when I learned the structure of a sonnet, the composition of prose, when I became familiar with the secrets and riches of our original past—and yet, at this moment I can see that little room, and that good, ugly, wrinkled face of Ms. Kissewetter, giving me tons of reading to do so that I would have to study for hours. It wasn't exactly a safe thing to be doing. I crept stealthily through the streets with my books, for which I could have been killed, hidden under my jacket.

The first winter of the Occupation came; it was bitter cold and snowy. From the window of our room, I could see white caps on the brick wall of the cemetery, and the meadows on which cows had been grazing during the summer were covered with a thick white blanket of snow.

In the summer of 1939, when most of the Polish population hadn't even considered the possible danger of an imminent German attack, my grandmother had predicted it. She had sent a huge basket full of our winter clothes from Poznan to my uncle's house in Lublin. I don't know how we would have survived that first winter of the Occupation without those clothes.

I finished the sixth and seventh grades of middle school. The only way to continue my education was to go to one of the trade schools that trained masters—even an average education was forbidden. My parents signed me up at the private Chemische Schule that was run by a Ukrainian cooperating with the Germans. This school was located in Adolf Hitler Square—formerly Freedom Square—in an old worn-down apartment building. Our school was on the second floor, a school of carpentry was on the third floor.

There weren't many classrooms, and the few there were were crowded. There were wooden floors—the strong smell of disinfecting solution still makes my nose itch. It was a strange school. They were supposed to teach us trade, but the teachers were mostly Lublin university professors and high school teachers.

The students were also an original and varied group. There were sons of the Lublin intelligentsia, boys from nearby villages—

we all shared a quiet, unspoken, but well-understood hatred of the German occupiers.

The teaching in that school also happened in such a way that could not have been foreseen by the occupying authorities. The physics course was very advanced—when I got into university after the war, I didn't need to study much. And so were math and chemistry. We didn't have Polish language lessons, only a course in "Polish correspondence." Despite this, our teacher, under the guise of teaching proper letter-writing techniques, drove Polish grammar and syntax into our heads.

The strangest thing had to be our German language course. We were taught by none other than one of the Polish submarine captains! We came to know everything about his past; he didn't hide anything, because he trusted us completely. Those lessons were pretty sad. They began with the reading of a textbook, and then after fifteen minutes our "teacher" completely changed the subject to what the Polish fleet was like before the war, how Polish submarines were still fighting on the high seas

He also taught us how to defend ourselves, how to fight. I have no idea what happened to him, if he even survived the Occupation, but I know that I gained a rather poor knowledge of German from his lessons—we hated that language—and in its place, got a hefty dose of patriotism.

There were two boys in my class from nearby Lublin villages. I remember their last names but not first. I know that one of them—tall as a young oak tree with a freckled face—was Tkaczyk, and the other—somewhat shorter but stocky and strong—was Golianek. They sat in the last school desk. The lessons were difficult for them, and they got mostly Cs. Golianek was a little brighter, but Tkaczyk had a lot of trouble. When he was asked to respond in German, he would lift himself heavily from his seat and say, "Ich mich nicht." That really can't even be translated. I remember their heavy steps, caused mostly by big, hefty boots that were always somehow crusted with Lublin yellow clay. They would often leave yellow marks on the floor that soaked up the black disinfecting solution.

Near the end of the week, they didn't show up for class. It was Sunday. My parents and I went for a long walk. We walked alongside the cemetery on Lipowa Street. The sun was shining on the old trees, and for a moment, you could forget about the nightmare of the Occupation and be happy about the warm spring day. We went past the city, passed by the last houses, and walked into a long canyon with light, shining walls that were covered here and there with clumps of grass. Higher, above the canyon, wavy meadows and fields spread far and wide. I looked all around, happy about the sunshine, the singing larks, and the smell of the green fields and earth. And then, I saw heavy boots that were dirtied with clay sticking soles-up on the slope. I looked quickly—yes, I recognized the boots—and was filled with horror. Two bodies lay there, dead and still—Tkaczyk and Golianek. They were both killed with a single shot to the back of the head. Later, it was said in school that they had been connected to the national underground army, and ended up being murdered by the Germans. Similar executions had been carried out all over in surrounding villages. I will never forget that day.

I already mentioned the cemetery near Lipowa Street—old, with large old trees, almost always drowning in dreary shadows, because the sun had a hard time getting through the large treetops. I liked to go there. It was quiet and calm—there were old tombs by the wall dating back to the beginning of the nineteenth century, if not the eighteenth century, tombs that had already been forgotten, often overgrown with weeds, with crooked crosses and headstones. You could feel deceptively safe in this place; it was a break from everyday reality—and then . . .

The Germans would often rush Jewish prisoners dressed in prison uniforms to all kinds of roadwork. These people looked awful, peering out dismally, with very thin bodies. They were usually guarded by a few plump soldiers with weapons in their hands.

One day, during the summer, I was looking out at the meadow and cemetery wall through the window of our apartment. Suddenly, I heard quick shots, a lot of footsteps, and wails behind the cemetery wall. Several people in prison uniforms had tried to escape, and the Germans were chasing them and shooting. Soon, the runaways fell in deathly stillness. The large group of Jewish prisoners had escaped to the cemetery, and the guards caught them and killed them on the spot. This was an unusual event, as the Jewish prisoners rarely geared up to escape; many treated their fates as a punishment for the sins of the Jewish people, those committed and not committed, and endured their sufferings and deaths in the silence of utter despair. It seemed strange that only a few soldiers could chase down a whole crowd of these prisoners; it was strange that the prisoners didn't try to throw themselves on the Germans so as to at least die fighting.

In the spring of 1941, the meadow by our apartment was infested with the German army. There were several thousand regular army men—the infantry. They trained, marched in perfect rows, separated, and then united again, creating a mighty wave of gray-green uniforms and characteristic helmets. They also trained in frontline attack, digging in, and storming forward. After a month of these preparations, which for us, the boys of the closest yards, had become an attraction of sorts, a group of German generals and an orchestra showed up, and the soldiers lined up in a long row and marched out. It was clear to everyone that this was a unit preparing for battle, but no one knew who their opponent would be. Throughout all of Europe, there were flags with swastikas, brown, black, and green uniforms ruled, and entire nations were stepped on, degraded, and ruined everywhere, treated like scum serving only to carry the burden of building a worldwide Nazi empire.

In June of 1941, the whistle of monotonous engine noise woke me up early. This noise spread everywhere, from the east to the west. My family and I, like most of the other residents of the apartment buildings, ran out to see what was happening. In the light, powder-blue sky, I glimpsed squadrons of bombers, flying east. One of the squadrons flew right over our heads; it was easy to see the bombs attached under the wings. There seemed to be an endless line of them from west to east.

Fierce joy washed over us. People started yelling and crying—

everyone knew that war had begun between the two greatest enemies of the Polish nation, Nazi Germany and Soviet Russia. This
flame of hope that had been so difficult to maintain in the days
of the Occupation, burst and burned with the thought that if the
criminals from the west and east would kill each other, Poland
and all of us might regain freedom.

When the news started reaching us of the lightning-fast forward advances of the German army in the depths of Russia, when
the Belorussian and Ukrainian armies had surrendered, and when
the tabloids of the Occupation starting spreading news of German
triumph, we didn't worry. We were sure that the army could get
very far, but that it would be much more difficult for them to leave
from the heart of Russia.

One winter day, confident soldiers appeared in Lublin dressed
in uniforms lined with fur. They were young and full grown; they
exposed their bare chests to the cold of winter. These were two
select divisions of the SS, the Hermann Goring Division and the
SS Viking Division. They were going to the Russian front to help
strengthen the still advancing German army. Sure of themselves
and laughing, they were certain that victory was theirs. At the end
of that winter, I saw them again—or rather, their corpses, lying on
straw in wagons. They had frostbitten hands, feet, faces, and bel-
lies. Supposedly, the Russians had maintained constant machine-
gun fire for forty-eight hours just above ground-level so that no
one could stand up. The crackling Russian frost did the rest.

The winters were freezing, especially from 1941 to 1942. The
German offense got stuck out in the ice-cold Russian steppe. At
the same time, terror grew more intense. Hundreds and thousands died in Gestapo prisons and in the Lublin Castle which had
been converted to a prison. A concentration camp was also built
in Majdanek. Transport after transport of prisoners went to the
death camps never to return. Black smoke from the crematorium
hung over the city day and night. Yellow lists—the lists of those
murdered—were changed almost daily, and the number of vic-
tims kept increasing.

Life was strange in those years. The goal of each day was endurance, survival, just to hold on a little longer, to arrive at that one desired day of freedom, in whose coming we all believed—adults, teenagers, and children alike. Awful information reached us from Majdanek, but the yellow lists of death inspired more hatred toward the occupier than fear. Everyone knew that, as soon as they set foot out the door, they might not return. Life went on every day at a rather normal rate—it is undoubtedly and obviously true that if you are alive, you must somehow live. Apart from the everyday fight for bread, for a piece of lard or butter, apart from working on the garden, which soon became the main means of supplying food, apart from all of this, there was some "normal" life—families visited each other, celebrated holidays together, and went to church, where they listened to notes of organ music and Polish religious songs.

We would most often go to the Wizytki church. At the time, there was a beautifully organized choir that was able to strengthen more than one falling heart; it refreshed and faithfully reaffirmed that, as a nation, despite the horrible losses, we would endure. Even today, I feel warm in my heart when I remember the well-lit altar, the ringing of the bells, and the Polish religious songs—those for Lent, full of sadness and regret, and those for Christmas, beautiful Polish carols, and those in honor of the Virgin Mary in May, when the sun's rays already warmed backs that had been numbed by winter.

I was growing up fast—the voice that once belonged to the soprano section started to crack, and eventually, I found myself among the baritones with a tendency for bass. My father finally took me to an ENT specialist, who calmly concluded that nothing was wrong with me and that I was going through the normal phase of puberty. In that time, the subject of sex was something unspeakably difficult for me. The Private Chemiche Schule that I attended was a coeducational school. Girls who were already mature went there, and undoubtedly many of them had a lot of sexual experience. Most of the boys were at the same level. Attraction to the opposite sex made me blush without much reason, and almost everything aroused me, whether the sight of a bent knee under a skirt, hair cascading down a back, glances, movements, or anything that was in any way feminine.

I didn't have the nerve to develop close relationships with the girls in my class. I just didn't fit in with them, even though the sexual attraction was clouding my head and was in some ways a nightmare.

As if that weren't enough, my two front teeth and left canine tooth didn't come in; they were stuck in the jaw. I had a huge gap in my mouth that looked horrible and made me even shyer. Because I also had a streak of gray hair, which showed up in my family from generation to generation, I was ironically dubbed "grandpa." The one good thing was that I was learning a lot; I put all my energy into studying in school and during my secret lessons with Ms. Kissewetter.

When I was about fourteen years old, my parents took me to a woman, an oral surgeon, so as to remove those unfortunate teeth and insert a bridge.

The operation, which consisted of cutting open the gums and removing the teeth from the jaw, was a big ordeal for me, though it wasn't because of any pain or fear. The doctor was a pretty blonde with a rather large bust and blue eyes, and the skin around her eyes shone from Vaseline (it was supposed to help prevent wrinkles). When she positioned me in the chair and then leaned over me, her bust lay on my chest, and I could feel her warmth on me. Her lips were right there, so close. I looked in those blue eyes, and I think I had my first sexual experience of contact with a woman's body right there, despite the whole paradox of the situation! That hour of surgery went by very quickly. When I recovered, the dental technician put in a bridge. I already looked a lot better, with a shiny silver tooth in the front, and I felt quite a bit better.

Around the same time, one chilly winter day during a lesson, we heard the noise of truck engines that fell silent in front of the school. Our teacher went pale, and silence fell. After a moment, we heard heavy steps on the creaky old apartment building stairs. Everyone could think of only one thing. Were they coming for us, or were they going higher up, to the carpentry school? In the silence, we heard footsteps pass by our classroom door and go upstairs, to the third floor. Soon we heard an awful tumult, yells and wails, then the sound of shoes on the stairs, German curses, and wails of those who had been beaten. Then, silence fell once again, an awful silence. With a trembling hand, the teacher picked up a book, but he couldn't lead the lesson. And we, too, sat in silence, horrified and stunned. Later there were rumors that some of the young boys in that school were part of the Home Army—no one saw them again.

In the year 1942, we got orders to leave our apartment on Piechoty Street. The building was to be occupied by the Gestapo. To "convince" us to leave quickly, the Gestapo organized inspections of all the apartments, beginning on the ground floor and working all the way up to the third and top floor. Our apartment was on the second floor, as were the books from my secret schooling of Polish history and literature—all of which warranted execution. The Gestapo agents were close, very close; we heard their approaching footsteps on the stairs. Literally, at the last minute, my mother threw the books into a box filled with Christmas ornaments that was on top of the closet. Two Gestapo agents came into the apartment. They searched every corner, threw our things around, and tore apart the beds. The younger Gestapo agent went into the kitchen where the closet stood. He looked at the box that contained the ornaments and forbidden books.

"*Was ist das?*"

My mother calmly replied, "*Weinachten dekorationen— mochten Sie ihr sehen?*"

"*Nein,*" fell the hard reply.

They left, slamming the door behind them, and went to the apartment to the left in which the Goreckas lived. I think he was a bank worker, and she was a doctor. After a moment, we heard the awful horrifying cry of a person being beaten mercilessly. A few minutes later, the Gestapo agents dragged him out, bloodied and half-conscious, and took him with them. Mrs. Gorecka stood in the doorway with horror in her eyes. He never returned, and Dr. Gorecka received the news shortly after that he had died. A few months later, she died of typhoid that she had contracted from the sick.

In this stage of the Occupation, the Jewish population of the Lubartowski region had been removed long ago; everyone died at the Majdanek camp. We were told to look for an apartment in those abandoned old apartment buildings. I remember empty dens with doors and often windows that had been beaten out and the remains of the property of some poor working class family who had previously lived there scattered here and there. Millionaires didn't live on Lubartowski Street. The poor lived there, small artisans and peddlers—these are the people who were sent off to die. Some of the rich saved themselves by bribing the Gestapo and fleeing to Sweden.

I can not fail to write at least a few words about the tragedy of the Jews in the time of German Occupation, which is called the Holocaust today. It has been commercialized in thousands of books, publications, and films that alter the truth and often border on libel.

It is an unquestionable truth that the Jewish population was sentenced to complete annihilation. The "final solution" to the Jewish problem was the insane politics of "cleansing the race" by Nazi deviants. It is also true that part of the pre-war Polish police, known as the navy police (because of navy uniforms), decided to cooperate with the occupier and capture Jews that were in hiding. It is also true that there was a Jewish committee in Lublin, created by the Germans, which cooperated with them. It is true that there was a Jewish police force armed with clubs that guarded Jewish prisoners and used those clubs to beat them. It is also true that for housing a Jew, a whole Polish family was murdered, and many, despite the awful danger, were saved that way.

More than half a century has passed since those days, and not many are left who were eyewitnesses; even they will soon pass into the world of shadows. The truth about the crimes committed against the Jewish population should never be forgotten, and it is right that means of remembering have been created in the form of museums and that materials have been collected to showcase the entirety of the crimes committed.

But something that was somehow strangely overlooked was the planned and well-organized genocide of the Polish Christian population. In the first phase, university professors, and others of the intelligentsia who really meant something in pre-war Poland, were murdered. But the extermination didn't stop with the intelligentsia. I remember a horrifying massacre that was organized in Zamojski—a train, packed tightly with children, was taken off the track so that the children would freeze to death. I remember entire groups of people being burned who were suspected to be cooperating with the National Army, as well as the mass transport of country people who sold their food in the city—which kept the city alive—to their deaths in the Majdanek camp. I remember this all very well.

I also remember Mr. Uszacki's visit to our house with his wife and daughter; he had been the chairman of the Department of Agriculture in Brzesc before the war. He was of Ukrainian descent, so he thought that he might be able to get a position in the Hitler administration that met with his level of education. How wrong he was! Just a few weeks after reporting himself to the German authorities, he ended up in Majdanek. He survived there only a few months, dying in terrible suffering. That's how it was.

One day, when we were still living near Piechoty Street, there was a knock at the door. I opened it and was shocked. Before me stood a man—or rather the ruins of a man—with a gray, horribly emaciated face and eyes that seemed almost crazy, dressed in dirty rags. He asked to see my father and said that he had just been released from Majdanek. I didn't know who he was, though he supposedly came from the same area of Poland that my father did. I also didn't know why he ended up in Majdanek or why he was released. Such rare cases of release from Majdanek sometimes happened when the prisoners were food merchants. We didn't know anything about this person except that he was close to death. He was loused up and stank unbelievably. My mother and grandmother undressed him, burned the rags in which he had shown up, then put him in the tub and scrubbed him for a long time. He put on something from my father's small wardrobe. He ate very greedily, silent almost the entire time, and said nothing about his experiences. A sugar bowl stood on the table—sugar was considered a luxury then. Thinking that no one could see him, he took some sugar with a trembling hand, spilled it, and put it in his mouth. He wasn't our guest for long. As it was dangerous to house him, my father arranged a quiet move to where he had relatives.

Eventually, my father found an apartment in an old apartment building on Okopowa Street, not far from Chopin Street. The apartment didn't have any amenities except for running water. The walls were very thin and the winter cold penetrated horribly. There were two rooms and a kitchen. The windows overlooked a dirty yard and outhouses, from which a disgusting smell arose. The sun never shone in there, because the windows faced north, and all the light was blocked by the apartment building in the front. Sometimes, you could catch the sun's rays moving on the walls, reflected off the windows that faced us. It was unbelievably cold. My father found an iron stove somewhere, well known then as a "goat." It had burners on top so you could cook on it. He put it in the middle of the apartment and attached a long metallic pipe that ran through the whole room into the chimney. Even at this very moment, I can hear the clinking of that pipe heating up when my mother turned on the oven in the morning and the overwhelming cold of the night was replaced by warmth.

In the winter of 1943 to 1944, just before Christmas, my parents received the news that on a certain day they were supposed to report to the Gestapo. Similar news went to a doctor we knew, as well as a lawyer, my uncle, and his friends. The one thing they had in common was that they all had higher education. Before leaving the house, my mother and father said goodbye to me, not knowing if they would ever come back. Yet, they came back rather quickly. The young Gestapo agent had ordered them to return the

"Ausweiss" that they had at that time, looked at their faces and then at some document in front of him, and then gave back a different booklet, also an "Ausweiss," with the only difference being that it was no longer gray but blue. No one knew the reason for the change or what it meant. We didn't have to wait long to find out. In May, half of the people who had received such a booklet were dead, killed in the prisons of the Gestapo. It became clear to everyone that a blue "Ausweiss" was simply a death sentence.

⁂

One Sunday morning, my uncle Wladek showed up unexpectedly at our apartment. His face looked gray, and his eyes were full of terror. I had never before and would never later see him in such a state. We soon learned what had happened. He had been sent to Warsaw by his German employer with appropriate documents with him that had been confirmed by the German police. In Deblin, he was taken from the train, as were others by the German gendarmes. They were searched for food, their documents were checked, and those "guilty of smuggling" were set aside. The train left, and the group of people was left on the platform not knowing what to do. Day was slowly turning into night. The only option was to return to Lublin, but the train arrived after the police curfew, after which no Pole was supposed to go anywhere. Most of the people got on the train and arrived at the station in Lublin after the police curfew. The Gestapo was waiting there for them. Everyone, including my uncle, was loaded into a canvas-covered truck and taken to the Lublin Castle, one of the three main prisons. There, they were rushed like a herd into a large room, where they were told to form lines in front of desks at which young Gestapo agents sat.

Each "delinquent" had to give his personal information, address and present personal identification. The Gestapo agent recorded everything on the appropriate form, and then a guard led the unfortunate person into the prison.

My uncle was standing in front of the desk as the Gestapo agent started filling out a form. All of a sudden, he heard in German, "What are you doing here?"

He lifted his head and saw a Gestapo agent who had been at his office of urban surveys of the city several months ago, ordering maps of land that could be used by the Gestapo to ride horses. He recognized my uncle, went up to the desk, pulled the partially filled-out form from the typewriter without saying a word, nodded his head at a seated Gestapo agent, and took my uncle out of the room. They went down a long corridor. Without a word, the Gestapo agent opened the door and said to go inside. The key screeched in the castle, and silence fell. There were a lot of people in the room, a nun, a fat individual, and still others. None of them had any idea why they were separated from the others and locked up, and that's how they spent the rest of the night, not knowing what fate awaited them at dawn. Around eight o'clock, a Gestapo agent showed up and led them almost to the front door before saying, "And now, go home, and quickly!"

Those that had not been freed soon appeared on yellow lists. They never went home again.

In the winter, when we were living on Okopowa Street, I got sick with infectious hepatitis. I was very sick, felt terribly weak, and my skin and the whites of my eyes were almost brown in color. The illness lasted a long time; after a few weeks, I could move around a little bit, but the great weakening lasted a good few months. In those days, infectious hepatitis was spreading like wildfire in Lublin. A lot of children died of that horrible disease, often spread through infected milk. Hygiene was very poor. Typhoid and typhoid fever were also spreading like a fire. I remember signs stuck on doors by the German Sanitation Service that read, "Seuchen Gefahr"—danger of infection. Those signs were supposed to warn Germans so as not to walk into a contaminated area.

Soon after, the Polish Underground printed many of those signs and used them to create some kind of protection for places hous-

ing the Home Army, places where people were hiding, as well as places where you could get radio broadcasts that played the BBC programs, where weapons were kept, and where communications were printed that were passed on from one hand to another.

I already mentioned that after receiving the blue "Ausweiss," half of those with that document were dead in less than six months. Engineers Ptaszynski, Sadownik, and Janowski were arrested, and after several days we got news of their deaths. Engineer Plominski was also arrested. Though he had been tortured and had broken bones, his wife got him out of the Gestapo by paying a bribe. People suspected that they had been "squealing," though these were only rumors that weren't supported by any facts. Still, the very notion of being released from the Gestapo prison was enough to raise suspicions that the prisoner was cooperating with the enemy.

One of those days a German engineer showed up in the *Ehenerungsamt* where my father worked. This man worked in the *Organization Todt*, which was a technical paramilitary organization that took care of building bridges, preparing land for army bases, building bunkers, etc. This engineer, whose name was Jakob, appeared to be a nice person. He supplied food to groups of workers whom he supervised. He came over many times and, strangely enough, became friends with my father. He told stories about secret meetings of the German administration and about frightening new directives that were to be incorporated into life. But these visits didn't last long. One day, he disappeared, and no one ever saw him again. We didn't even utter his name again.

After the deaths of my uncle's colleagues, it became clear that his days were also numbered. And so he moved his family to live with my aunt Jania near Warsaw. With his family settled he ran away, roving from one village to another. This was in May.

My parents decided it was necessary for me to stop my schooling. My mother and I left for my aunt's house, and my father stayed in Lublin for a few more weeks.

My uncle ran away just in time; a few days later, the Gestapo showed up at his apartment on Gliniana Street. They surrounded the building and asked for him. The thoughtful neighbor, the wife of a pre-war major, told the Gestapo that if engineer Mikulski (my uncle's last name) wasn't home, he was probably at the Subczynski house—with my parents.

My father was alone. In the middle of the night, he heard a banging on the door—he opened the door half-awake, and Gestapo agents came into the apartment. One of them, who led the group, fell into a chair and started interrogating my father. They had a Jew with them who served as an interpreter, but my father figured out that it was better to reply to the questions himself. After a brief period of watching him, the German paused for a moment, hitting his shiny boot with a crop, after which he waved his hand and said, "Well, we still have time." My father was left alone, not believing his good luck, as he had been preparing himself for death.

He went to work in the morning not knowing what to do, only hoping that it would draw any attention away from my mother's and my departure. In school, he arranged for me to get my diploma finishing my education with the condition that all my grades were lowered. I still have that sheet of paper with me in the United States. I look at it with a strange feeling, as the past resurfaces, as does that fight for survival.

After about a week, while he was at work at the office, my father suddenly got a call from a German telephone operator—I remember that her name was Foemers—with the following directions, "Leave immediately through the back door!"

My father understood. He got up from his desk calmly and slowly went out. The Gestapo was already at the main entrance. He wandered through the streets to the winding road that led to Warsaw. In his desk, he had hidden several bottles of vodka, specially prepared for an occasion like this one. In exchange for that vodka, he got himself on a truck with the German army retreating to the west, and that's how he escaped.

The eastern front was quickly moving west, the German administration was more and more chaotic, even the Gestapo was losing a good deal of its unity, and escaping to another place offered a chance for survival. Our escape from Lublin to Brwinow outside Warsaw was our chance to be saved. Danger threatened us all, not only my father but also my mother and even me, as I was already a grown young man.

Our trip to Warsaw that memorable day in May was to a certain degree a revelation for me. Two lorries full of sand were in front of the locomotive, and behind it there were cars, with armed guards in the last one. On the route between Lublin and Warsaw in 1944, you could see the devastation caused by the diversionary tactics of the Home Army. You could see the remnants of explosions—piles of metal, broken train cars, broken-up military equipment. The whole route was surrounded by outposts of the Wlasow troops— a division of Belorussian. General Wlasow had gone over to the German side. He particularly distinguished itself with inhuman cruelty that became infamous during the Warsaw uprising. All the stations were surrounded by military ready to fight.

I will never forget an incident that terrified my mother and me. We had brought bread and hard-boiled eggs with us. It was a beautiful warm May day. The compartment was empty except for us. The window was open, and I kept leaning out, admiring the efficiency of the Home Army's actions. I peeled an egg and, not looking, threw the shell out the window. Almost immediately, the door to the compartment swung open. A German officer in a Wehrmacht uniform stood in the doorway, nearly frothing at the mouth. He was furious and yelled and threatened my mother and me, huddled in the corner. It turned out that the unfortunate eggshell had hit him right in the face. His pride didn't allow for an *Untermensch* (subhuman) to offend him, a representative of the superior race of men. But he wasn't a bad guy. When he saw our shock and heard my mother's apologies, he said something or other and slammed the door behind him.

We arrived in Brwinow, at my aunt Jania's house. She lived there with her husband and three sons. My uncle Wladek was already there—the same one who experienced a "trip to the Lublin Castle"—with his wife Nata, their eight-year-old son

Andrzej, and the last descendant, one-year-old Stas. Jania's husband, Mieczyslaw, also a civil engineer like my father, had been the head of the Warsaw municipal surveying team. He of course didn't admit to his level of education or position that he had occupied in Warsaw and instead took a job as a glass worker.

The home was rather spacious, wooden, with a large yard in which scrawny tomato bushes grew. There was also a potato patch there, as well as a row of onions and other vegetables. A few fruit trees and clumps of weeds by the fence made up the rest. In front of the kitchen door, there was a large yard dirtied with chicken poop, and a sty connected to the chicken coop where a goat lived that was the only source of milk. There were a lot of chickens, and a cocky rooster was their leader.

The house didn't have any amenities. It was located on the periphery of Brwinow just next to a peat bog that stretched all the way to Zbikow. There were a few other houses nearby occupied by locals.

After escaping, my father also arrived there, unshaven, with black stubble on his face, tired from his trip from Lublin. These three families, together with my grandmother who was already living there, found themselves without any means of survival, without work, and—what's worse—without any documents that would be credible to the German authorities. And yet we had to survive somehow, to eat something, and to protect ourselves from danger. The location of the house was advantageous in that when we heard about the possibility of "roundups"—the Germans' choosing people at random so as to take them to dig trenches or to kill them—we would go spend the night in the peat bog, where you would need dogs to find anyone. I remember that one of those nights I had a terrible cold because of the penetrating dampness and chill.

We had some fruit in our possession, mainly plums, and the children would each get an egg every few days. The goat's milk was reserved mostly for little Stas.

Wiecek, the owner of the nearby mill, agreed to hire me so that

I could have some kind of working papers. My father and uncle, not to mention the rest of the family, didn't have any documents except the dangerous blue Ausweiss.

My getting hired at the mill was a fiction; I would sit there bored out of my mind for a few hours, filling out forms, though it did have one additional advantage. Mr. Wiecek sold sacks of flour to my father and me that we would then load on wheelbarrows and take around to the nearby shops, making enough money so as to be able to make noodles for peasant soup, which, besides the noodles, also consisted of potatoes and roasted onion. I waited the whole day for that soup for we only ate once a day. I was always hungry. I lost a lot of weight, and my skin was covered in pustules from severe malnutrition.

I found a recipe somewhere for making soap. I got to work with my older cousin, Bohdan. We got lamb lard and the necessary ingredients for the production of that then valuable merchandise. The soap turned out well, though truthfully, it wasn't the best quality and lathered poorly. Still, it became a valuable product in such poverty.

With a suitcase full of cut-up pieces of soap, I would stand at the market in Brwinow many times hoping to make some money. I didn't sell much, as no one had any money, but I made enough to continue production and to be able to occasionally buy a piece of bread and sometimes even a piece of sausage. I can still see one-year-old Stas in Aunt Nata's arms with a piece of dark rye bread in one hand and a tiny piece of sausage in the other, eating as best he could. That particularly luxurious feast undoubtedly did him good.

In the shade of a big tree standing near the house, we dug out a big pit measuring two-by-two meters. We covered it with wood, to make a roof, over which we poured dirt. The entrance to it was a narrow opening that could be closed with a trap door, and then covered with dirt on the outside. It was a shelter for the men and for us teenagers in case of a sudden search by the German police. Fortunately, we never had to use our hiding place.

I also almost became a victim of the German terror. One day, during our peddling efforts at the Brwinow market, I found myself in a "crowd" of armed soldiers who were gathering groups of people into canvas-covered trucks. The goal was to frighten the local population. I immediately understood that I was in danger. They hadn't noticed me yet, so I began to move stealthily off to the side of the cordon. I looked over and saw an old German in a *Volksturm* uniform—the last German reserves, called up near the end of the war—near me. We looked into each other's eyes. He saw my horror and took pity on me.

"Raus!" He shook his hand, motioning for me to escape. He didn't have to do it twice; I ran straight ahead and turned into the first street I saw. I could still hear the yells and sobs of captured people.

The summer was passing by quickly. The news in a secret newspaper of the AK (*Armia Krajowa* or Home Army) that Uncle Mietek brought home was encouraging, as the eastern front was moving to the Vistula River. It was obvious that the Hitler-supporting Germans were finding themselves at the beginning of a catastrophe. Although we would be glad to be rid of the Germans we waited in fear for the Soviet troops from the east. We had heard about massive send-offs of people from eastern Poland to Siberia, where murder and other horrors were committed by the "Soviet authorities." The Home Army took up the practice of "standing with arms at the ready." Its divisions were then quite numerous; it has been estimated that about a million people made up its branches. I never found out if the number was really that high, but I do know that the work of those divisions on the territory of the so-called *General Government* was significant.

The Germans continued dishing out more and more terror, executing masses of randomly captured people or sending people off to forced labor, digging trenches under the threat of death. I have a sheet of paper in front of me that my mother received, ordering her to report for digging trenches. If she didn't show up, she would get the death sentence. The mess was getting bigger and bigger, and the chaos was growing. My mother didn't listen to the order, despite the even greater danger to the whole house and everyone in it. My grandmother, always eager to fight, put a heavy scythe next to the kitchen door.

When I asked, "Babcia, why are you doing that?" she responded, "The first German who sets foot in here will get his head knocked open, and only God will decide what happens after that!"

On the first of August, my father was planning to go to Warsaw to look for some kind of job to help us all survive, but for some reason he didn't go. And on this memorable day the outbreak of the Warsaw uprising took place. Engineer Wloczewski, an old colleague of Uncle Mietek from the Warsaw administration, brought "Bor" (the assumed name used by General Komorowski in charge of the Warsaw uprising) communications to us every day. We all listened to them, concerned, full of shock but also hope. The uprising didn't erupt spontaneously. A lot has already been written about the mistakes made, about the endangering of the civilian population of Warsaw by the Polish government-in-exile in London.

I know with full certainty that the Warsaw uprising was instigated under Stalin's orders by the Soviet army. The Home Army, which was despised by the Russians, was accused of not helping to rescue Poland. Stalin insisted on creating an uprising in Warsaw to make the Soviet Army's crossing of the Vistula River easier. The Red Army, however, was already in Praga, where there were groups gathered on the right side of the Vistula River, and Berling's Polish division was also there with the Russian army.

The first days of the uprising were successful. We listened with joy to the communications about gaining the PASTA building (a famous skyscraper built before the war) about the effective battles in the city center, and about the defense of the Stare Miasto neighborhood (old town). Days went by, and the Germans in Warsaw reinforced their strength by adding the Wlasow division to the fight; Horrible acts were also committed by German criminals under Kaminski's leadership. Black clouds of smoke and fire overshadowed the city, but Soviet aid didn't come. Berling's Polish divisions pleaded for permission to go help the uprisers, but they were categorically forbidden from doing any such thing. Divisions of the Home Army tried to get to the beleaguered city of Warsaw, but they couldn't get past the German cordon.

One day, we saw a squadron of four-engined "flying fortresses" of the Allies high in the sky; they were dropping weapons and food for those fighting for Warsaw. These airlifts were not very effective, and in many cases, some of the supplies got into German hands. An awful truth was becoming more and more obvious. The Soviets had purposely led everyone into the wrong so as to destroy Poland's capital and, with the help of German hands, to eliminate this bastion of national identity and resistance.

The extent of German and Russian hatred for Poland and Poles became evident in the final stages of the war. Even though they were engaged in deadly combat, they both worked together to destroy everything Polish. There is photographic proof of Russian and German officers exchanging intelligence useful to annihilate Warsaw. This is a barbarism against Poland without equal in human history.

And yet we had to live . . . and survive.

In July, before the outbreak of the Warsaw uprising, my cousins and I were busy digging in the peat bog. We would carry wet brown chunks home in wheelbarrows, then form them into muddy paste that we then put into a wooden mold. We dried the peat in the sun, and after a few days, it became a rather hard block in the shape of a large brick that we used as fuel in the kitchen and then to heat the house. The peat didn't light easily, so we had to use some wood as well, of which we also didn't have a lot. It smoked and clouded, but it did enable us to cook the meager, yet necessary, peasant soup that became the staple of our food supply.

From that period, the two things that stood out the most were hunger and boredom. Hunger is something despicable, as the feeling of not being full, the emptiness, consumes every thought. The other hardship was boredom. Despite some dramatic moments, the days rolled from one to the next incredibly slowly. There were no chores to be done, no work, and no school. I worried about this all the time, because I saw education as a way to fight against the occupier, as a means for a haughty teenager to resist the plans of the Third Reich.

There were a lot of books of beautiful literature, Polish history, and poetry in my aunt's house.

I made legs from four little poles for a trunk that had been turned upside down, and then I had my own table, at which I spent long hours trying to absorb everything within reach—even my grandmother's old illustrated magazines from before the First World War in which the *Trilogy* had been published in chapters. I remember the advertisements in those magazines, especially of women's corsets—this particularly interested me as I was going through puberty. The "beauties" presented in those ads were full, big-busted, and similar to Rubens's women with the only dif-ference being that they were thin in the waist, pulled in to near unconsciousness by a corset.

Reading literature gave me something that stayed with me for the rest of my life. During that difficult period, I got to know the literature and history of Poland, much more than I ever would later at the PRL (*Polska Republika Ludowa*, the People's Republic of Poland) high school. I felt a quiet satisfaction as I was able to recognize the lies and falsification of facts surrounding the past and richness of the original Poland.

The uprising began to settle down. Thousands of people ended up in a concentration camp in Pruszkow. Each day, we saw people taken west from Warsaw in beastly wagons.

Many managed to escape, whether from the camp in Pruszkow that wasn't that heavily guarded or through the fields after leaving the ruins of Warsaw through the sewers.

People who were able to extricate themselves from the hellish uprising started coming to the house at the edge of the peat bog. These people stank terribly, as they had reached freedom through the sewers. The first to show up was a family with two small chil-dren, then two men, then again some family. They would stop for a night's lodging but often ended up staying a few or even a dozen days, not having anywhere to go. There were days when three or four families other than ours were mingling in our home, and all shared in our main meal of peasant soup.

Autumn was already well under way; the peat bogs and fields were covered in the silver-white garment of frost. The piercing cold was getting to us more and more. The home was heated by an iron stove. At night, the fire would go out, and the cold would penetrate every rag and blanket that could be used as a cover. From one day to the next, life was getting harder and harder—and the poverty more frightening. News reached us of the systematic destruction of Warsaw by the so-called *Vernichtungskommando* (troops designated for total destruction), whose mission was to level the Polish capital so that it could never recover. The Germans started dismantling telegraph poles and electric train equipment, preparing for their withdrawal.

At the end of November and beginning of December, my father and I took sleds and a saw and went toward the train tracks at night so as to cut off a piece of a fallen pole to get some valuable wood for burning; the peat would not light without it. It was a dangerous game because the Germans had surrounded the train tracks with guards. Quietly, with thumping hearts, we moved in the direction of the tracks over the white covering of snow. We finally reached the desired pole. We began cutting off pieces fever-ishly that were just the right size so we could load them onto the sleds. We were successful. We rushed back so as to get away from danger as quickly as possible. One of the guards noticed us, and some bullets whizzed by our heads, but we had already gotten pretty far away, and he wasn't able to hit us. He also couldn't chase us, because he wasn't allowed to leave his post. After we returned, Uncle Mietek and Bohdan went out again the same night to bring back the remaining piece of the valuable pole. They were success-ful; so now we had enough wood to light the peat, make soup, and somewhat heat the house.

Finally, Christmas rolled around. All I remember is that we shared our bare shelter with other refuges. And then the bitter cold of January began.

In the middle of the night, we suddenly heard the rattle of engines in the air, then several bombs—twenty-five kilo ones— fell all around us. All the panes flew out of the windows, and our neighbor, who had gone out to his outhouse, was torn apart by shrapnel there. In the morning, when it was again silent, we went outside. Strangely, it turned out that our outhouse had also been hit and was partly broken up by shrapnel. If someone had been out there, he would have certainly been killed. This bombing was carried out by pilots of the Red Army with two-winged *kukuruzniks* (Russian planes); they were slow and not suited for battle. Why these two huts in particular that stood practically in the fields were scattered with bombs will always remain the sweet secret of those wielding power in the Soviet alliance.

After this nighttime attack, chilling wind and snow wailed through the whole apartment. Luckily, my uncle still had a reserve of glass somewhere; he worked all day to replace the glass panes, and we boarded up some of the remaining window gaps.

The Germans were withdrawing in full force, destroying bridges and gathering their logistical supplies; the wave of the army was moving west. We knew that the long-awaited Soviet army offensive had begun. I don't remember how many days had gone by since the nighttime attack, but I remember hearing the hum of tanks that turned out to be the first-line divisions of the Red Army. In the midst of so many soldiers sitting on the huge tanks, I was surprised to see women, dressed and armed like all the rest. The Kalmuk column reached the market on tanks—the army poured out over the entire area. Soon, we heard several rounds fired from machine guns—someone came into the apartment with the news that the Russians were shooting an entire group of German army marauders. Supposedly, they didn't do this very neatly, as you could hear the wails for many hours, though no one was in any hurry to help them.

All of a sudden, a few days later, there was an army in Polish uniforms and four-corned caps. The soldiers were greeted enthusiastically. I had a red-and-white ribbon in my coat lapel. I pushed my way toward a large wagon harnessed to healthy horses where someone was yelling something. He was a propagandist who was in favor of freeing Poland from the Germans and the bourgeoisie, and who praised the Soviet system. This speech didn't really concern me or anyone else. We were looking instead at the supplies in the wagon—it was full of loaves of bread! Soldiers started throwing these loaves at the crowd—everyone tried to catch them. In the tumult and chaos, I was able to catch one of the coveted loaves. I went off to the side and devoured that bread, tearing off pieces with my teeth. I delighted in its taste, and for the first time in a long time, I fully satisfied my hunger.

6

"Liberation"

WARSAW LAY IN ruins, bare, covered in snow, and abandoned. The January frost penetrated into your bones. There was no fuel for heating, no food, and no work. The Soviet divisions pushed forward quickly. We soon learned that another large town, Lodz, had already been taken and that battles were occurring all around Poznan.

Everyone wanted to go back to their former work as quickly as possible so as to rebuild ruined Poland. Despite the presence of Soviet hordes, we all had false hope that Poland could rise again, that we could salvage the country's so-called independence. We were counting on Western allies. Truthfully, we already knew about the Lublin Committee formed by the Soviet occupant. On the other hand there was talk that Russia had agreed to free elections and to the creation of a coalition government made up of a pro-Russian group together with the Polish government-in-exile in London. The very fact that we were parading around with red-and-white ribbons strengthened our spirits and reinforced our false hope. We didn't know yet that, on the other side of the Vistula River, the NKWD (*Narodnij Komissariat Wnutrennych Del*, the Soviet Secret Service) had organized concentration camps, that soldiers of the Home Army were being captured and murdered or sent off to Siberia, or that a Polish equivalent of the NKWD was created in the posture of the UB (*Urzad Bezpieczenstwa*, the Office of State Security). We didn't know about any of this and lived on in hope.

We didn't have anything to burn in the iron stove—even peat was lacking. My father and uncles, like many other people, went to Warsaw with sacks attached to their belts. The main goal of these excursions was to collect charcoal that had been left over in the basements of destroyed homes. Sometimes, you could also find some food in these basements, though this happened rather rarely. I remember seeing my father when he was coming home from such an excursion with a sack of charcoal on his back. A week went by, then another. It became clear that something had to be done, and sitting at home didn't lead to anything.

My uncle Wladek, his wife, and kids moved to the right side of the Vistula River and settled in Radosc. Preliminary structures of administration were already being organized. As an engineer, he found work that helped them survive this period. My father wanted to go back to Poznan to resume his position as director of agricultural surveys of the province of Poznan. Everyone was told to return to their pre-war place of employment so as to recreate an administrative structure and rebuild life—and the nation—as quickly as possible.

My father went on his own at first. He wanted to reach his sister who lived in Zdunska Wola with her daughter, Zosia. She had a large house and several hectares of land. He was counting on having his family live there for a while before going back to Poznan to our former life. He was gone for a week and returned horribly worn out. He made the trip either on Russian transports or on foot. He did reach his goal and decided that we could survive at my aunt's place for at least a few weeks.

During his wanderings, he had encountered a Russian battalion that was going to the front lines without weapons and surrounded by machine guns. These were soldiers of the punishment regiment who had been sentenced to death. The Russians created numerous such punishment regiments, to be used in the front lines of attack. They got weapons at the last minute, were ordered to go forward, and machine guns stood behind them to kill everyone who made any move to retreat. The death toll in these battalions was over ninety percent. Those who were able to survive were immediately incorporated into the next punishment regiment. These soldiers made a great impression on my father; they were completely indifferent and resigned to their fates, knowing that their days were numbered.

A few days after my father came back, we set out on the road to the west—my parents, my grandmother, and me. We had bundles of food and a few warm rags. I was dressed rather peculiarly. I was wearing shoes that my father had found somewhere in Warsaw, though they were at least two or maybe even three sizes too small. I could walk in them only by stepping down on the backs. My grandmother had sewn me some knickerbockers from an old gray German army blanket that I found somewhere. This was the best part of my outfit, for they protected rather well against the cold. The whole thing was completed by a too-small blazer, an overcoat from I don't even remember where. I wore also a *Volksturm* cap on my head. The symbols had been ripped off, and I decorated it instead with a red-and-white ribbon.

What was the journey like? We walked along the railroad tracks and waited for the next army supply transport. A crowd of people waited in the cold by these tracks; sometimes some were let on, sometimes not. There was no way to get into the train cars, not even the most beastly ones. People curled up and cuddled into one another, sitting in the open lorries exposed to the piercing, icy wind of the January night. And such was the trip to Lodz. When the train was moving, despite the cold and the misery of it all, my spirits didn't falter, but when it stopped in an empty field and stood there for many hours, my legs got so numb that I practically couldn't feel them, and I would begin to lose all hope.

Near the end of the German Occupation, we got a dachshund—I don't know how—who was named Bary. The name I took from the Jack London novels which I was very fond of. He was my loyal and good companion. He survived the poverty and hunger of our stay in Brwinow and wandered with us now, hidden in my backpack, as he was in danger. People were hungry, and they wouldn't have hesitated to eat him! As if aware of the danger, he sat on my back without moving for over twenty-four hours, even warmed me a little, and that's how we meandered through the new Poland.

We arrived in Lodz at night. There was a lot of shooting in the city, and bullets whistled here and there. We went into the basement of some building, where we huddled up on the cement floor until the morning. I don't remember how we got on the winding road to Zdunska Wola from Lodz—probably again on some army transport. I only remember that when we finally found ourselves on the road in the morning, it was thickly covered in snow. It was a beautiful sunny day, the frost eased up, and the sun's rays warmed not only our backs but also the snow that started to soften underfoot. It felt strange, as though we were walking on some springy mattress. I couldn't understand what was happening. After a moment, I glimpsed a human hand sticking out from the melting snow. We were walking over the ground covered with the corpses of German marauders. The Russians had placed two tanks next to one another and flattened everything and everyone on the road.

After long hours of walking, we reached a hamlet. We were so exhausted that we walked into the first house we saw asking for a night's lodging and some food. We were warmly welcomed, though the people seemed afraid. They gave us food, as they had quite a bit on their well-preserved farm. Night fell. Suddenly, we heard a banging on the door. Our host went pale, but he did go and open the door. Two soldiers wearing Polish four-corned caps with an eagle without the crown came inside. Their faces were red from vodka, and they were carrying guns. They swore at the farmer, using the most vulgar words. One of them was a Jew with a thick, dark beard; the other spoke in a typical Belorussian accent that I knew well from my early childhood years in Brzesc. They threatened the terrified family, the father, mother, and two daughters, and then sharply turned to us, asking who we were and what we were doing there. My father explained that we were on our way to Poznan so as to go back to work and start a new life. Then the Jew replied, "Well then, we won't hurt you; you just have to listen to what we say!"

And to the host he said, "So, now you have to pay for your German 'citizenship!' You'll pay now. First, we will rape your daughters, so that they have something to remember us by, and then we'll take care of you. We were having guests over in the village, and the good people told us that you were Volksdeutsch (from German nation) 'citizens,' so we came over to straighten you out."

They chased us out, along with the host and his wife, to a big hall that divided the house in two. They took the girls into the next room and slammed the door. We stood in the front room—full of terror and fear. From the closed room, we could hear beds shaking, as well as cries and moans. After I don't know how long a time—it seemed like ages—one of the daughters came out. I remember her ripped dress. She pushed her bare breast back into her bra with her hand and then ran out of the house into the darkness of the night. After a moment, a soldier came out and said in a Belorussian accent, "So, you see, I took care of your daughter, and now it's time for you."

Then he fell into a litany of profanities. He looked all around him. A thick, knobby stick stood in the corner. He threw his pistol into his left hand—I saw how he released the safety—grabbed the stick in his right hand, waved it around a few times, then turned to the host, "Get undressed and put your nose to the floor! If you don't do it, I'll shoot you like the worthless scoundrel you are!"

The unfortunate man started pulling off his clothes and was left standing in only his underwear. The soldier beat him with the stick. He did it meditatively, slowly, so as to hurt him as much as possible, hitting him in the kidneys and back. The beaten one didn't even wail; after each hit, you could hear a painful inhalation of breath. His horrified wife was wailing in the corner. The executioner's face showed only beastly desire to kill. My mother started pleading for mercy for the beaten one, and my father pulled out his watch and wedding band, offering them in exchange for stopping the execution. The soldier agreed to it. The beaten man couldn't stand up on his own; his wife got him out of the front room. Shortly after that, the second girl came out of the bedroom, and the Jew walked out behind her, pulling up his pants. They went to the doorway and warned as they left, "We'll be back, just you wait!"

I will never forget that awful night as long as I live. Looking at such torment of people, I knew that Satan really existed.

We finally reached Zdunska Wola and my aunt Maria. She was a large woman with crooked, almost manly, eyebrows; she didn't resemble my father. She welcomed us very warmly. Joy radiated through the house, as her daughter, Zosia, had returned from a long absence. She had been taken into forced labor for the Germans, and luckily, greater harm didn't find her there. She was placed with a German peasant, worked in the field, and was treated decently. She was still very young, about twenty years old, and petite and thin, not at all like her mother. There, for the first time in a long time, we found ourselves in humane conditions. There were normal beds with linens, homemade bread, potatoes, kasha, cow's milk, and even lard.

For the first few days, we simply tried to get our strength back, but my father decided it was best to go back to Poznan as quickly as possible, even though there was news going around that the Germans were still defending themselves in the citadel.

I remembered Zdunska Wola from before the war; I had visited my aunt there with my parents. It was a city in which about half the population was made up of Orthodox Jews in yarmulkes with long black cloaks and curled sideburns, speaking in yiddish. How different Zdunska Wola looked at the end of January in 1945! You didn't see any Jews, their neighborhood was empty—you rarely saw anyone in the streets.

In those days, there was an incredible rush to reorganize normal life as quickly as possible, to mobilize the administration and open schools. My father went to Poznan, but he signed me up at the newly opened high school in Zdunska Wola. It occupied a massive, old brick building that had been built on a German model. I had to pass an entrance exam to qualify for the appropriate class. I was supposed to go into the eighth grade, but it turned out that because of my education at the chemistry school and particularly my lessons with Ms. Kissewetter, I qualified for the ninth grade. My Polish literature teacher was a pedagogue who still remembered having my father as his student.

And so, I started my education from scratch again. It lasted a very short time before my father brought us to Poznan.

One event sticks out in my mind from those days in Zdunska Wola. To get to school, I had to cross through a rather large market. I would go out early, to be there by eight o'clock. I gaped at the sky, the surrounding buildings, and the bare, leafless trees. Suddenly, in the corner of my eye, I saw something just next to my shoe and shuddered in fear. It was the bloody face of a dead person that had been blown off by machine-gun fire. The corpse lay on its back, and on the chest was a sign with a shoddily written statement: "traitor of the people." I never found out who this person was or what he did.

We got to Poznan. The city center was nearly destroyed. The streets were covered in rubble in many places, and bombarded apartment buildings stuck out here and there displaying ruined interiors that contained the remains of people's possessions. Besides in the city center, the damage to buildings wasn't severe. Traces of rifle bullets were visible in many places, and a hole had been blown out here and there by artillery fire. In the citadel, the Germans were still defending themselves, and sounds of battle could be heard from there.

We were assigned to a temporary apartment in the buildings in Jezyce surburb—our old apartment near Asnyka Square had been occupied by someone else. We were able to recover some of our old furniture, a few kilims, and the piano—my mother's greatest treasure.

The apartment in Jezyce was large and comfortable, full of beautiful Gdansk furniture. We settled in there as best we could. My father reported to work; the Germans in the citadel surrendered. We experienced the last bombardment of the Second World War, carried out by Luftwaffe; it was rather weak and didn't cause much damage.

Everyone got involved in rebuilding. Energy was high, as everyone wanted to rebuild ruined and stepped-on Poland so that it could come back to life. In a flash, schools were opened, and the Poznan University was reorganized with the help of a very thinned-out staff.

I got into ninth grade at Marcinkowski High School. The curriculum was shortened but extremely intensive. In my class, there was a mix of guys, teenagers of all ages and all kinds of life experience. There were also soldiers from the Home Army, though they didn't admit to it. There was already a sense of the beginning of Bolshevik terrors. Among others, one of my friends was a lieutenant in Tito's army. How he ended up on the territory of Yugoslavia during the war remains his secret. He described the terrors of battle in that region, and in particular, remembered that after a trip to the villages cooperating with Germans, baskets were brought to the camp—full of human eyes, so as to prove the extent of massacres that had been committed.

There was also a young guy from Warsaw who was two years older than me—a blonde with blue eyes—who with thousands of others had been taken from Pruszkow to Germany. He escaped and lived in hunger and cold. He tried to get back to Poland somehow, but he couldn't speak German. He finally reached the railroad yard in Berlin. An older German woman was almost the end of him, as she saw the miserable boy and tried to help him. He escaped from her and got into a train that was heading east. It was a Pullman car. Before the train left, several guards got on and started checking documents. The train was moving. He knew that he was lost. He stood in the corridor by the window and watched as the gestapo went step-by-step into each compartment. He noticed that when the first one was in one compartment, the other one would go into the next. So when the first one went into the compartment to his left, he moved over slightly to the left. The second guard walked past him, thinking that his documents were already checked, and went into the next compartment. That's how he made it.

We all shared one thing in common—a desire for learning, for gaining knowledge, and education. When after all these years I hear that young people have problems, because they "cannot find themselves," when I listen to the stories of dilemmas that families and children face—I go back to those days in my thoughts. None of us had such dilemmas; everyone just tried to fill up the void that had been created by the war; everyone was working directly toward their goals.

The principal of the school was officially a "Red" Latin teacher. It's certain that he joined the PPR (*Polska Partia Robotnica*, Polish Workers Party) to advance his career, though he was a good teacher. He walked around the class carrying a volume of Livius about the Punic wars and clapped us on the head with it when we didn't know what *ablativus absolutus* meant as opposed to *accusativus cum infinitivo*. This treatment didn't appeal to me, so I studied Latin grammar intensely, memorizing hundreds of words and translating Caesar. It served its purpose; I don't recall ever being tapped on the head by that massive tome.

Professor Navratil taught Polish literature. He was a tall, older man with a lion's face, a high forehead, bushy brows, and a milky white mane that fell down to his back. He came to class in a well-worn overcoat with a scarf wrapped around his neck that hung down almost to the floor. At that time, I could draw caricatures pretty well; he was just asking for a sketch. During a break, I drew him quickly in chalk on the blackboard to the amusement of the whole class. Then, I wanted to erase it, but they wouldn't let me, and the Polish language lesson was about to begin. Professor Navratil came into the classroom, looked at the board, turned to the murmuring class, and asked, "Which rascal created such a work?"

"It was him, Subczynski," they replied in unison.

He looked at me harshly, but his eyes were smiling. He said, "Well, you just might make something of yourself!"

I sat there beet red not knowing what to do.

I can't say that Professor Navratil led an organized course in literature. He was a born chatterbox. He sat down at the desk that served as a pulpit and with a calm voice, almost unintentionally, began talking about the old days, his memories from Krakow, about Young Poland, Wyspianski, Rydel, Przybyszewski, and the "Green Balloon" (a hangout for artists, actors and painters). After a few minutes, the noisy class quieted down, riveted by his memories. You could really see those people and those times; the whole rich past became real before our eyes. He jumped from one subject to another; from Young Poland, he somehow managed to move on to Romanticism and his skepticism about Classicism, and then told anecdotes about the sexual verses written by Rej.

No one could read the Kochanowski elegies like he could. He not only taught but rather fostered a love for the Polish language and its beauty, fluidity, and richness. His classes made you want to tear into classic Polish literature as soon as you got home. I grew very attached to him as only a student can to a great teacher.

Professor Rzecki taught German. I found myself in his class by accident, as I supposedly knew the language, whereas I knew nothing about French, which was also a language option. My situation was rather difficult. So, besides Blaszczynski—the Warsawian who escaped from Germany—I, an A student and self-confident to some degree, was the worst student. Almost the whole class could speak German fluently, and the German literature course didn't give them any trouble. I, however, sat there terrified, as if at a German sermon.

The figure from those years that stuck not only in my mind but also in my heart was Father Marcinkowski. Supposedly, he was part of the family after which our school was named. He was an intelligent person, kind in his actions and, most of all, good. He taught us the history of the Church. His lessons were very interesting; he would illustrate not only the intriguing and tumultuous events in the Church's history, but also give us an impression of the entire epoch, the customs. He didn't leave anything out, spoke objectively, and at the same time, knew how to convey a supernatural feeling of the Church's worth. He didn't try to convert anyone.

He spoke in a calm, clear voice about the fact that doubts are one of the attributes of life, that faith is a gift for which you have to pray, and that despite all the warnings, difficulties, and upheavals of life, it was necessary to continue the religious tradition of our fathers, grandfathers, and great-grandfathers—all the ancestors who had gone before us. He advised us to look for support in the Gospels, in the teachings of Christ.

The priest was able to reach me and many others in my class. You could feel the power of conviction in his words; it wasn't just repetition of platitudes, but instead confessions and advice given from the heart.

Near the end of the ninth grade, the possibility arose of learning the English language. After seeing the teacher, everyone wanted to attend those classes. No, it didn't just have to do with expanding our knowledge; it had to do with looking at our teacher during the hour-long lesson. She was a very pretty young woman with a terrific figure and a kind smile. Though she wasn't inclined to flirt, her femininity and charm made a great impression on all of us. Sensitive, she blushed at our unwavering stares. And we looked at her greedily, up and down, down and up. I felt sorry for her, because she didn't know what to do with herself in the presence of such sexually deprived young men. She couldn't stand the pressure, and after a few weeks, her lessons ended.

During the first few weeks of our stay in Poznan, when we were still temporarily living in the wonderful apartment in Jezyce surburb, Mr. Syrewicz suddenly showed up at our place. He was an engineer and an old colleague of my father's from Brzesc. I remember him well from the pre-war years. He was a fat gourmand, a connoisseur of culinary arts, obviously from the consumption point of view. His wife seemed to serve as his antithesis. She was a tall woman, with a strong and just character, and my mother's closest friend. During the Occupation, they ended up in Warsaw in the region of Wola.

When the uprising began, he escaped to the city center, but she stayed where she was. She went through hell. Together with many others, she and her little daughter found shelter in the church on

Wola. At night, German criminals of Kaminski battalion came and ordered groups of men to go outside. When the first group left the church, those remaining heard a short round of machine-gun fire and then silence. There was no doubt that they had all been shot. The Germans showed up again, ordering another group of men to go outside. They said that if they didn't do it, they would use their weapons to kill everyone in the church. The men walked out in groups, and shots were heard, and so the next group had gone to their deaths. That lasted until the morning. When at dawn, the women went outside with their children; a pile of corpses lay near the entrance to the square. I know about these ordinary people, average Poles, and about their agonizing deaths from an eyewitness—Mrs. Syrewicz. She and her husband were both taken to a concentration camp in Germany. She was sterilized by radiation, while he sat in the camp. Finally, he was able to get out.

When he came over, he looked terrible and thin, with skin hanging off his once fat face. He still didn't know what had happened to his wife and daughter; they found each other later. We were all so happy to see him that we had to welcome him somehow. We had some bread, flour, and sugar—and my father got some yellow, already rancid lard. After so many years, I can still see this party—thinly sliced lard, elegantly laid out on a plate, bread, and something to drink. I think we also had some milk. So, the gourmand sat down in front of the feast and ate the stale bread and rancid lard, delighting in the taste.

My father finally got an allotment from the Office of Housing for an apartment near Gorczynski Street; the name had already been changed to Rokossowski Street. Located just next to the railroad yard, the apartment was on the third floor with a large balcony. On the other side of the street, the Russians buried their dead.

We were able to keep some of our furniture, linens, and the piano. We lived very modestly. It was a luxury when my father managed to get us a chicken during his work travels.

Time passed quickly. Spring came, then summer. We high-school students worked Sundays doing "community service," cleaning up the ruins of bombarded apartment buildings. I remember those Sundays well. After early Mass, we went to a meeting and then got to work. The physical labor didn't scare us off; there was also a lot of fun to be had with pleasant company.

I finished ninth grade with good grades, with the exception of German, in which I got a B. But, I did qualify for lyceum. We were divided into two groups, the first made up of older kids; it was supposed to move at a faster pace in a ten-month course leading up to the final exam. The lyceum did this so as to send them off to university as soon as possible. We, the younger ones, qualified for the full two-year course, so I was to complete lyceum a year later than the first group. I had a year extra anyway, because I had made up a class during the Occupation. I was beside myself with this injustice, that those who were below me in knowledge were going to get their lyceum diploma before me. I was an A student and also wanted to get into the university sooner.

After the list of students was announced, I went to the principal asking him if I could be allowed to go into the faster course because of my good grades.

"No way!" he cried, "Get out of here and stop bothering me!"

Not fazed by this less-than-warm reception, I tried twice as hard. He threw me out of his office several times, and finally said, "I have nothing to do with this; it's in the hands of the superintendent of the school district. Go there and bother him!"

I listened to this good advice and the very next day found myself in front of the superintendent. The discussion was very brief. I think he threw me out the door three times, and after the fourth, when I was still bothering him, he exclaimed, "Get out of here and do what you want!"

After this exclamation, not supported by any document, I went to the principal and told him that the superintendent didn't have any objections to my going into the advanced class. I guess he had already lost all his energy because he didn't object and, murmuring something under his breath, signed me up on the desired list.

After winning my private battle, I got into a special lyceum course that would speed up my education by two years. This made a big difference on many levels. The Bolshevik system, at least in the first year of "the people's government," wasn't yet developed properly, and students were still being accepted into the university according to the old pre-war system. Besides that, brainwashing in lyceum wasn't well organized yet, so I got a pretty truthful basic history class. Polish literature was still taught by Professor Navratil. He liked me and gave me A's on tests; he also scolded me from time to time: "Subczynski, for God's sake, don't write so much; I mean, then I just have to read it all!"

Near the end of lyceum he suggested that we should all choose some epoch in literature, whether Romanticism or Classicism, Renaissance or Baroque, and write a long essay based on primary sources.

I don't know why I chose Rococo. I set out for the already functioning library and started poring over thick volumes trying to gather appropriate sources. I had some idea about the strange and overloaded Baroque period of Rococo in architecture and sculpture, but I knew less about the literature, and nothing about the way of life.

Reading historical materials, I found several interesting things about the unraveling of those times and customs, bordering on licentiousness.

This interested me greatly; I organized all the data in a twenty-some-page report and then read it aloud during the Polish lesson. The class listened enthusiastically, especially to the frivolous parts of my work; Professor Navratil kept saying I was digressing, but I still got an A+.

As I already mentioned, my grandmother's brother was a priest in the province of Vilno. He christened my mother and also conducted her wedding ceremony. During the war, his and my grandmother's sister, Jadwiga Wiszowata, lived with him. Her husband was an Uhlan cavalry captain, and during war dealings in 1939, he managed to get to Romania, from there to France, then through Dunkirk, and finally to England, where he trained to be a pilot, serving in Polish squadrons.

Father Stanislaw Klimm (that was my grandmother's brother's name) stayed in the province of Vilno while we were starting our new life in Poznan. The Polish population from the former eastern areas was resettled en masse into the so-called *Ziemie Odzyskane* (the recovered territories) that had been abandoned by the Germans, but he didn't move.

Because we knew about the persecution of priests under the Bolshevik regime, my father concluded that a formal invitation was probably needed to get him out of the Soviet paradise. And so he sent out such an invitation. He and my grandmother's sister came soon after. It turned out that without that invitation, they were meant to barely exist there without the right to leave.

The apartment got crowded. Father Klimm immediately reported to the bishop's curia, looking to take over some parish; Jadza waited anxiously for the return of her husband from England, but this homecoming didn't happen. I was preparing for my final lyceum examination resulting in award of the maturity certificate—it wasn't easy, as the apartment was crowded and noisy, and to my protests that I had to study, "Aunt" Jadza responded impatiently, "But you will pass anyway, you already know your stuff, so why all this fuss?"

In some sense, she was right, because I was well prepared. For Latin, I had memorized Cicero's entire speech against Catiline, some charming poems of Horace, and finally a large section of Ovid.

I didn't have any trouble with the scientific subjects, as I had learned a lot of math, physics, and chemistry in the private chemistry technical school during the Occupation.

My one Achilles heel was German. Together with my tutor, a miserable little student, we pored over German literature. To this day, I sincerely hate *Nibelungenlied*, have no kind feelings toward Schiller, and cannot stand *Hermann und Dorothea*. These are examples of German classics. But, of course, the final exam for German would touch on German literature.

There were only two more months to the final exam. My tutor came to the pessimistic conclusion that despite all my efforts, I wouldn't be able to write anything that made even a lick of sense.

But we didn't give in to despair. After thinking long, he figured out that the final exam usually revolved around a rather tight focus, so if I could memorize six of the probable subjects, one of them would have to be right. And, in the worst-case scenario, I could pull together one that made some sense out of those six.

We got to work and wrote six compositions. Under his supervision and with his corrections, I memorized them all and sat down at the school desk with a trembling heart to write my final exam in German. I opened the test; my subject was "Wilhelm Tell." I had that subject entirely worked out! I saw how others were struggling and thinking, but I wrote without hesitation, calmly, and quickly. A shadow fell on the writing paper—the shadow of Professor Rzecki, my teacher. He stood and looked, not able to tear his eyes away from my work. Finally, he said, "You know, son, I have been a teacher for forty years and I have never seen anything like this! I can see that you're not cheating; I know you don't know German, and I also see that you are writing a good composition in proper German. I have never before experienced such a feat in a high school class!"

On my final, I got a B in German!

Now that I had my final examination all wrapped up, the question arose as to what kind of studies I should pursue. Professor Navratil wanted me to study Polish literature. I couldn't go to engineering school, because they weren't accessible in Poznan, and studying in another city was impossible because of our difficult financial situation. Law wasn't really a good idea, as it was becoming clear that their main role was preparing a group of Bolshevik servants. Only medicine remained. When Professor Navratil found out that I was planning for the exam in that field, he fell into a rage and called me names, from criminal and murderer to butcher. Well, needless to say, it didn't change anything.

The entrance exam in 1946 wasn't yet controlled by the authorities, so the old methods of testing intelligence and knowledge were used. I was accepted and could begin my studies in the fall.

The first post-war Christmas was rather nice. There was a Christmas tree, fish for Christmas Eve, some kind of cake, and carols played on the piano. We were together, with my beloved uncle (Father Klimm), Jadzaa, and the small dachshund Bary, who had experienced the whole harrowing trip to Poznan with us.

The apartment building we lived in was old, spacious, and solidly built. We had a large, bright apartment with a balcony that led out to the street. There was also an annex to the apartment and a large yard. You could smell the acrid scent of urine in the entranceway, because, unfortunately, a lot of those leaving the train station, mostly soldiers, relieved themselves there. Some young ladies lived in one of the annexes who worked in the oldest profession in the world, and once in a while you could hear drunken cries from there at night.

One day, I was staring out the kitchen window at the yard. Suddenly, a window shattered loudly in the ladies' apartment, and a Soviet soldier fell onto the pavement in the yard. He didn't move, and a growing puddle of dark blood formed around his head. I felt sick and fainted at the sight.

On New Year's Eve from 1945 to 1946, we heard commotion on the street. I went out on the balcony to see what was going on. There was a drunken Russian soldier there who was yelling, swearing, and singing in a hoarse voice, swaying from wall to wall. He wasn't causing anyone harm, apart from the inhuman noise. And then, a Soviet army police patrol car pulled up. They ordered him to approach the jeep, said something, and he responded vulgarly. I watched the scene carefully. I saw how the Russian soldier to the right of the steering wheel slowly opened the chamber of his gun, then just as calmly removed the safety, and shot the unfortunate Russian in the head. Then, the jeep went on its way. They didn't even glance around. The still figure stayed on the street in a pool of blood.

7

Medical School

I N THE FALL of 1946, I started medical school at the University of Poznan. The Medical Academy didn't exist yet; much later, the medical department was separated from the university and made into its own academic unit.

I registered in the dean's office and got the schedule showing the location and hours of my classes and labs.

I remember the first day of my academic career. In the large auditorium that had been somewhat shot up, about two or three hundred students sat down. I looked around the room, curiously looking at future friends and pretty girls. Everyone was happy and restless, and commotion filled the room. Professor Rozycki came in and sat down at the pulpit. Silence fell. He said, "Well then, you are candidates to be future doctors, and today, in this moment, you must decide if you are suitable for this role or not. A doctor lives his life in the shadow of the unshakable companions of pain, illness, suffering, and death. They will be with you in every hour of every day. You cannot forget that."

Then, he turned to the orderly who transported cadavers. "Bring in the body."

The side door of the auditorium opened, and a nurse brought

in some still form covered with a sheet on a gurney. He took off the sheet; I saw a man's body, fully naked, brown, with well-preserved facial features. The biting smell of formaldehyde filled the air, burning the eyes and tickling deep inside the nostrils.

Professor Rozycki went up to the body and told everyone to come down to the podium and touch the cadaver's hand. We went down one after another. When it was my turn, I carefully touched the dead body. It was stone cold and stiff. I didn't feel aversion, but rather curiosity and at the same time pity that this person had lost his life.

⼁⼁

The next day we began learning about osteology. A stone table used for dissecting cadavers stood in the huge anatomy prosectorium along with running water. In the first stage of our education, we didn't work with a complete human cadaver, but only the bones—the skull bones, the spine and pelvis, arms and legs. Each one of us had a brown book in which the proper structure of the skeleton was outlined; the students had to study each section and take a test given by the assistant professor. In the beginning, I got the skull, which is really quite difficult. You not only need a good memory but also the ability to see three-dimensionally, so as to put all the countless fragments of the structure in the right place. I didn't have an anatomy textbook; I learned from a borrowed one.

I was sure that as an A student in high school, I wouldn't have the least bit of trouble. I flew through all the material and became familiar with the details of the skull structure, not trying to remember it all—and, convinced that I had done what I was supposed to do, reported for the oral exam. I remember that the assistant's name was Szkopek. He was a big guy with a calm phlegmatic nature. When after three or four days of school, I went to him proposing an exam, he looked at me rather strangely but didn't refuse. A few minutes later, he said calmly, "Go and study more; you are not ready."

I felt shattered. I, the number-one student, had failed—and failed miserably. My ambition suffered greatly. To this day, I am grateful to Dr. Szkopek, as he gave me invaluable advice. He taught me that you couldn't start something if you weren't prepared enough to see it through. He also instilled the conviction in me that medical study was not a joke; you really had to learn and cram it all in—not just "study." I had the good fortune to understand this early on. Those that only "studied" either failed altogether after the first year or had difficulties during their entire medical educations.

Professor Kurkiewicz taught histology; he was bald with a hunched back and a choleric disposition. He had a sense of humor with everything and was very likeable. In his class, I stepped into a completely different world, the world of the microscope. I had to be able to distinguish various tissues by looking at their microscopic structure, to become familiar with different kinds of mucous membranes, to be adept at distinguishing between a specimen of heart muscle and a specimen of body muscle. All of it was really interesting and at the same time not easy, for the differences in structure were often very subtle. I didn't have a histology textbook, but somewhere in a used old bookstore, I found a German atlas complete with descriptions for a few cents. The language didn't bother me, and I could learn from it.

Professor Krause taught inorganic chemistry. He was tall and straight as a reed, an elegant man who always wore a bowtie at the collar of a clean shirt. In those days, it was the style to dress like "Comrades," and so without a tie, "à la the working class." This style was propagated by the "people's government," even though Comrad Bierut still wore a black coat with a fur collar.

Professor Krause didn't take new trends that had been propagandized by Soviet collaborators into account. Just as before the war, he came to the room elegant and clean and lectured on the appropriate division of chemistry in a clear voice. He was a great teacher.

We had a lot of other lecturers who I don't remember nearly as well as those I have named here. They didn't have the individuality to make an impression like those three did. From the beginning of my studies, I ran into a serious difficulty. I didn't have an anatomy textbook, which was just indispensable, and I also didn't have a watch so as to get to classes on time. You could buy a "Bochenek" on the black market—a many-volume textbook of anatomy published before the war that had been composed by Professor Bochenek; it was terrific, very clear, with good illustrations. But the price was, for our means, astronomical. And the most basic watch, even used—only those were on the market—considerably surpassed my father's budget.

One day, I came home from lectures. I saw my mother standing in the doorway with light, smiling eyes. Not saying anything, she brought me over to the table, next to which my father stood, similarly smiling. I couldn't believe my eyes. I saw all of the Bochenek volumes, somewhat worn, and a nice little watch with a black strap. Tears filled my eyes; I was so moved. I could see my parents' joy and their sacrifice!

Now, years later, when the past lives only in my memory, I am still moved and feel an unbreakable bond to my parents. They have been gone for many years, and yet in the moment I write these words, they're right here with me, so close, looking at me through kind, joyful eyes. And this is something nothing and no one can take away.

In a way it was a happy period of my life. I didn't know that at the same time I was learning chemistry, physics, biology, and anatomy, thousands of soldiers of the Home Army were being tortured and killed. While I was thriving on knowledge, horrors were taking place in the infamous Wronki prison, the jail on Mlynski Street the UB dungeons (Office of Security) on Kochanowski Street and in many, many other places. Concentration camps were open even for teenagers. The terror was made all the worse because it was quiet and spreading more and more. Only rumors leaked out to the public which heightened the terror.

Granted, we were barraged with primitive pro-Soviet propaganda, but no one thought much of it. The very fact that I could learn and move forward, dreaming of a better future, was enough of a reason to live each day optimistically. And I was young, healthy, and full of energy.

I recall several facts from that period of my life that affected me individually and that cast an eerie shadow on my life.

The long-awaited Mikolajczyk finally came to Poznan. Stanislaus Mikołajczyk had been premier of the Polish government in exile in London in 1943 and was leader of the faction opposed to the communists. We all hoped that a coalition government would arise in Poland that would be made up of those who fought for Poland in the west. We knew about the bravery of the Second Corps in Monte Cassino, the tragic death of Sikorski[3], and the massacre in Katyn[4] that was only whispered about, as it was carried out by Soviet agents.

So when we heard that Mikolajczyk[5] was in Poznan, I went with a whole mass of students to the little hotel in the Stare Miasto neighborhood where he was staying. We chanted, "Mi-ko-lajc-zyk, Mi-ko-lajczyk," and then, "Where are the rest, where are the rest?"

Mikolajczyk came out onto the balcony and waved his hand at us. We were incredibly excited, full of hope, and completely unaware of the awful danger we were putting ourselves in—informants of the UB were in that crowd! Soon after that, like a flash of lightning on a clear day, we got the news that Mikolajczyk had escaped just before being arrested and that Korbonski[6] was in prison!

At about the same time, Mrs. Wisniewska, a good friend of Aunt Jadza from the time when both of their husbands were cavalry captains in the Tenth Uhlan Regiment, and who had also been waiting for the return of her husband from England, showed up at our apartment with her husband full of joy that he had decided to come home. But this joy didn't last long. Just a few weeks later, cavalry Captain Wisniewski completely disappeared—there was no trace of him, no sign that he had ever existed. His wife went

---

3. Polish General in charge of Polish army in the West. Murdered in clandestine way at the demand of Stalin

4. Extermination of Polish officers, POW's taken by the Russians.

5. The Prime Minister of the Polish Government in exile in London.

6. Member of Polish government in exile.

from prison to prison, then to the Office of State Security—every place told her that they didn't know anything about him. There were a lot more of these disappearances, but this was one that I experienced myself. I remember how Aunt Jadza would say regretfully that Wisniewski had returned to his wife, while her husband, Ryszard Wiszowaty, was in no hurry. It wasn't until the disappearance of cavalry Captain Wisniewski that her eyes were opened—her husband couldn't come back, because suffering and death awaited him.

When I was in high school, I had a friend who was much older than me, a quiet fellow who had a lot of trouble with school. I offered him my help. He would come over to our home, and I would try to hammer math, Latin, and foundational texts of Polish literature into his head. He passed his final high school examination with Cs. When I had already been accepted for university, I saw to my wonder that he was also among the students in the first year of medicine. He was smiling, sat up straight, and wore in his lapel a badge for the Fighting Youth, a communist organization. Much later, I learned that he had sent information about me to the party organization indicating that I was "politically suspect," which in all practicality closed the door for any medical specialization. That's how he paid me back for my good deeds!

In that time, Poznan was still full of Russian army members. They made an announcement that a cemetery would be created for "Soviet heroes" just next to the citadel, complete with a beautiful memorial of gratitude from all of us Poles for our freedom and for the sacrifice of their lives for us.

The small cemetery in front of our apartment building was exhumed. The awful stench of decomposing bodies, now being taken to their new resting place, stayed with us for many days.

My father, together with a group of other engineers, like Grodzki, Surman, and Wloczewski, went back to work enthusiastically to rebuild Polish life. But they had trouble from the very beginning. The assigned communist boss didn't help and, instead, made their work more difficult; when anyone had a positive idea he immediately twisted it so that nothing would come of it. My father didn't understand this, and neither did the others. When a few engineers were arrested, among them Surman, for no apparent reason other than to create greater chaos and disorganization, my father realized that the "authorities" didn't have normalization of Polish life on the agenda so much as disorganization so as to then institute Soviet collectivization!

Engineer Surman, an older man, sat in prison for over a year. He was never told why he was arrested, and I am not even sure if he was ever interrogated. He sat in a cell with others, and after he was released and he came over, he looked old, totally ruined emotionally. He said that the only thing that saved him from going insane was chess. Closing his eyes, he would continuously try out different strategies in his mind.

After the sad experience of my first failed test in osteology, I learned well. I had to study a lot, and the material was difficult, particularly because we didn't have textbooks. After the first year, I took only two exams, as most of the subjects were two-year-long courses.

I got so nervous about my first university exams—as did my grandmother, whose unfulfilled dream had been to become a doctor. Perhaps it was because of this fear that I got a B+ in chemistry and a B in physics. The next exams, with few exceptions, were all A's.

Meanwhile, Father Klimm and Aunt Jadzaa left for *Ziemie Odzyskane* (the recovered territories). I don't remember the name of his first parish there, but I know that a lot of people from the province of Vilno had been transferred there and that the standard of living was rather primitive, making life difficult. An old Protestant church had been converted into a Catholic church. The curia started publishing a pamphlet that was stopped in a short time by the "people's government." Because the history of Poland was already being misshapen terribly, fragments of a shortened and simplified history of Poland, beginning with the Piast dynasty and ending with the period prior to the country's partition, was printed in that pamphlet. I wrote that history. I didn't get very far, though, as halfway through the Jagiellonow epoch, the pamphlet was eliminated.

A year went by, and my second year of medical school began. The second year of medical school is the hardest. We had tons of lectures, chemistry labs, and anatomy lab classes.

A lot of people quit, usually about one third of those studying. After finishing that year, you had to take exams in all the basic science courses, in anatomy, biochemistry, biology, histology, and pathology, as well as anatomical pathology. The material covered was very extensive.

At the beginning of the academic year, we were divided into two groups. The first had chemistry labs early in the morning in the laboratory until 11 a.m.—usually with a brief oral exam. The second group had anatomy in the afternoon that went on into the late evening. Lectures were throughout the day.

I and my closest friends, Jozek Wagner, Stas Woyke, Ola Krygier, and Stojalowska—the wife of Professor Stojalowski and our friend—got the idea to sign up for both groups in the first two semesters.

This was quite difficult, because we had to participate in chemistry labs in the morning, then rush to lectures, and then be prepared to go to the prosectorium. This hurried pace created the possibility of studying for exams during the second half of the year and preparing all the better in that time.

Not really in accordance with the program in place, we signed up for both groups. No one checked up on it; no one even thought that students might choose to tire themselves out like that.

My day started at seven a.m. in chemistry lab, and then I ran to lectures. I would go home briefly to eat dinner, while at the same time, flipping through the anatomy textbook, and then rush to the anatomy auditorium to make it for anatomy lab. When I got home, I would have supper and then study chemistry until midnight to prepare for the next day.

This effort was fruitful. During the second half of the year, after completing the prosectorium and chemistry lab, we had time to properly study for the exams, while everyone else was still busy with their other courses.

I remember Professor Rozycki's anatomy lectures from those years; the lectures were rather atypical, because he would come into the room and begin talking about various aspects of human anatomy. His lectures weren't organized in any rigid system; he liked to talk to his listeners. A game he played was to challenge us to guess what he was talking about before it was clear, thus showing him that we knew the material. I did this with pleasure and would specially prepare so as to "shine." Rozycki indulged my pride and the pride of those who did the same. He also had a lot of fun catching us in mistakes.

Because you had to take an exam in all of anatomy after the second year— a huge amount of material was covered—and Rozycki wasn't easy and would often throw students out, we would go up to the sanctuary door to find out what it had really been like from our older friends who had already taken the exam. These trips to the anatomy auditorium door weren't very helpful, and it would have been better just to study, but no one, especially those least prepared, could stop themselves from going.

Even I went. We stood in the hallway, actually by the stairwell. It was quite large; there was a glass wall on one end with doors leading to the anatomy auditorium. On the right side, at the end of that straight corridor, where it met the one perpendicular to it, was the place of torture that terrified us—Professor Rozycki's office.

The delinquents were called in by the orderly who transported cadavers. They went inside and the door slammed—and after a while they came out red-faced wearing a not very intelligent expression. Many of them had to make that trip again.

One day, Professor Rozycki's son showed up for the exam. We all stood there waiting to see what would happen, and he was boasting, "Well, what then, maybe this or that guy, but the old man won't throw me out." After a moment, he went in feeling good, with a smile on his face. Not even five minutes had gone by when we heard a yell, an anguished commotion, and the door flew open. The young Rozycki was running away at full speed with fear in his eyes, and Rozycki senior was running after him with his white jacket blowing open and the femur bone in his hand. "I'll kill you, scoundrel!" he yelled.

Well then, young Rozycki finally did learn anatomy and later became a psychiatrist.

After completing all the necessary work during the first half of our second year of medical school, my friends and I had a lot of time to prepare for the exams that would encompass the entire first two years of biochemistry, anatomy, histology, general pathology, as well as anatomical pathology, microbiology, and immunology.

We each studied individually, but we would quiz each other in groups trying to find any areas of weakness. Jozek Wagner was sort of a phenomenon in our group. He had the ability to memorize entire volumes almost photographically. When he went to take an exam, he usually did very well, because not many other people could remember so many details. He was already very interested in internal medicine. Absorbed in that field's textbook, he would familiarize himself with diagnostic methods. Ola Krygier was a quiet, calm young woman with no desire to show off in any way. She was usually silent but always well-prepared—no one had better notes from lectures than she did. Stas Woyke was a nerd—learning was more difficult for him than for Jozek Wagner, but once he learned something, he never forgot it. Stojalowska was very smart; studying was easy for her. I didn't really distinguish myself in any particular way in the group except for the fact that my interests were more diverse and not so limited to medicine. I was going to English language lessons, and during my first year, I had gone to music lessons, though I had to give them up during the hectic second year of medical school. When I had a bit of free time, I would go see concerts of the Poznan Philharmonic together with my high school friend, Dziewulski, who was studying economics. The concerts took place in a hall that was still littered with bullet holes.

I took the exams one after another and got A's on all of them.

Then, it finally came time to take the exam for anatomical pathology and general pathology, which we had to take in a hospital auditorium with Professor Skubiszewski. The exam took the entire day. In the morning, each student had to perform an autopsy on a deceased man and identify the cause of death. During that time, the professor would ask questions to one or another of the five taking the exam. That part of the exam lasted until the afternoon.

An essential thing to find out before the exam from the orderly who transports cadavers was what the clinical diagnosis of the deceased had been; that made the identification during the autopsy much easier. For a small bribe, you could usually find out that information. We found out that the sick man had had a severe hemorrhagic stroke from which he died soon after.

I was the one who ended up having to do the autopsy of the brain. The skull was already open; the dura matter was untouched. I opened the dura matter, waiting to see blood under the subarachnoid space; it should be there if the sick man had died of a ruptured artery in the brain. But you couldn't see any blood. I thought that maybe he had had a massive arteriosclerotic hemorrhage in the region of the internal capsule, the nuclei of the brain stem and in the brain ventricles. I made a horizontal incision of the brain after the top of the skull had been removed. I still didn't see what I expected. I was filled with panic. It was already clear to me that the clinical diagnosis had been wrong and that the sick man had died of other causes. Repeated horizontal incisions into the brain didn't reveal the cause of death. Finally, one of the last incisions revealed a hemorrhage in the brain stem that was undoubtedly fatal. I breathed a sigh of relief, having found the real cause of death.

It worked out oddly enough that during that exam, everyone was able to answer all of the questions. And when, for example, I couldn't answer some question, it was given to Stas Woyke or Jozek Wagner, who answered correctly—and vice versa—when they couldn't answer, the question was redirected to me, Ola Krygier, or Stojalowska.

In the afternoon, the second part of the exam took place, which involved identifying different illnesses in microscopic specimens. We managed to do fine with all the specimens. Then, there was an oral part of the exam, but that didn't last long; each one of us got an excellent grade.

Professor Skubiszewski did us an unfortunate favor. He put up the names of the five of us as an example for the other students. This made the party members furious, for they were supposed to be the ones to advance, not the offspring of some "rotten intelligentsia." They decided to ruin our lives. They didn't have any formal reasons for taking us out of medical school, but they could close the doors to any kind of specialization. The only remaining options were being ordered to go work in some countryside in the middle of nowhere with no opportunity for further education, or being called in to the army, which was even worse.

We understood this very well. Professor Stojalowski and his wife moved to the newly opened Medical Academy in Szczecin. Ola Krygier and Stas Woyke also went with them. Jozek Wagner and I were left, without the opportunity for any such move, because we didn't have enough money. Complete defeat threatened us. Jozek fell ill with tuberculosis and had to go to the sanatorium; everybody knew about it, so the threat no longer existed for him. I was left alone as the only remaining target.

I thought long and hard about what I could do in this situation; I knew that the very next day after receiving my diploma, I could be sent to a village in the middle of nowhere or into the army. I remembered that there was a regulation, honored by the regime, that students could not be drafted into the army before finishing their studies. They also could not demand work if someone was a student. So the one thing that could save me would be to begin studies in another field. The division between the University of Poznan and the Medical Academy had already occurred. So I put together the appropriate applications to the heads of both schools, asking for permission to study psychology at the same time. After many difficulties, I finally got that permission. I also got credit for the first year of study in the discipline of psychology as I had completed the appropriate courses in medical school. No one knew about my studies at the philosophy department at the University of Poznan. Often the lectures took place in the evenings, and I didn't go to most of them, as labs were regularly scheduled in the late hours of the afternoon.

The third year of medicine had a much lighter workload than the second, and it served as a sort of introduction to clinical practices, focusing on internal diagnosis and surgery on animals. There were lectures from all kinds of clinical specialties, mainly internal medicine, surgery, and obstetrics and gynecology.

Thus, my psychology studies didn't interfere much with medicine.

The passage from second year to third year in medical school was memorable for me and decidedly influenced the shape of the rest of my life. In July of that year, already after finishing all the exams for the first two years and grasping the basic theoretical issues in medicine, my grandmother, who with my mother had raised me from the time I was an infant, suddenly got sick. One afternoon, she got severe chills, her temperature jumped up, and at the same time she felt a sharp pain in the upper right quadrant of her abdomen. My father immediately called in an internist, supposedly a good one, who concluded that my grandmother suffered from neuralgia and that the fever was the result of a cold. The next day, her condition had already worsened considerably. Her abdomen was distended and sensitive to pain, she began vomiting, and the high fever persisted. The same internist diagnosed peritonitis and didn't offer any hope for recovery. He also concluded that it didn't make sense to send my grandmother to a hospital as they couldn't help her. I didn't know enough then to be able to recognize severe cholecystitis with secondary peritonitis. She should have had surgery immediately; with the absence of antibiotics, the chances for recovery weren't great, but there would have been some hope. The first trials of penicillin were then taking place—though it was very difficult to get and could only be gotten in small amounts. She died consciously, and she was happy that I had completed the two foundational years of medical school, so she knew that I would be a doctor, which was her unfulfilled life dream, as she had gotten married after high school.

My grandmother's death had a significant influence on the shaping of my personality. I was terribly shaken up by it. Even though I had seen death many times during the German occupation, even though I had seen such horrors unfold during my childhood, I hadn't yet lost anyone close to me. Through all the dangers, difficulties, and lacks, we had made it through together—my father, mother, grandmother, and me.

The shared poverty and the shared fight for survival tied us very closely together in one unbreakable knot. And then suddenly, in one week, the entire sense of my life, the support, and the feeling of stability despite existing odds fell into an abyss. I looked with horror at the brown coffin, found the silence of the house very strange, and felt deafened by my own, individual tragedy. I walked with all the others in the burial procession, but I didn't hear the Holy Mass and for many years to come saw only that brown coffin being eased down into a deep hole, and then the rustle of dirt as it was shoveled on top.

The apartment got empty and quiet. My mother didn't even go near the piano. I walked around sad from corner to corner, not knowing what to do with myself. My father took us for a week's vacation to Karpacz, a mountain resort, thinking that a change of scenery and new sights might help us get past the shared tragedy. It didn't do much good. The return trip to an empty home filled with a deafening silence was as awful as the departure.

Luckily for me, I had to study hard to continue my studies at the Medical Academy as well as at the university.

I had to take two initial exams in psychology: the first one in philosophy (we learned from the textbook of Tatarkiewicz), as well as an exam in logic. I didn't go to lectures, because I couldn't, so I would teach myself at home. I did well on the exam for the first part of psychology that I took with Professor Blachowski, an old pre-war professor, as I had forced myself to understand the thoughts and ideas of the ancients as well as the later philosophers.

Philosophical concepts and the effort to understand and make sense of life and its essence fascinated me. My deepest desire was, after meeting death face to face, to understand and explain what no other philosopher had ever been able to put into words.

I was disappointed. I didn't find what I was looking for in any of them. I wasn't convinced by Aristotle, Plato, or Descartes. I read the description of Socrates's death with great interest, but even that one didn't thrill me with his method of reaching the truth by asking questions. Leibnitz only amused me with his concept of "the best of all possible worlds."

In their estimation, you couldn't find any way to make sense of life. I resisted as an arrogant young rebel and looked for an answer but didn't find it, though I did do well on the exam.

I then had to take an exam in so-called "great logic." I went to Professor Wigner's lectures several times; he was also a pre-war professor from the University of Poznan. He was a small, older man in tattered clothes and a crooked tie that had clearly been worn a lot. His gray hair was disheveled; he completely ignored his appearance. And yet this person was able to influence me significantly. I remember a lecture during which he calmly that our thinking is deterministic, that the whole deductive system on which science is based and all our knowledge can be narrowed down to four axioms which were accepted a priori and four definitions accepted the same way.

After we settled resignedly into the cage of determinism he calmly asked the question: why should we not rise above these deterministic constructs? After all, no one was stopping us from creating other logical constructs which would give rise to limitless possibilities, possibilities that at this point our minds couldn't even imagine.

I saw that he had opened up a vastness before my eyes that wasn't recognized but still existed, and I also understood the rather laughable position of those "philosophical proofs." I was fascinated by the incredible possibilities of knowing through broadened logical systems that deviated from so far accepted forms. After many years, I convinced myself that my feelings were right—presently, in astronomy they are using not only the fourth, but also the fifth and sixth dimension, and the relationship between "cause and effect" is not one-directional, but rather, at least, two-directional. Understanding these things significantly changed my awareness of human physiology and the integral bond between a person and his environment.

Wigner had a huge influence on me, so huge that in those years I was actually considering whether I shouldn't just drop medicine to become yet another "guru" in a field that in those days didn't have any meaning, but that today, in the epoch of computers, is one of the most avant-garde tools for progress.

Unfortunately, I couldn't go to Professor Wigner's lectures because they coincided with my medical studies. Luckily, the professor had published a logic textbook; it wasn't the greatest quality publication, but it encompassed the whole course. I bought that little book, looked through it, and didn't understand anything. There were only some strange equations, with almost no clarifications, from the first to the last page. I didn't want to give up. With the stubbornness of a maniac, I would go back to the same equations often. Slowly, I began to understand what it was about, and the later pages became a little easier. I solved one problem after another, though I got terribly stuck on several pages, not understanding anything. It came time to go to the exam. Professor Wigner, knowing that I hadn't gone to his lectures, asked how I had learned the material. I responded that I had studied his whole book but that on this and that page, I didn't understand a thing. He asked me to show him exactly which pages I was talking about. When I told him, he asked me for my personal grade book and wrote: "Excellent!" I looked at it completely dumbfounded. He looked at me, smiled, and said, "You may not know this, but you're the first person, other than me, to discover the printing mistakes in my book."

Contact with death and biological knowledge about the functioning of the human body called my faith into question. The mechanical interpretation of human behavior and the role of the brain in determining our emotions and thoughts completely fascinated me. During anatomy, I came to the conclusion that the time allotted for dissection of the brain in the prosectorium was really insufficient. From the textbooks, whether Bochenek or Reuberkopsch, I couldn't create a three-dimensional image in my mind of that most important organ. And so, I bought a human brain illegally from the orderly who transports cadavers and brought it home in a bucket of formaldehyde—every night, with the anatomy atlas in my hand, I would learn its secrets. The smell in my room was awful, and you could smell the formaldehyde in nearly the whole apartment, but at least my parents were understanding about it. When the brain was finally all cut up into small pieces, it had to be destroyed. I couldn't bring it back to the prosectorium for obvious reasons, so we burned it in the oven.

In connection to that, I remember another thing that happened in anatomy. Professor Rozycki had created a wonderful museum of anatomical specimens that made learning much easier. They were preserved in pure alcohol. But then, despite the preservation, one after another started to go bad. It turned out that the main orderly who transports cadavers of the anatomy department drank some of the alcohol and diluted the rest with water. I remember him like it was yesterday, with his red-blue face, moving through the Anatomicum's corridors with a somewhat swaying step. He soon died of liver cirrhosis.

My world was becoming more and more complicated. Tradition, faith, and the Church didn't fit in to my newly acquired knowledge. That which I was taught led to a materialistic understanding of human existence. We were taught that our emotions were controlled by a specified structure of the brain—the hypothalamus and limbic system (the part of the brain determining emotional reactions). In that teaching, there was no place for the soul, for a spiritual perspective of human existence. The logic lectures, however, greatly shook up this mechanical view of people. I came to see that all our knowledge, as great as it was, uncovered only a tiny fragment of the vastness of reality. Einstein's theory of relativity or

Planck's quantum theory enabled a better understanding of certain physical phenomena that, up to that point, no one had been able to make into a logical whole, but they were still incomplete views of a reality that we were still unable to fully understand. As I write these words, science has made tremendous advances, but it still rests on the same four axioms and definitions that were accepted thousands of years ago!

This understanding of human limitations turned me into an agnostic—a person who doesn't know—at the age of nineteen. I didn't discard my traditions or faith and, though full of doubts, didn't leave the Church. I read somewhere that in the history of the Church, they wanted to burn agnostics at the stake. I also don't remember which pope finally settled the matter. The conclusion was interesting: It was not a sin to claim that one didn't know, because the Church rested on faith, which is obviously a grace. That really cheered me up and comforted me.

Several events, from which I had been isolated up to that point, occurred during my third year of medicine. The Soviet dictatorship was becoming more and more brutal, there were accounts of the "heroic" destruction of armed reactionary groups of the WIN[7]-u in the press. People disappeared and there was talk of prisons overflowing with members of the Polish intelligentsia, National Army soldiers, and pre-war officers. But my life was somewhat isolated from these incidents; it revolved closely around education, both at the university and at home.

My father, a survey engineer, like his colleagues, wanted to rebuild Poland. But from nearly the very beginning it became obvious that the "authorities" were shooting down any efforts to make things better, and, instead, purposely harmed and sabotaged them. And that's not all. A terror action began against the workers in the department of agricultural surveys. I recall the fate of engineer Surman, an older man with gray hair, a heretic-atheist, and a decent and honest person. He didn't have a family and often came

---

7. Underground independence organization, Wolnosc I Niepodleglosc, Freedom and Indepence.

over to our apartment. And then, one day he disappeared without a trace. Only after weeks had already gone by did my father find out that he had been arrested and put in jail. Engineer Grodzki was also arrested, though he was released after a few weeks. He was a survey engineer, while Surman was an agricultural engineer. The difference was significant, because just then, a regime was beginning to form collectives and government-subsidized farms, based on the Soviet model, and the goal was to create maximal chaos so as to then "improve" the situation through the Sovietization of Poland. Surman's arrest deeply shook me up; for the first time, I saw the whole danger of the situation, understood the baseness of the system that had been put upon us, and saw that, though it was under different circumstances, we were again in an occupation.

Years later, when I was already in America, a document came into my possession that had been sent to Bierut[8] from Moscow. It presented the demonic plan to destroy Poland in bullet points.

We were filled with contempt for the West for betraying Polish interests, for turning against us at Yalta. Poland, the unappreciated ally of the West had shed so much blood during the Second World War.

At the same time, in schools, students had to absorb all kinds of communist poison. Even at the medical academy, as well as the University, I had to take an exam in "Marxism-Leninism," with the only difference being that at the University it encompassed more extensive material.

In bookstores, the beautifully published writings of Marx, Engels, and Lenin—the famous *Short History of the WKPb*—appeared with red covers. We were forced to read it all and remember it. I read the history of the Russian communist party very quickly; it was so poorly written and full of mistakes that it nearly aroused pity. And I knew history rather well; during high school, I had even written historical essays. The writings of Lenin fascinated me extremely. For the first time, I had pure, clear, open satanic literature in my hands. Lenin was undoubtedly a good

---

8. Bolestlaw Bierut, a Colonel of the Soviet secret service imposed as President of the Polish Peoples Republic.

strategist and, at the same time, a Satanist without limits. And Satanism had something to it that drew you in.[9]

When I went for my exam, I was confident in my knowledge of the forced reading. The reading of Lenin's writings didn't go to waste. I understood that Lenin had emphasized in them a whole plan of action, a plan to destroy humanity and transform it into slavery. It was Lucifer's perfect plan, a plan for a horrifying utopia in which a wonderful new world would rise from an ocean of blood.

Later in the United States, I would often hear that Russian communism was warped, that "pure communism" is ideal, not self-interested, and even compatible with Christ's teachings! I never fell for such garbage. Because I became very familiar with its theory and its practice, I could always refute such destructive nonsense.

In the third year of medicine, clinical work began—the first contact with sick patients, the first experience of suffering, pain, and human frailty. We were young, and young people don't understand suffering the way that older, more experienced people do. Youth is in a way cruel and at the same time not resilient.

I was fascinated by everything from the first moment, when the stethoscope was in my hand, when I heard the beating of a human heart for the first time. When I walked into the operating room, I saw sick people being wheeled in on gurneys, blood on the floor, and the figures of surgeons bent over the operating table—all of this excited me, but I didn't give much thought to the suffering of the patients.

I remember the internal medicine lectures led by two professors, Roguski and Kwasniewski, with different personalities and teaching methods. I can't forget Professor Drews, the chief of surgery, and his associate professor Borszewski, who spent most of his time in surgical wards and operating rooms. He remembered the names and problems of all the patients, and there were about sixty of them!

---

9. Pope John Paul II said the following at one of his general assemblies: "Evil possesses a mighty power of attraction."

I also remember my friends from that time, those with whom I kept in close contact. After the departure of Ola Krygier, Stojalowska, and Stas Woyke to Szczecin, and Jozek Wagner to Zakopane, I was left rather alone. From time to time, Leon Konieczny would come over; though he was drafted into the army after getting his diploma. I kept in touch with my high school friend Dziewulski, who studied economics.

With Dziewulski, I would often go to concerts of the Poznan Philharmonic. The hall was still riddled with bullet holes, the seats were hard, and the orchestra was still being completed, but it was always full—mostly with young academics and the remains of the intelligentsia who were able to survive the Occupation. Classical music wasn't new to me. My mother, though not a concert pianist, played most of Chopin's pieces very well, as well as Beethoven's sonatas, and Mozart's music. She loved Scarlatti and didn't like Bach.

In the first year of medical school, I started going to music lessons—late, as I was supposed to start lessons when the war suddenly started. My mother took me to a professor at the conservatory, Mrs. Finklow, in 1938. She was a Jewish woman who at that time was also teaching my mother. The war disrupted everything, and only God knows what happened to Mrs. Finklow. Though I was a young boy, I remember well how she would play chords and ask me to describe them. She concluded that I had good tone recognition and would make a good student. When we recovered our piano that the Germans hadn't taken away in Poznan, we returned to music again. And that's how I began my lessons with an old retired woman, a professor at the conservatory. She taught very well, though after the first year I had to stop learning—I just didn't have time for it. I did manage to go, at least once a week, to the Philharmonic. The tickets were cheap, and the music overjoyed and enraptured me. To this day, I remember how I felt during Brahms's symphony; it was so romantic, and even now as I play the piano version of the main movement, my thoughts drift back to those days.

The quality of life was getting more and more harsh. The regime forced upon us by the Soviet occupant with the help of Polish traitors was getting worse, but I was young and full of eagerness, wanting knowledge. And that's how nearly all of my friends were in my class. It was a strange group, younger and older, those who had come out of the underground, of course not admitting to their past, those who had survived the war in Poznan as citizens of the Third Reich, and those whose fate it had been to be exiled from the Eastern region of Poland, deceptively stolen by the Russians and covered in the blood of millions of people. Each one had some past, but the common denominator was the desire to gain the knowledge for which we had fought.

It might seem strange to also have good memories from the period of the Bierut era, a period of terror and poverty. It may simply be that young people can find a handful of happiness even in the most difficult circumstances.

One colleague who would come over often was Mietek Wender. He was a little shorter than me and had a thin nose that was red at the tip and always moved a little, like a rabbit's did. His hair was a nondescript reddish-brown color, and his eyes ran all over the place. I knew him from high school. He was a good student. He quickly joined quite deliberately the PPR (Polish Party of Workers). He did it on purpose, hoping to better his career. He liked to come by, mainly to see how I progressed so that he could compare with his own advancement.

My grandmother couldn't stand him, but he would come by, often despite that, even when uninvited. I still tolerated him then; I discovered his true character later when I had finished medical school.

In that time, maybe because of the intensity of the work and schooling, and the desire to reach the goal I had dreamed about, I wasn't especially interested in the opposite sex. At the dissection table, I had a good friend who I liked and with whom I danced at a few of the academic parties. It was great to dance with her, because she was small, light, and thin. Still during medical school, she married a friend from the same prosectorium group. Much later, I found out that the marriage wasn't that great and that her life wasn't easy.

I remember another friend, Basia, who was full of sex appeal and charm. She had a big influence on me, made me feel shy and excited at the same time. But it never came to anything. Years later, when I was an assistant in neurosurgery and she was a doctor, married with a child, she would call me late at night terrified that her son had a brain tumor, because he was vomiting. I told her that she was talking nonsense and suggested that she go to sleep. She would always thank me, being reassured.

There was also a couple in our class that was impossible to forget. She was a light blonde with beautiful classic features and a wonderful, somewhat full, figure; he was tall and dark-haired with black penetrating eyes and a bouncy hairdo, maybe a bit too bouncy for those times and circumstances. This couple, as opposed to others, officially manifested their bond. They didn't do very well in school, just barely passed with C's. After getting his diploma, he dumped her, and I don't know what happened to him. She, not having any specialty, worked in a regional outpatient clinic. She gained some weight, and her light blue eyes lost their former luster. She certainly experienced something awful.

Jozek Wagner finally returned from his treatment. He had always been fascinated by internal medicine. Because he had an incredible memory and knew German—those textbooks were then the easiest to obtain—he soon advanced in clinical diagnosis of internal diseases

In the later years of school, I was interested in two fields—neurology and oddly enough, obstetrics. As part of my training I was shut in with a group of other older students in a hospital for women's illnesses for several weeks. That hospital, whose name I unfortunately can't remember, was a large complex of somewhat-blackened red brick built in a German style. The inside was clean and bright, and it smelled strongly of antiseptic. Our chief was Associate Professor Ryglewicz, who was tall with broad shoulders, red hair, a ruddy complexion and large, red hands. He actually

anti-abortion

gave the impression of being a huge, just-delivered newborn. We slept in special rooms for students, four to five in a room, on bunk beds. Every other night, we were on-call in the delivery room. There was no talk of sleep, because during the night someone was always either coming in or going out, turning on the light, and not even bothering to whisper. More than once, sitting on a high metal stool in the delivery room, vis-à-vis dozens of women in labor, despite the yells, wails, and noise, I was able to doze off. The delivery room made a great impression on me. That act of a new life coming into the world, the pain and suffering, the fear and sweat, and then the cry of the newborn and the joy of everyone, not only the mother but also us, who shared in this wonder of nature. The delivery room is usually a place of joy.

There were, however, some tragedies. One of the women, in a very late-term of her pregnancy, developed sepsis. The fetus was dead, and it had to be removed. I watched in fear as Associate Professor Ryglewicz forced a sharp tool into the child's head and removed the brain from inside out so as to decrease her size and get the unfortunate little body out. The partial-birth abortion of the newborn left an awful impression with me—even though the fetus was in fact already dead. Now, when I hear "liberal" American arguments against prohibiting abortions in the third trimester of pregnancy, when the child can already survive, and the abortion happens in exactly the same way, by the partial birth of a live and moving newborn, I am filled with horror at how far people can go on the road to evil in justifying crimes.

Ryglewicz, with his imposing build, also distinguished himself with a deep, booming voice. It was his vocation to be a doctor. He saw patients in a small office with glass doors that divided the examination room from the small waiting room. The panes were matte, though it wasn't difficult to hear the associate professor's statements. First, there would be a shy, quiet female voice and then a loud declaration, for the whole world to hear, "My dear, I don't do that!" Truthfully, it wasn't difficult to figure out what they were talking about.

Ryglewicz was killed in a train accident; he fell under the train's wheels, which cut off his leg at the part of the pelvis. He was conscious and said, "Don't do anything because I'll die anyway." Death came quickly after these words. It was a shock to me; it was hard for me to accept the fact that he was gone—he who was my idol, healer and truly all around good man.

My dreams of a career in gynecology quickly ended when I worked in the female oncology ward. It was an awful ward—dying women, burned from the radiation treatment with all the possible complications in their abdominal organs that you could imagine. In that stage of development in Polish medicine, there was no mention of Foley catheters, which are put into the bladder when the patient has a loss of bladder control. In the cancer ward, the stink of urine, excrement, and rotting flesh hung like an ominous stench of incoming death in the air.

How many years have passed since those days! And how therapeutic possibilities have changed! Still, even today, a lot of young women die from late-stage cancer, maybe in a better environment but in the same shadow of a slow and painful death.

Besides Associate Professor Ryglewicz, two other mentors left clear imprints on my life. The first was Professor Dowzenko, a neurologist, and the second was Associate Professor Borszewski, who I have already mentioned, a surgeon in the first Surgical Clinic in Poznan.

Professor Dowzenko was a small, thin man with graying hair and piercing eyes that looked out through the thick lenses of his glasses. He spoke in a calm, quiet voice without any particular emphasis, but he could fascinate hundreds of listeners such that no one even coughed. He would walk into the auditorium and stand at the pulpit; in the room there was the usual commotion and conversations. He didn't pay much attention to the students or their behavior, just began his lecture in a quiet, calm voice. After a few minutes, silence fell; I can't explain how he achieved this. Maybe it was just the way he lectured that made a difference. Or maybe they were very well written and thought out, but in any case, that's what happened. His favorite saying stuck in my mind, sounding rather pessimistic. When he named neurological illnesses, one after another, mainly degenerative ones, he said, "The cause is unknown." Indeed, in those years, little was known about genetically triggered neurological syndromes, not to mention that no one had any precise idea about the endocrine function of brain tissue.

Neurology fascinated me with its logic. The nervous system can be compared to an unspeakably complicated electrical network controlled by a supercomputer. Logic and a good thorough neurological examination can lead to a rather accurate localization of the lesion. This logic really fascinated me, so I studied neurology happily and would regularly come well prepared to Professor Dowzenko's lectures. Once that preparation for a lecture created a bit of a complication. I knew that the next day various kinds of epilepsy would be discussed, such as grand mal, petit mal, and other seizure activity from different foci of the brain.

The lecture began. It happened that I was sitting in the last row, high up in the back. Because I already knew what the lecture was going to be about, I amused myself by mimicking various epileptic attacks as they were being described by Professor Dowzenko, much to the amusement of my friends. When he finished, he calmly and quietly said, "If you don't remember my lecture, then ask that guy to show you every attack again."

He said this without a smile on his face, but in his eyes flashed what seemed like a giggle. I easily got an A on the neurology exam.

I lived with my parents first near Gorczynski Street, renamed Rokossowski Street, then in the very city center in an old apartment building in which one large apartment had been divided into a few smaller ones. The building was on the corner and passing streetcars made a characteristic screeching sound as they turned toward the city center. That screech woke me up early. I would take those streetcars to the clinical hospital. It was rather far to Diakoniski, and you had to transfer from one streetcar to another.

One day in the early sunny morning, we arrived at Grunwaldzki, where the streetcars stopped. The cause was an accident on the road. So, I looked over the internal medicine exercises. When I caught up with my group, the young, boastful, "red" assistant yelled, "You're late; there's no place for people like you here. Get out of here; you won't complete internal medicine."

My explanations that there had been an accident were to no avail. The assistant threw me out of the rotation with a yell. I had to go to the dean of the department to get permission to continue the internal medicine rotation and also to continue my study of medicine. I got this permission without any trouble, as the dean knew about the accident I had described.

In a strange twist of fate, many years later, I ran into that unkind individual. I was already a neurosurgeon then, when we got word over the phone that one of the professors in Szczecin had suddenly fallen ill and was unconscious. The neurologist had ordered a neurosurgical consult. At that time in Szczecin, there was no neurosurgery clinic yet. My chief at that time, Dr. Powiertowski, sent me to do the consult. We went in an emergency rescue plane. The trip in the small plane was interesting; the pilot was a Polish air-force pilot who had participated in defending England. He, of course, couldn't admit to his past, as he would be in danger of prison and a painful death. We flew low in the sky, so that, once in a while, a herd of cows would scatter in the meadows upon hearing the engine noise.

I finally reached the clinical hospital in Szczecin and the patient whom I had been called to see. He was that same assistant who had treated me so badly during my internal medicine rotation. He didn't need surgery; he regained consciousness while I was standing over his bed. I'll never forget the look on his face! Human fate certainly takes a strange turn sometimes.

After the fourth year of medical school, I really wanted to go on vacation, but there was no money to do so. Camps for kids were being organized then, and medical students were hired to handle first aid and maintain appropriate sanitary conditions in the camp. I applied and was accepted. I went to the Owl Mountains with a group of guys, teachers, and women who would be running the kitchen and washing the kids' clothes.

We arrived late and it was already dark by the time we reached the formerly German school in which we were staying. The children were tired, and we had to take care of their sleeping arrangements and give them something to eat and drink. When they finally got into bed, sometime around midnight, I and the head of the whole affair, a "red" teacher who was there to lead ideology classes, and one other teacher went to a local tavern to get something to eat. We were hungry and tired. There, a group of drunken young hoodlums tried to beat us up. We ran away under cover of darkness back to the school. We were young and weren't directed by healthy reason so much as by anger that we had been treated in such a way. The rest of the teachers joined us along with some of the teenagers from the older grades, and armed with sticks, we went back to that tavern. A fight broke out. I remember that I hit one of them in the back with a board torn off a fence. He fell and didn't get up again. I also remember and can still picture at this very moment how that "red" teacher pushed one of the rogue's heads into a toilet and patiently waited until he saw the air bubbles had ceased.

We beat them up terribly. We took one of them back to the school as a prisoner and locked him in one of the classrooms on the second floor. Late at night, he jumped out the window and supposedly twisted his leg. Our triumph, however, didn't last long. In the morning, agents from the Office of State Security/UB showed up. An interrogation began, full of insults and warnings. Our "red" commander told us, "Don't admit to anything. We were all just sleeping here at the school and don't know anything about it.

We listened and despite threats to "beat us down" in jail, we didn't admit to anything. The interrogations lasted two days. The fury of the UB officer was completely understandable—it just happened that we had beaten up none other than the entire active local party group.

Still at this moment, I think in horror of what could have happened. I could have ended up in prison in the worst times, could have died there in suffering. My hopes and dreams would be finished once and for all, and if I survived, I would be a nobody. Our "red" commander gave us a good pep talk and raised our spirits. He filed a complaint at the local province party committee, and the UB was called off. We all breathed a sigh of relief.

I remember that camp well. The beauty of the Owl Mountains in the summer sun's rays, the silence, the peace, and the company of children made it possible to relax and forget about that first unwelcome party. We had been given food for the children, mainly flour and kasha, and there was a lot of it. We came to the conclusion with the cooks that we could sell some of these products at the local market and, with the money from the sale, we could buy vegetables, fruit, and some meat. The cooks had been transferred over from the Eastern region of Poland, and they could cook very well. Everyone was thrilled with the dishes they prepared; there were terrific soups, meats, vegetables, and fruit. My work was limited to putting on bandages for minor cuts. Fortunately, none of the children got really sick.

A few kilometers from our camp, there was a similar camp for girls. A medical student worked there with similar duties to mine. One day, she came over to our camp. I was of course polite and hospitable, and she ate some of our delicious dinner and stayed until dusk. She asked me to walk her back, as she was scared to walk by herself in the forest. I agreed happily, and we went on our way. We reached a small clearing where a tree had fallen over. She wanted to rest there for a little while. We sat there for about fifteen minutes, and then finally reached her camp. I said goodbye and walked back at a quick pace, as it was already very late. A few days later, I found out that she had called me a fool. Why? It's not easy to answer that question. The lesson I learned from that experience is that of course one must oblige the ladies' desires if one wants to avoid their wrath. I never repeated that mistake again.

The fourth and fifth years of medical school went by quickly— between clinical work, studying at home, and trying as hard as I could to memorize a tremendous amount of material. I took also the philosophy examination with Professor Blachowski. The last volume of Tatarkiewicz's textbook was not accessible, because it "deviated away from party lines." The mumbling of the party poured more and more over life like murky, dirty drain water. It was hard to get away from it, as all the newspapers, the entire press, were overflowing with "ideological" articles written by Russian propagandists—Jews that had been specially trained in this discipline in the Soviet Union. The same party mumbling poured out of radio speakers and children's textbooks, reaching even the pre-school level. Parents couldn't speak freely at home, because small children were trained to be informants. Life went on as if in a state of schizophrenia—that which was false was heralded as truth and truth was made false, and you had to pretend constantly that you believed in it. Everyone kept silent, except for those who had sold their souls to the devil. They were loud and dangerous.

Sometimes, the party members who screened the press didn't do their job well. I'll never forget the theater section, "The Green Goose," in *Przekroj* magazine, written by Galczynski. In one of them, this kind of action takes place. The people walk onto the stage. They call out, "The regime, the regime!"—Silence.—"The regime, the regime!"—Silence. The curtain falls. The Regime does not respond to the people.

This constant Stalinist indoctrination combined with the persistent extermination of thousands of Polish intelligentsia did not break the Polish spirit nor the silent resistance.

I was taking clinical exams. I was well-prepared and regularly got A's. It didn't happen without some adventures. I studied pediatrics from a German textbook. Aside from the sheer vastness of the subject, it was also full of additional material to memorize, such as recipes for various formulas essential for feeding infants and the periods of development of infectious diseases in childhood. I hated this dull cramming of material that didn't follow any larger logic, but I gave myself the task of memorizing all the data, if not for the rest of my life as a doctor, then at least for the period of taking exams.

Armed with this knowledge, I went to Professor Jonscher to take the exam; he was a very kind person with a rather large head covered with a small amount of hair and blue eyes, looking at the world with kindness. He reminded me, though I really don't know why, of a big somewhat-grown baby. When I showed up for the exam, it turned out that the professor had left, and his associate professor, Rafinski, was giving the exam. It began with those unfortunate dormant periods of measles, rubella, pertussis, etc. Because I had it all in my head, I recited it in one breath, without hesitation. I heard in response, "Wrong, you're giving the incorrect data."

This upset me deeply, because I had gotten the data from a good textbook.

"No, my information is true; it is supported in this and that textbook."

He got red in the face, and his eyes flashed with anger. "Oh, well, if you're so smart, let's see what you really know!"

He started asking me about material that wasn't even included in the program. Of course, I wasn't able to answer.

"See," he said, "it's better not to argue with professors. I'm not writing a grade for you in your grade book; come back in two weeks."

Well then, I went back home, studied like mad, flipped through other textbooks, and went to the retake I had been given. When I came to the pediatric clinic, I asked the secretary to please have Professor Jonscher examine me and not his associate professor. He heard me through the open door however and called me into his office. I told him that I would like to be examined not by him but by the director of the department. He was embarrassed and pretty much forced me to agree to take the exam with him. I didn't have any way out. He asked me a few ridiculous questions and said, "Well, you got a B."

When he opened my grade book to the right page, where exams from clinical subjects were recorded, and saw only A's, he gave me the same A in pediatrics.

My last exam was in forensic medicine. Before we even got to the exam, we were required to perform a specific number of autopsies on corpses in the prosectorium of forensic medicine— of course under the supervision of an assistant or an adjunct.

The material was very diverse, from murders to accidents. It was winter, and I was wearing my one warm wool suit, which I wore to lectures. We didn't change in forensics; over your own shirt and pants, you put on a rubber apron and did the autopsy. I reported to "perform" my autopsy.

The assistant told me to do an autopsy on a rather young woman, who had been found in her apartment when the awful smell of decomposing flesh had spread into the stairwell. She had to have been lying there dead for at least a week. If I did her autopsy in my wool suit, that awful smell would stay in my clothes forever. I said this to the assistant, who barked back, "I don't care; you're to do it, and that's that!"

I refused and reported to the director of the department and explained what had happened. He acknowledged that I was right, but wanting also to support his assistant, he told me to do not one but three autopsies. I had the opportunity to do them the next day. Three Polish air-force pilots crashed from the height of seven hundred meters. It was really a strange thing to see. The bodies weren't crushed, the facial features were almost intact. Extremities were deformed by the multiple fractures and discolored by the bruises in the area of impact. When I opened the chest and abdomen, however, there wasn't a single organ that hadn't been completely crushed. The incredible force of a collision with the earth at such a high speed became so obvious. I then made an important discovery, at least for me—that our skin was unbelievably elastic and resistant to breaking.

I completed the autopsies and could then take the exam. I already had all the other clinical exams behind me; this was the last one before getting my diploma. I didn't feel like studying, but the time for the exam was quickly approaching. On the critical day, I determined that I didn't know enough. I didn't have any more time to study, so I just flipped through that part of the textbook that touched on the legal side, trusting that I would somehow be able to manage the medical section. The first question was about those legal paragraphs. I recited them without mistakes, and the rest was just a formality. I got an A, though I really didn't deserve one.

On December 28, 1951, I finished medical school and got my diploma. It was a diploma with honors, luckily still in an ordinary blue cover, and not how it would be the next year, in a red one for the valedictorian.

UPON RECEIVING MY MEDICAL
DEGREE WITH HONORS IN 1951

8

Surgical Intern and Residency

IT WAS A time of propagating "honorable workers," or "Stachanows" (named after a Russian worker, Stachanow, who supposedly worked much harder than required), a period of wrongfully emphasizing the "leading role of the worker and peasant in the party." I remember a joke from that time—the only defense of a subjected nation. In that joke, there was talk of a village leader who intended to fart and accomplished 200% of norm!

During that time, party members were hired for all the young assistant positions at university clinics, while the rest were forced to go to the country where they were sentenced to a slow dulling existence, cut off from knowledge and literature, or drafted into the army, an even more horrible fate. The general of the medical corps of the People's Army of Poland was General Ogorkow, who a few years later was diagnosed as an advanced-stage schizophrenic and put in a mental institution.

As I already mentioned, the only defense against such a fate was further study. I was protected by the fact that I was a fourth-year psychology student. So, no one bothered me at the moment. But my situation still wasn't great, because I absolutely couldn't get into any kind of specialty training. I sent applications everywhere and received rejections almost immediately. It became clear that with my "political orientation" I wouldn't get work anywhere in Poznan. I traveled all over Poland to no avail. All the doors were closed to me. I sat at home, studying for my psychology exams, filled with despair.

Suddenly, my colleague from high school and college, Mietek Wender, showed up. He had become a party member early on. He came supposedly to visit me, but the purpose of his visit was just to boast. And so, I found myself in a situation from which I didn't see a way out, while he was already an assistant in the Neurology Clinic of the Diakoniski Hospital. He would talk grandiosely about what he did and what he planned to do, and said incidentally that the party leaders took all the young assistant positions in surgery and gynecology and that supposedly the same thing was happening in the internal medicine clinic. He didn't cheer me up, and I only grew to hate him more. His cynicism and surrender disgusted me, and I wasn't even jealous of his success, despite the fact that my situation was a lot worse.

Motivated by despair and determined to fight until the end, I went to Warsaw, where my aunt lived with her husband and sons, and went to see the Minister of Health, hoping to force my way into his very office. I didn't get there, but instead reached his secretary, who turned out to be a very kind and cultured lady, and not a "regime supporter." She listened with interest to the story of my difficulties and asked if I had a diploma with honors. When I confirmed that I did, she informed me that the Russian military authorities had ordered the Ministry of Health to train seventy doctors with high-honor diplomas in neurosurgery. In that time, the Soviet Union didn't have any neurosurgeons, while in Poland, there was a Neurosurgery Clinic in Warsaw that was directed by Professor Jerzy Choróbski. In Krakow, Professor Kunicki opened a similar clinic, and Professor Ferenc was in the process of organizing a neurosurgery ward in Wroclaw.

The reason that Russian military authorities ordered the training of Polish doctors in the field of neurosurgery is quite simple. In a time of unspeakable tension between the East and the West and the famous period of the "Berlin bridge" when allies brought food to Western Berlin by air, war hung by a thread. The Russians wanted to have a neurosurgical service.

The Ministry of Health had created the appropriate fellowships, and that lady already had the proper forms on her desk. She asked me if I wanted to be one of those who received such a fellowship. She added that the Russian authorities didn't care if the candidate was or wasn't a party member—he just had to have a diploma with honors. I seized this opportunity like a drowning man grabs at the tiniest thing. I filled out the form on her desk.

She suggested that I wait patiently, because she had several documents that the "Colleague" minister would have to sign. She also said incidentally, "I'll put your application inside; this nitwit won't even know what he's signing."

With a thumping heart, I waited for her to return. After a moment, she came out of the office with a smile on her face as well as the signed document. I don't know her name, but I have the deepest possible gratitude toward her. In just a few minutes, I had gotten a fellowship from the Ministry of Health in neurosurgery, with a salary of eight hundred zloty a month (one meter of good-quality material for a suit cost seven hundred zloty). I was happy, as the nightmare that had haunted me during the last months of 1951 lifted the way a fog does, and a new road stood open before me.

Neither my uncle nor my aunt could believe I had gotten so lucky.

The very next day, I went to the Neurosurgery Clinic in the Medical Academy of Warsaw, finding myself at the university hospital by Oczki Street. I went there after a sleepless night. I had stayed the night with my uncle's family in Radosc, where they had a nice apartment on the first floor; I slept on the convertible bed in the living room. Thoughts raced through my mind as did feelings of joy and fear.

It was January 1952. The hospital pavilion was located in a big park that was covered in deep snow. On the mat by the entrance, I wiped off my snow-covered boots as best I could and went inside.

I reported to the secretary, told her my name, and asked to see Professor Choróbski. This woman rather critically evaluated me, but after a moment of waffling, she brought me to the professor's office. I then met my future master/teacher. He made a big impression on me—small, with a thin, almost sharp face and piercing eyes. His ears were thin, almost like a monkey's, and his voice was rough and impatient.

"What do you want here?" I heard.

This wasn't very encouraging. Without a word, I gave him the invaluable document. He glanced at it, frowned, and said, "Well, if they've sent you already, there's nothing I can do. Go to the ward and get a white coat."

I got the impression that Professor Choróbski took me for a "regime supporter." And that's indeed how it appeared, but he soon figured out that I had been formed from a very different mold.

I reported to Mrs. Jadza, the head nurse—an attractive blonde with a nice figure fully aware of her somewhat faded attraction. She also evaluated me rather harshly while giving me a white coat and told me where I was supposed to go. On the ground floor, there was a long corridor perpendicular to the entrance that stretched out in two directions. On the right were Professor Choróbski's office, the adjuncts' room, and the operating rooms; while on the left were patients' rooms. At the very end, past the corridor, was a large, bright room with a ton of windows and a long table in the middle surrounded by rows of messily placed chairs. It turned out that this was the physicians' lounge. I don't remember who I met there, whether Stefan Banacha with black curly hair from his Jewish mother, or Zbyszek Szlaminski with the thick lenses of a near-sighted person and a cigarette always hanging off his lower lip, or Associate Professor Sierpinski, with gray hair and a reddish nose.

All of this got mixed up in my memory. I was shy, lost, and uncertain of what would happen. Someone introduced me, and someone brought me to the operating room where Choróbski was beginning surgery on an urgent case. In the hall, I saw an orderly wheeling out a gurney on which a still figure was covered with a white sheet. The stillness of that figure filled me with horror. I found the operating room. It was spacious, covered in olive-green tiles. The ceiling was painted black and was almost invisible in the light of the operating lamp.

I saw only the gray-green silhouettes of two assistants and the hunched-over figure of Professor Choróbski in the middle. I heard moans. The patient was undergoing surgery with local anesthesia; anesthesia technique was at such a low level that it was safer to give the patient oxygen and local anesthesia. I walked up closer and glanced at the operative field. I was filled with horror. I saw a huge wound with a torn-up brain. Blood was pouring out and dripping down on the green surgical drapes. The patient was a young soldier who had happened to shoot himself with a rifle in such a way that the bullet entered under the chin then lodged itself deep inside the brain, massacring the face on its way. His state was very serious, near death. Despite the efforts of the surgeon, the irregular, rattling breathing stopped. This first experience of the drama of the operating room and death at the hands of the surgeon shocked me completely. Shocked, I walked into the dim hallway blinking my eyes to see the corpse of yet another patient being brought out.

My first day at Warsaw's neurosurgery ward was also the worst day that clinic ever saw. Six patients died on the ward, and the seventh was that soldier. Neither before nor after was the death toll that high. I returned to my uncle's home in Radosc feeling shattered. My aunt Nata comforted me as best she could, gave me something to eat, and tried to talk about other things. In the evening, Uncle Wladek came home. He, too, though a survey engineer, had dreamed of going into medicine when he was younger. He listened with interest to the news of my experiences and didn't say anything or try to cheer me up, for which I was grateful. My teenage cousins, Andrzej and Stasek, were rather preoccupied with their own lives. Night fell. I was left alone on the convertible bed in the living room. I couldn't stop myself from crying, but I told myself that I wouldn't give up, that I would make it through everything and just had to keep going.

For the next two weeks, I went to the neurosurgery clinic regularly. I didn't have anything particular to do there; I participated in rounds, assisted in examining patients, and watched autopsies of the brains that Professor Choróbski performed with the whole team on Saturdays after grand rounds.

There was a large library there of neurosurgery monographs, but they were all in English. Before World War II, Choróbski had been trained in the United States in the neurosurgery department at Northwestern University in Chicago under the direction of Professor Bucy as well as at the McGill Institute in Montreal where the chief was Dr. Penfield. He brought an entire neurosurgery library back with him; it was really a treasure in those days, because literature on this subject didn't exist in the Polish language. He also regularly received the *Journal of Neurology,* from which assistants had to translate certain articles selected for them by the professors and then present them at the appropriate conferences.

Luckily, English wasn't completely foreign to me. During my education, I had gone regularly for lessons to Mrs. Guzy, where I also learned grammar and syntax. But the English medical terms, especially in such a specialized field like neurosurgery, were completely unknown to me.

Choróbski gave me a huge volume called *Brain Tumors* for personal use; it was written by the famous American neurosurgeon, Dr. Bailey, and said that in the beginning I had to read it. I took that volume bound in dark blue fabric gently into my hand and, with a dictionary within reach, started reading. The first page took me two nights. I had to look up just about every second or third word in the dictionary and even then uncovered the meaning presented there with difficulty. The later pages were a little easier, and when my problems with the language lessened, I became more and more fascinated by the style of that book. I had never read anything like it before. It was a classic describing the clinical progress of brain tumors, including classifications and surgical options. The novelty of the book was that Dr. Bailey didn't generalize about particular syndromes but rather presented them in the form of concrete clinical cases. When I read those descriptions, I felt as though I was right there, as if I were going to decide the patient's fate.

Despite the incredible advances in neurosurgery and the teaching disciplines associated with it, despite the sea of literature and information, Dr. Bailey's book is still treated with reverence today as a classic.

Warsaw neurosurgery in those days brought together a large group or more or less talented people. The head and chief was of course Professor Choróbski, and his right-hand man was Rudnicki—tall, thin, intelligent and somewhat arrogant, who almost didn't notice someone in a position as low as mine. There was Wislawski, below Rudnicki, who had light blue eyes and a shining blonde head of hair and was roundish with small, plump hands. This last fellow also took care of the laboratory. Easygoing, while at the same time off-putting, he, unlike Rudnicki, was an active party member. Next came Szapiro, a Jew with black hair and a dark complexion, who was of course a banner-waving party member and quite loud and arrogant. He was not, however, one of Professor Choróbski's favorites.

One of the stranger figures was Dr. Sierpinski, previously named Margulec. He was Jewish, a pre-war psychiatrist, and a member of the Polish Communist Party, which incidentally was made up by roughly eighty percent Jews. He was destructively intelligent, analyzing and negating everything and not reaching any positive conclusions. He could see and evaluate his colleagues well, familiar with their worst sides and shortcomings. He himself was an honest person, an idealist pre-war communist, for whom the People's Republic of Poland stood as a parody of his beliefs. He treated most of the members of that regime informally, and though he could have taken a high position and found himself in a leadership position, he didn't do anything of the kind—he only occasionally used some of his connections for the good of the Neurosurgery Clinic. He wasn't an exceptional surgeon, because he didn't have that cold skill of unwavering concentration that was essential for carrying out the difficult and tiring, physically demanding surgeries. He diagnosed very well, however, and had a good rapport with his patients and his colleagues, despite that he knew them very well and enjoyed making fun of them at every opportunity.

He had an interesting past. During the Occupation, together with most Jews, he had landed in a transitional camp, and then was jammed into a beastly train car with a horrified and screaming crowd. The destination of the trip was Treblinka, a then well-known death camp. During the trip, Sierpinski and another young Jew didn't surrender to the hopelessness of the situation like the others did and instead tore off planks from the floor so as to escape, risking being crushed by pieces of the train that were sticking out.

The ones who would be left behind started warning them that the "Germans would be enraged!" But this didn't do anything. They dropped down into the dark hole. The train went by, both survived, and they became part of a guerilla fighting group.

Doctor Sierpinski was probably the first person who treated me decently and showed me some warmth. The second was Toczek, a huge guy with somewhat Tatar-like facial features (I don't know where they were from, as he came from an average Polish village.). He was calm and careful in his movements, a skillful and quick surgeon. He also treated me decently, "noticed" me, and warmly engaged me in conversation. Many others also worked in the clinic. Dr. Kozniewska, who I would call a "saint" of the People's Republic of Poland, was a loner, not especially attractive, and full of complexes—she also got pregnant without a husband and boasted about it at every opportunity. A banner-waving Stalinist, she spoke quietly and calmly but was full of confidence and inner arrogance. When a surgery didn't work out well for her—which happened rather often—she would fall into hysterics and cry.

Finally, there was also Dr. Powiertowski, who was bald, muscular, and easy to get along with; he was a neurosurgeon who had been fully trained by Choróbski. He was supposed to create a neurosurgery ward in Poznan. After a brief discussion, it was decided that I would be delegated to him, because I was from Poznan. The ward there didn't exist yet, and Powiertowski often negotiated with the Medical Academy in Poznan, having to travel back and forth. Because the specialization in neurosurgery requires training in general surgery and neurology, Professor Choróbski decided to send me to Poznan to Professor Drews, the head of the first surgical clinic in the Medical Academy of Poznan. I was to spend six months there, after which the neurosurgery ward should already be set up. So I said goodbye to Aunt Nata and her husband, grateful for their hospitality, and returned to Poznan.

It's worth mentioning as an aside that in that time, thinking it was necessary to stay in Warsaw, I looked through the classifieds for some kind of room for rent. I got many offers with the condition, however, that there would be a marriage involved.

The next day, after getting the proper directions, I found myself in Professor Drews's office; he welcomed me very warmly.

"Well, my dear, if you are going to learn under my supervision, then it's going to be well; go to the ward and report to the head nurse to get a white coat. I'll try to get you into the surgical cases that will be helpful to your future specialty."

I got a freshly starched and pressed white coat and went to the ward. The surgery clinic in the Diakoniski hospital made an admirable first impression—beautiful, large operating rooms, spacious rooms for patients, vast corridors. I reported to Dr. Borszewski, who would be my chief. After this introduction, I went for a lonely trip through the ward. And then, I ran into a group of my colleagues from medical school, staunch party members. When they saw me walking in a white coat, they became as speechless as if they had seen Lot's wife.

"What are you doing here? What's going on?" I was supposed to have been "eliminated," but here I was wandering through "their" clinic, acting like a doctor!

I understood them very well, and then a thought flew through my head in a flash—these base people only understand base and violent behavior. I am not ashamed of my behavior or language, and am instead proud of it.

"And what did you think, you sons of bitches, that you would be able to eliminate me? It's not that easy; you'd better take care of your own asses so no one hurts them," I said.

I turned on my heel and confidently went on my way. They didn't say anything, and during the whole year, they couldn't understand that no one stood behind me, that I didn't have any "connections" or appropriate "contacts." During my surgical training, they never bothered me and rather, kept their distance.

My father was the director of agricultural surveys in the province of Poznan. That department was part of a larger department of agriculture which was made up of divisions of drainage, agriculture, and many others besides surveys. The head of the department was a Jew named Jagielski, who was, of course, a party member and tightly connected to the communist administration in Warsaw; he was the same person who later led negotiations with the leaders of the "Solidarity" movement in Gdansk.

After the period of terrorist arrests in the department of agriculture, some kind of peace settled. One day, my father didn't come home until eleven p.m. He looked awful, and it was clear that he had been through something very difficult. He told my mother that there had been a very long unexpected conference. These "conferences" started occurring every few days. My father was wasting away, becoming a ball of nerves, and my mother couldn't figure out what was going on, which made her even more upset. After one of these late-night homecomings, he confided in me, so that my mother wouldn't hear, that he was being called in every few days to the UB/Office of State Security, that awful prison near Kochanowski Street. He would receive a phone call that he should report there after work. When he got there, a worker of that institution would lead him to the basement, without saying a word, to a little room without windows in which there was only one chair. He would lock the door and leave. My father didn't know if he had been arrested or not, and the worst possible thoughts were running through his head. After three or four hours, the same worker came back, opened the door, and said that he could go home. This hellish psychological torture lasted several weeks and ended without a word and with no explanation. My father was convinced the entire time that they would eventually lock him up for good, and he wanted me to know what had happened to him if one day he suddenly didn't return. His health declined quite a bit, but he didn't stop working.

I started my surgical internship. I rode the streetcar early in the morning. In the physicians' lounge hung a schedule of the day's surgeries and the names of the assistants who would be helping the surgeons. I had an interesting experience the first time I "scrubbed in" with Dr. Borszewski. He was good man, completely devoted to the vocation of being a doctor and surgeon, but of course, he didn't have much patience for a novice like me.

"Don't lean your head in so much, because you won't find anything important there, and you're blocking my view." That was the first warning that stayed in my mind.

"Calm down and hold the retractors." And that was how the minutes, quarters of an hour, and hours went by.

After shaking off my initial fears, I started to look more sensibly at what was happening and helping as much as I could in the said case. Soon, I learned the surgeons' habits and could adapt myself to their operating styles and actually be useful. Each of them had a somewhat different technique, different temperament, and different approach to solving the problem. Participating in surgeries, I learned to proceed on the most appropriate and least traumatic path to the site in question, learned how to make incisions so as not to harm muscles or mistreat the skin, and learned how to stop bleeding, put a clamp on an artery and larger veins, and how to use cautery for smaller bleedings. I understood that a well-performed surgery should look like the image in the anatomy atlas during each of its stages. Soon, I was allowed to close up the wound after the majority of the surgery had been performed by the surgeon.

One day, as the second assistant, I participated in a surgery of a neurofibroma that was growing out of the nerve root in the thoracic part of the spine and then through the intervertebral foramen (opening between two vertebrae) into the chest, forming a tumor there that was slightly smaller than a human fist. After opening the chest, the surgeon removed the tumor; he was also able to remove the part located inside the spinal canal. Nowadays, this procedure would be considered horrendous, as it was almost tantamount to ripping out the spinal cord and could have caused paralysis. Fortunately, nothing happened; the surgeon left the operating table as did the first assistant to have a cigarette. I, however, was left with the huge open wound. I had to sew in layers, one after another, to recreate the normal anatomical structure. After a moment, I noticed that I had one layer too many on one side; I had to take all the stitches out and fix it. The young, seventeen-year-old girl came out of that surgery without any injury and fully recovered.

I was also given patients on the ward whom I had to take care of, whom I would see every day a few times and also be on call, for whom I would write out prescriptions for the medications ordered by the chief of the ward, and for whom I would change dressings. One of these patients was a roughly fifty-year-old man. His name was Olenderek. He had undergone surgery for esophageal cancer. Such an operation is difficult, because not only the abdomen but also the chest has to be opened. You remove the upper portion of the stomach and most of the esophagus are to be removed. This connection must heal—the life of the patient depends upon that. On the third day, after surgery, the anastomosis (connection) did not heal and whatever the unfortunate patient was trying to eat spilled into the pleural cavity. All attempts to induce healing of the fistula through the elimination of oral feeding failed. Mr. Olenderek died right before my eyes. He was a good and patient person, the kind that no one would notice in a crowd. His agonizing death and the suffering he endured heroically lodged like a splinter in my soul and remained there forever.

After a few months, I was assigned to take care of smaller procedures. It began with work in the surgical ambulatory service, where various cases were brought in right off the street. I remember a hefty individual with a big belly and nose, indicating that he was somewhat partial to alcoholic beverages. He came in with purulent cellulitis of the hand. The whole palm was red, swollen and puffy, and incredibly painful. It was necessary to make several incisions so that the pus could flow out. We had penicillin then, but it was used in microscopic doses. It was just that no one really knew yet how it was supposed to be administered. I explained to him that I had to make an incision in the palm, but because it was a painful procedure, he would get some light anesthesia. He asked how much the anesthesia cost. When he found out (the cost was minimal), he said, "Doctor, just wait a minute, I'll be right back, but I don't want any anesthesia."

Indeed, he showed up shortly thereafter, already well loaded with alcohol, held out his hand, and said, "Well, now you can cut."

He got through the whole thing without budging!

From the period of my surgical internship, I remember a motorcyclist who was brought in from a cinder track competition. He was wearing a boot through which his shin bone was sticking, his boot stained with drying blood. It was impossible to save the leg, because the muscles and blood vessels were crushed and torn. To save his life, I had to perform the first and last amputation of my career. It is a mutilating procedure that completely goes against my nature. I performed the amputation below the knee, so that his crippling wasn't so completely severe. That procedure was so sad for me that I felt as though I had performed something wicked.

The time went by quickly. Dr. Powiertowski got a small ward on the very top floor of the clinical hospital with an even smaller operating room. About twenty or thirty patients could stay there. The windows of the rooms were really small, and there was a long corridor—on one end was the nurses' station, straight ahead was the operating room, and near it was the physicians' lounge and room for the surgical nurses.

By the time I finished my surgical internship, I was allowed to perform hernia repairs and some appendectomies. Doctor Powiertowski was not working alone. Feliks Tokarz was with him, who was a few years older than I. He had minimal training in neurosurgery, because he had worked with Dr. Ferenc in Wroclaw. Ferenc had died suddenly when he was mistakenly given a much higher dose of heparin than he was supposed to get. The mistake was made because the brand of the ampoule had been changed. It was different from the ones that the nurse was accustomed to using. By the time anyone figured out what had happened, he had already bled to death.

Feliks had been his assistant and wanted to stay in neurosurgery, so he joined Dr. Powiertowski in Poznan. I was the next doctor in line in the newly opened ward. Dr. Powiertowski was the chief and main surgeon, Tokarz had the second highest position, and I had the third. Soon, more assistants came to work with us—Jas Solawa, Tadzio Wenzel, Bronek Stachowski, and Jurek Rostek. This group became the core of the developing Neurosurgery Clinic in Poznan. After a year or two, Kukla and Huber also joined us.

Dr. Powiertowski wasn't affiliated with any party, and neither were Feliks Tokarz, Tadzio Wenzel, Bronek Stachowski, Jurek Rostek, and I. Jan Solawa was a party member, but he wasn't active, and we never felt his party allegiance. I think he joined the party so as to get into the university. Kukla and Huber already belonged to a different category of people. They showed off their party membership and made clear to the rest of us that they were "on a different level."

As much as the first group was compatible, and there were no particular secrets among us, whenever those other two came by, we all fell silent.

Dr. Powiertowski had a lot of trouble getting even the most basic equipment; the red tape in the bureaucracy was just unbelievable. During the second year of neurosurgery, he suddenly had to go to Warsaw to get essential instruments, primarily a new apparatus for the cauterization of small vessels that was of Czech production; it was essential for brain surgery. His departure coincided with the time when Dr. Tokarz was home with the flu, so I became responsible for the patients during the two days that the chief was gone. I was young and full of confidence in my abilities. Powiertowski, who knew me well, categorically told me that I should not try to perform any kind of surgical procedure.

The next day, walking proudly through our area, I made rounds, changing bandages and taking care of medications. There weren't any patients who were in a very serious state, so everything was going smoothly—smoothly, up until a certain moment. Around eleven o'clock, Soviet officers suddenly showed up with a very sick, unconscious man on a stretcher. A colonel led this group. He demanded to see the chief of neurosurgery immediately. I told him that I was the oldest assistant and responsible for the whole ward, for the director was in Warsaw. He couldn't believe it at first—I looked so young—but he soon figured out that I was telling the truth.

He pointed to the patient and said, "This is our general. He had a terrible car accident and requires immediate attention. Do you know what to do?"

I did a brief examination. The general was unconscious and was barely sensitive to pain; one pupil was dilated, the other narrow. His blood pressure was high, his breathing rattling. I concluded that he had elevated intracranial pressure (pressure inside the skull) and that the pressure was so high that it was causing compression of the brain stem. If he were to stay in such a state, he wouldn't survive for more than a few hours. The most probable cause of the brain compression was a hematoma formed from the bleeding large vein under the dura matter, compressing the cerebral hemisphere and pushing the brain down, resulting in compression of the brain stem.

I explained all of this to the colonel and clearly stated that the general needed immediate surgery, that his skull had to be opened on the side of the dilated pupil and, if there was indeed a subdural hematoma, there would be a chance to save him; if, however, the surgery was not done, he would certainly die.

"And are you capable of doing it?"

I responded that I was but that the situation was pretty hopeless.

"So, operate immediately; I'll be standing behind you."

We immediately took him to the operating room and without general anesthesia, just local, I got to work with Bronek Stachowski. I made a semicircular incision on the shaved head on the side of the dilated pupil, and then we clamped the bleeding blood vessels with forceps and separated the whole flap of skin and the muscles together with the periosteum. I drilled four holes and, using the Gigli saw, sawed the bone between the holes and removed the square piece of bone. The exposed dura matter (external meningeal membrane) was tense and black from the venous blood that had accumulated underneath it. I incised the dura matter, and the huge subdural hematoma, pushed up by the increased pressure, began to progressively come up through the incision. I opened the dura matter wide—most of the hematoma was already coagulated and reminded me visually of the liver, but there was still quite a lot of liquid blood. I found the bleeding vein and coagulated it. The brain started to pulsate as it should, according to the action of the heart, and slowly expanded in the space which had before been filled by the hematoma.

I had only anesthetized the general locally. Once I relieved the pressure on the brain stem, he began to regain consciousness. It's worth mentioning that he was quite drunk, and had supposedly forced the chauffeur out of the way and decided to drive the car himself, causing the accident.

I experienced some unforgettable moments when a torrent of the most awful vulgarities in the Russian language came from beneath the surgical drapes. The most wonderful Chopin concert couldn't have sounded better than these curses; it was clear to everyone that the general had been saved. The colonel, who was still standing behind me, murmured in my direction, "And he's so young!"

With Bronek, we calmly closed the skull and brought the patient to the ward. His condition improved very quickly; the next day he was already feeling like himself, and the smell of alcohol drifted out of his room.

The colonel almost didn't leave his side. Once the general was conscious and feeling better, he said that he wanted to move him to a Russian hospital. Despite my warnings against it, he did it. He also asked me right after the surgery if the general didn't need some medication or bandaging materials. We were suffering then from a lack of all the most essential supplies, including surgical gloves, gauze, antibiotics, etc. I didn't think long before writing a long list of our needs. He looked at it, smiled, and said, "Well, our general needs a lot."

The next day, everything that I had asked for was brought over. When Dr. Powiertowski returned and found out about everything, he grabbed his head in horror. It did help, though, that the supplies from the general lasted us for almost a month. I wonder sometimes what would have happened if the general had died on the operating table. I'd rather not think about it.

My father suddenly got joint inflammation of the right shoulder. The pain was very intense, and his sedimentation rate was very high. Salicylates didn't help much. Gradually, the inflammation decreased, but he developed heart problems, fatigue, and pressure in the chest. The sedimentation rate continued to be very high. He didn't have a fever. My mother had essentially studied medicine with me and read Orlowski's textbook of internal medicine from cover to cover. She and I concluded that my father must have a source of infection manifesting itself in varying ways. My mother reminded me that in 1937, he had had acute appendicitis and had gone to a surgeon who said they should operate. He had gone to another surgeon who said the same thing, but hesitant to operate, he also said that there were indications for surgery but that he could wait. My father obviously picked the last option and recovered. My mother and I determined that he had a source of infection in the peritoneum.

I went to Professor Drews and asked if he would do a laparotomy and look for a source of infection. He thought I was a lunatic, but when I described the medical history to him, he considered it and said, "Well then, the chances of finding anything are minimal, but if you insist and your father is having such recurrences, we can do a laparotomy (open the abdomen) and see. The risk is minimal. I will use local anesthesia."

Despite his protests, my father was admitted for surgery and Professor Drews operated. I was present the entire time. It turned out that he had developed multiple adhesions where the appendix was and that he had a retroperitoneal abscess behind it! After the surgery, he recovered very quickly, the sedimentation rate returned to normal, but the damage to his heart muscle had been done.

In the early 1950s, during the Stalin and Bierut years, it was difficult to get the equipment necessary for the neurosurgery ward to function properly. Dr. Hieronim Powiertowski made superhuman efforts so that the ward would somehow function and be able to help the patients that came in; it was, after all, the only neurosurgery ward in all of Poznan and the surrounding areas. The working conditions of both the doctors and nurses were tough; infections that arose from improper operating room conditions and lack of antibiotics were common, and more than one patient died from complications that could have been avoided under better circumstances. We didn't have any anesthesia equipment, and it was safer to operate using local anesthesia—you can imagine the horror of a surgery in which you open the skull and operate on the brain of a conscious person. Fortunately, the brain is not sensitive to pain and only the dura matter has nerve endings, so the most important part of the surgery was done without the patient suffering. Death, as a result of surgery, was common, in a way not thinkable in today's conditions. There were many deaths on the operating table.

For us, the young doctors, who after all wanted to do good and to help and who, instead, saw a sea of suffering and despair, everyday life under such conditions was undoubtedly a factor that shaped character and personality, as well as one's outlook on the world, life, and death.

I studied the whole huge volume of brain tumors written by Bailey that I had gotten from Professor Choróbski. I knew the contents of that book almost by heart, because the language barrier (it was, of course written, in English) meant that many times I had to go back to the beginning of a sentence to understand the meaning. I ended up learning neurosurgical terminology in English, which helped me greatly later in life. I brought that volume back to Professor Choróbski in Warsaw, then got another from him, possibly even thicker, written by Bailey, Buchanan, and Bucy about brain tumors common to childhood. I got through that book a bit more easily.

Because I was more familiar with neurosurgical problems of childhood than the rest of my colleagues, Dr. Powiertowski put me in charge of caring for children who had undergone surgery. Two events stick out in my mind from that period.

A four-year-old boy was admitted to our ward with severe headaches, vomiting, and edema of the optic disc, indicating that he had elevated intracranial pressure. The child was also experiencing balance problems. This indicated that he had a tumor in the cerebellum in the posterior part of the head.

Dr. Powiertowski performed the surgery, and I assisted. The tumor was large, soft, gelatinous, and was blocking the flow of cerebro-spinal fluid. It was a malignant tumor—medulloblastoma. We removed as much of it as we could, trying not to kill the child or damage the brain. After the surgery, his symptoms went away, but the basic problem hadn't been solved, and the improvement was only temporary. Because the tumor was radio-sensitive, we did radiation therapy. The technique of radiation therapy was primitive then, and the skin darkened and somewhat atrophied. But even radiation therapy would only help for a little while. Six months later, he had to have surgery again to remove another huge piece of the tumor. The child went through hell that year, and I with him. I felt sorry for the little boy who behaved so calmly during the whole awful ordeal, as if he knew what was going on. Finally, death came for him. It was very hard for me, because I had become quite attached to the little one. The parents were young, and he was their only child; it nearly broke them.

A few years went by. My training in neurosurgery was progressing, my life was rolling along at a steady pace—work, overnight call, studying. Spring came. The day was beautiful and pleasant, the sun warmed my back and, with its rays, turned the scratched up apartment buildings and walking people a golden hue. I was on my way home from overnight call, tired, and full of thoughts of what had happened on call. And then I heard, "Doctor, doctor!"

I lifted my head and saw the parents of that child in front of me. She was pushing a stroller in which a small, maybe one-year-old little kid was sitting. They were smiling, kind, and polite. I felt something completely irrational. Seeing them, I could see that little suffering boy again whose pain, illness, and death had left a deep gash in my heart. The parents had not only rebuilt their lives but were even able to feel normally happy with their next child. I felt something like betrayal, something shameful, but, of course, I was wrong. They hadn't forgotten about the other child, but they had to live somehow. And the new child helped them do this. I, however, wasn't able to forget. Now, when decades have passed since that moment, I still see the light curls and blue eyes of the little boy, his head deformed from surgeries, that whole sea of suffering.

The ambulance brought a six-year-old boy to our ward. He looked awful. His whole head was bloody, covered with an incredible number of stab wounds. It turned out that his schizophrenic mother had experienced a severe attack of rage and had cut up her own child terribly with scissors and then thrown him out the window into the snow.

Luckily, the wounds were superficial—none of them penetrated to the inside of the skull. The child bled a lot but was conscious and didn't have neurological damage. It took a long time to repair the torn-up scalp—plastic surgery had to be done. After the surgery and transfusion, he felt completely fine. Because his bandages had to be changed often and his healing process had to be observed constantly, he stayed on the neurosurgery ward for a long time. He didn't lie in bed but rather ran all over the ward. Everybody loved him a lot; he would sit at the nurses' station and even in the physicians' lounge. He was a child of the streets, literally without any upbringing. So, he had to make do as best he could. He smoked cigarettes, figured out a way to make money; he walked from one bed to another and asked if patients needed anything from the store that was located in the hospital hallway downstairs. He collected money, did the shopping, and delivered the merchandise, keeping the appropriate percentage of the money for himself. When caught smoking a cigarette, he would throw it on the ground, stepping on it with his foot, and vehemently deny that he had been smoking. He was quite arrogant, but we all liked him.

When new patients were admitted to the ward, he would go to them and ask about their symptoms. When they told him that the headaches were localized in the front part of the head, he would comfort them and say that everything would be fine. But when they complained of pain in the back, he calmly said, "Ah, well, nothing can be done." The worst part was that he was very often right, because the tumors in the back of the head often had a much higher risk of death.

When he had finally healed, he was adopted by an older, kind, quiet couple. This woman and her husband made a nice impression on me. He went with them into a new life. And then, after a few years, we happened to run into each other again. I didn't recognize the little rogue. He was now a well-behaved child. When he saw me, he got shy and hid behind his adoptive mother's skirt.

I often claim that there are no bad children and no bad dogs—only people can be bad who treat these defenseless beings in a cruel and base way. Of course, psychopathy can occur in both people and animals, but it is a rather rare occurrence.

When I was already working in neurosurgery, I finished up my studies in psychology, receiving a diploma of Masters of Philosophy (in psychology). To get that diploma, I had to write a Master's thesis. During that time, I was interested in speech deficits that were caused by damage to the left side of the brain. I had ample material with which to work, because many such patients came through the neurosurgery ward with speech impairments caused by brain tumors or other events. These types of speech impairments (dysphasia and aphasia) can be presented in a variety of ways depending on the site of damage and its extent and nature.

Additionally, by analyzing speech, both perception and vocal expression, you can determine the type of impairment almost exactly and administer the appropriate rehabilitation. The brain distinguishes itself with a certain ability to adapt to deficiencies; other parts of the brain can partially take over for the deficient areas.

In the evenings, I would often spend many hours with patients who had these problems. They were pleased to see me working with them—you can imagine how a person can become desperate when struggling to express himself and be understood. The work went very slowly, for I didn't know much then about the mechanics of these impairments. I didn't know how best to get through to my patients, what to do so as to make contact, so as to better communicate with them.

The Christmas holidays came. There were no holiday decorations or even a cross, as such things were strictly forbidden. When I was struggling with my aphasia patients, the idea suddenly came to me that, while I couldn't reach them with words, maybe I could reach them through the Christmas carols that were deeply ingrained in every Pole. So, I started humming, "When Christ is Born." The unfortunate people came to life, and though they often couldn't speak at all, they were able to sing the carols together with me. Apart from both of us feeling moved the emotion of mutual communication and the very fact that they could sing, lifted their spirits. They were often even able to sing words that in normal circumstances they couldn't say.

The psychology department of the University of Poznan approached me about my work with aphasia patients and asked me to accept psychology students for sessions with patients suffering from speech impairments. I learned a lot from that work, and it also resulted in my good friend Bronek Stachowski meeting his future wife.

One of the students was a young woman who had miraculously gotten out of Soviet paradise. She could speak Russian fluently and without any foreign accent. One night when she was going home after evening lab, Soviet soldiers started bothering her with obvious intentions on a dark and empty street. The situation was dangerous, as there was no one around, it was dark, and the soldiers were drunk. But, she didn't lose her head in this dif-

ficult situation. She turned to the soldiers chasing her and starting swearing at them in the foulest Russian words. They stopped
dead in their tracks hearing such a litany of words, and they were
shocked, "She's so young—and such vulgarity!"

By doing that, she saved herself from likely being raped.

The Berlin crisis had long since passed, though truthfully the
"Cold War" was still in existence, and the Russians lost interest in
training fellows in neurosurgery. Still, something had to be done
with me. The easiest thing would have been to give me a position
as a senior assistant. But the problem was that I didn't belong to
the party, and my old "friends" from medical school already had
quite a bit of influence in the politics of the personnel department
of the school. How to solve this dilemma? They turned to me so
that I might "declare my allegiance" and join the party. I didn't
refuse right away, but I did say that I was still "ideologically unpre-
pared" for such an undertaking. Though he himself had problems,
because he wasn't a party member, Dr. Powiertowski, my chief,
who I respect and whose memory I will always cherish, resolved
the situation. He categorically decided that I was absolutely necessary for the proper functioning of the ward. And so, that's how,
despite regime opposition, I got the position of the senior assistant at the Medical Academy of Poznan.

My situation wasn't easy. During that time, my former colleague, Mieczyslaw Wender, quickly advanced in the Neurology
Clinic and became an adjunct. He was a banner-waving regime
supporter—everyone feared him, and rightly so. We had minimal
contact then, but there was some, because neurosurgery and neurology were tied together as close specialties.

This was a period in which really no one, practically speaking,
could do a doctorate without joining the party. In our ward, Kukla,
Huber, and Solawa belonged to the party, and Huber was even
very active. Wencel, Stachowski, Tokarz, chief Powiertowski, and
I were not affiliated with the party, so, of course, we were looked
down upon.

At about that time, it was decided in Moscow that Russian
education should be the best. They heralded Stalin as a polyglot—

as far as I know, he could speak Georgian and Russian. Miczurin was the next pillar leading Russian education ahead, but another pillar was still necessary. They dug up Pavlov and his theory of conditioned reflexes. It's worth noting that Pavlov was a religious person, and it's because of him that the nearby Orthodox church wasn't closed down. His work was undoubtedly scientific, focusing on behaviorism. His findings were worthwhile, and they sparked a whole series of tests that focused on gaining a better understanding of brain function. Still, Pavlov's interpretations were often naïve. Yet the results of his experiments were quite valuable. Personally, I value Pavlov much more than, for example, Freud, whose personality analysis and theory of dreams caused such controversy in science. Still, Freud's work was undoubtedly associated with the development of psychiatry.

Because Pavlov and his teachings became a pillar of knowledge and everything was to be explained according to his theory, "the authorities" ordered all doctors to be trained in Pavlov's theory. This training was mandatory; we were given a huge textbook that was, incidentally, well written. I got these materials, and, motivated by curiosity, I started learning them. I understood immediately that treating this experimental work as an argument in support of Marxist dialectic was really lunacy. The work was objective, and the conclusions were somewhat naïve and often far-fetched—but it was mainly from a lack of foundational knowledge that really had not yet been discovered. The material was based on concrete experiments and therefore had undoubted value.

My "red" colleagues were not in any hurry to study the rather difficult material, but in accordance with orders "from above," someone had to be selected to lead the Pavlov training properly. And then, I got a terrific idea—I would go for this training, wouldn't be tainted by it, and maybe they would leave me alone and stop pressuring me to join the party. So, that's what I did. It certainly caused some surprise and joy that someone had been found who, kindly put, was naïve, and who would take that additional weight on his shoulders. Dr. Powiertowski was very happy that he didn't have to deal with the problem anymore, and signed me up for the central training held in the Medical Academy of Warsaw. I was then also made the lecturer on Pavlov's teachings in the Neurosurgery Ward at the Medical Academy of Poznan. Once a month, I would go to Warsaw for training that was led by the following professors: Haussman, Selecki, and Szapiro (all Jewish). Professor Haussman, who was called a slut in Warsaw for her frivolous behavior at the pulpit, was a major in the Red Army. She came to Poland on Soviet tanks together with her sister, Professor Jablonska, who was also a major in that army, and took over as head of neurology in the Medical Academy of Warsaw. Comrade Jablonska, who also signed death certificates for Home Army members who had been shot on Rakowiecka Street, "took care of" the old dermatology professor, Grzybowski. He was arrested and put in the UB prison where he quickly died and she took over as head of the department after him.

Wald from Tworki, the Jusow couple and "Frania" (I don't remember her last name) also belonged to this group of Jewish communists. Frania fought like mad against Professor Konorski (whose real name was Kohn; he had been one of Pavlov's pupils), accusing him of Trotsky-ism. He somehow survived her pursuit and continued to be the chief of neurophysiology at the Nencki Institute.

This very group took over my training. I remained silent, trying to focus only on Pavlov's texts, and because I easily understood his theory, I didn't have much trouble. I would pass on my knowledge to bored and mostly "red" colleagues, who "persisted" in pretending that this interested them. Because I had finished a degree in psychology, I was considered by the Medical Academy to be specially qualified to lead training in Pavlov theory.

I quickly figured out that while Haussman, the Jusow couple, Wald, and Kozniewska were simply Stalinist regime supporters, Professor Konorski, who was then being condemned and passionately destroyed, was a real man of science. He was concerned with seeking and finding the truth, not spreading propaganda.

My role leading training in Pavlov theory influenced my entire life. I was left alone, at least for a little while, in terms of joining the party; I also met the "people on top" of the Medical Academy of Warsaw in the neurology division; this became quite helpful later. I want to emphasize here that Professor Choróbski never disgraced himself with even a bow toward the regime and didn't praise his "red" assistants. They didn't bother him, though, because he was necessary.

My wish was to become a good surgeon as quickly as possible. I studied and assisted in surgeries that my chief performed, but what I really wanted was to learn how to operate on my own. When I look back, I am proud of my own arrogance—or not so much arrogance as working to achieve my goal and having some youthful, naïve faith in my own strength.

Dr. Powiertowski was a reasonable and good person. He understood me very well and allowed me to open the skull for brain surgery on my own. I was already performing ventriculography, which was then considered an essential diagnostic method. Besides the X-ray and the neurological examination, we did not have any other methods of localizing a brain tumor. Cerebral ventricles could be filled with air through an injection via lumbar puncture (spinal tap), but this was very dangerous under conditions of increased cranial pressure. Only ventriculography remained an option. This method required the drilling of two holes in the occipital part of the skull, incising the dura matter, coagulating the exposed brain, incising it and introducing two cannulas to the lateral cerebral ventricles, releasing some of the cerebro-spinal fluid, resulting in brain decompression, and then filling these ventricles with air. Then ventricles were visualized on the X-rays, and their dislocation indicated the localization of the tumor.

Dr. Powiertowski always emphasized that the brain ventricles well with air, because if they were not completely filled, the X-rays obtained would be unclear and would not have the necessary diagnostic value.

A young woman was admitted to our ward with symptoms of highly elevated intracranial pressure—headaches, vomiting, and papillary edema on the examination of the fundi (back of the eyes, visualized during an ophthalmologic exam). She did not have any localizing symptoms or signs.

Early the next morning, I was supposed to perform a ventriculography, and then a radical surgery was planned.

With the patient under local anesthesia in a sitting position, I drilled holes into the occipital part of the skull and, after properly incising the dura matter, I introduced cannulas to each of the two lateral cerebral ventricles. The pressure of the cerebro-spinal fluid was very high. It flowed out in a stream from both ventricles. I started to inject the air. Because there is a connection between the lateral ventricles through the third ventricle, located in the middle, the injection of air to one ventricle results in an automatic outflow of the cerebro-spinal fluid from the other. When the ventricles are properly filled with air, the air flows out through the cannula of the other ventricle. I injected air into the right ventricle, but I did not see any increased outflow of cerebro-spinal fluid from the left. I injected more and more, and finally there was a sudden outflow of cerebro-spinal fluid and air from the other ventricle. The patient endured this brutal procedure well.

Then I went with her to the X-ray department; the X-rays showed a smooth, round cyst in the very middle of the brain in the third ventricle. The surgical technique in those years was still primitive, so Dr. Powiertowski thought that the case was inoperable and informed the family that, unfortunately, the young woman would die. She didn't die, however, and the next day she felt a lot better, the third day even better, and she insulted my chief, saying that he didn't know what he was talking about. She went home feeling fine. What had happened? She had what is known as a colloidal cyst in the third ventricle of the brain; my brutally forcing in air ruptured the cyst and restored the flow of cerebro-spinal fluid. Ventriculography cured her, because such cysts do not usually recur.

I was proud of my achievement, though it was the result of stupidity and chance rather than sound judgment.

Dr. Powiertowski decided to test me. He allowed me to perform a lumbar sympathectomy alone with only a younger assistant to help. The procedure involves the cutting of the sympathetic nerves at the lateral-internal surface of the spine. One gains access to this area through an oblique incision, parallel to the ribs, and then through the retroperitoneal space to the targeted site of surgery.

Full of pride that I was now an independent surgeon, I made the incision quickly, reached the retroperitoneal space, and began to make my way toward the spine. But I couldn't reach it. I got lost in a muscle mass, not knowing where I was. Sweat covered my forehead from anxiety; all my efforts were futile, as I couldn't figure out where I was in the area's anatomy. I didn't have any other option but to ask the chief to come into the operating room to help. He came immediately, looked, and showed me calmly that instead of retracting the ileopsoas (hip-lumbar) muscle off to the side, I had inserted the retractor underneath the muscle. In a few minutes, he reached the sympathetic ganglia and performed the appropriate cutting of the sympathetic nerves, or rather their partial excision. He left me to close the wound. All my confidence as a surgeon was ruined; I felt so small that it's sad to think about it. Right after the surgery, I went to the prosectorium and performed four such operations on corpses. Today, I am already old and haven't operated for three years, but I can perform a lumbar sympathectomy right now with my eyes closed.

That upheaval of my confidence and reputation was an invaluable help in the rest of my life. I understood very well that if you take a scalpel in your hand, then you have to know exactly what you're doing, why, and what the complications and difficulties might be and always be prepared for them. It was one of the most important lessons of my life. I understood that this condition applied not only to surgery but to everything a person did. I also understood that the operative field was a bit different in every case, that there were no two cases that were identical, and that you always had to be prepared for every eventuality.

I don't remember now where I first heard the phrase "constructive pessimism." It is an unfathomable perspective, in which at

Chapter 8 · Surgical Intern and Residency

every moment, you expect the worst and are completely prepared for what that worst might be. If it doesn't happen, it's a cause for celebration.

I am convinced that that's exactly how every surgeon should think. This position protects against many complications and tragedies on the operating table. It requires, however, years of experience and often having many difficult cases.

At around the same time, the Neurosurgery Outpatient Clinic was opened. I worked there with Feliks Tokarz; he would work one month and I the next. We admitted patients from the afternoon into the evening.

I have a few memories that stuck in my mind from that outpatient clinic. The patients were usually well-behaved waiting for help, which we provided the best way we could.

One evening, I heard what sounded like a quarrel in the waiting room, some raised voice, then the door to the office opened and a fat individual with a bullish back and angry, red face rolled in.

"I don't have time to be waiting here, Comrade Doctor; I have rather important affairs to deal with for the committee. You have to take care of me immediately!"

I wasn't thrilled with this greeting, but I didn't react in kind—that might have been dangerous. I asked what was bothering him. It turned out that he suffered from trigeminal neuralgia. The condition is characterized by frequent attacks, sometimes every few minutes, and a very intense pain, usually on one side of the face, in the area of the affected branch of the nerve. I identified this quickly, as the pain seized him right then. His face twisted up, he got even redder, and he started wailing. After a minute, the pain went away. In those days, the emergency treatment involved the injection of pure alcohol to the respective (relative to the localization of pain) branch of the trigeminal nerve, and therefore, destruction of the nerve and elimination of the pain. Such a procedure, performed on an outpatient basis, was very unpleasant, because during the injection, which lasted for about 15 seconds, the patient felt excruciating pain.

I calmly explained to him what he was suffering from and what the treatment was. The ugly, small eyes became big and round; all his arrogance disappeared. He stopped calling me Comrade Doctor and even uttered the word "sir." I injected the alcohol, and the pain went away and with it all the arrogance and conceit of the regime supporter.

I also can't forget the day when a tall guy came into my office with a gloomy face and broad shoulders. His eyes were sunk in beneath bushy eyebrows. He didn't say much. I was sitting behind the desk with my back to the large window in the office, which was located on the fourth floor; the patient sat opposite me. There was no one else in the office; we didn't have any nurses.

The patient sat down. I asked what was bothering him. He leaned in to me a little bit and put two huge vein-covered hands on the desk. He started talking.

"I have these attacks that begin with a strange feeling and an unpleasant smell, then both my hands shake, and then I don't know what happens. Supposedly, I break and destroy everything."

I listened to this story and looked with horror as he was leaning in more and more and his hands were starting to shake. I thought that I couldn't even escape, because he was in my way, and behind me there was only a fourth-floor window. I started speaking in a calm voice, shyly petting the huge paws. Slowly, he calmed down, and the danger passed. He suffered from temporal epilepsy.

I had taken care of the last patient and was getting my things together, feeling tired and ready to go home. I knew that there was no one left in the waiting room. But then, someone knocked on the door. I said, "Come in." Through the slightly open door, a woman with a nice figure came in. She was about forty years old and looked elegant and pampered.

"Excuse me," she said, "that I'm coming at a time like this; I am the head nurse at this hospital, but I have a problem that, if you'd be so kind, I'd like to discuss with you."

Of course, I didn't protest. In a kind and warm voice, she started talking.

"I am married, have three children from the ages of seven to fourteen, and my husband is an engineer. Lately, I figured out that my husband has been cheating on me; he acts very strangely at home, sometimes looks fixedly at one point, and I know for sure that he has auditory hallucinations, hearing some voices. I am also convinced that he had visual hallucinations. His whole personality has undergone a radical change, he treats me badly, and he ignores the children."

It sounded like a classic case of schizophrenia. There was no doubt that this was the case. And yet I had a strange feeling that something wasn't right about all this. I realized what was bothering me. Why did an intelligent and educated woman come to a neurosurgery clinic with an issue that should certainly be handled by a psychiatrist?

I showed a lot of kindness and understanding and said that she should take this matter up with my psychiatric colleague. I gave her his name and the hours of admission. She thanked me and left. Immediately, I picked up the phone and called the psychiatrist. He agreed with me that the whole situation seemed a bit strange.

A few months went by, and I had forgotten about that visit, when I happened to run into my friend. "Listen, Janusz, I want to tell you what I found out."

That head nurse indeed went to him with the same story. To confirm the truth of the facts she had given him, he asked that the children also come in. All three of them confirmed exactly what the mother said. Then, he asked the husband to come in. He absolutely refused and was deeply upset about it.

But the matter was not resolved. He got an idea that would be unthinkable today. He admitted the whole family into the psychiatric ward. After two days, the children changed what they had to say, the husband was almost furious with suspicion, but that lady still calmly claimed the same thing. The psychiatrist politely explained to her that he was very busy during the day, and gave her paper and a pen to try to describe everything. He would read the information at night. She started writing and writing and writing.

She was the schizophrenic, and the children had developed induced psychosis under her influence.

Two new procedures completely changed our situation at work. The first was giving general anesthesia with intubation using the appropriate apparatus, and the second was the introduction of urea as an agent for lowering intracranial pressure. General anesthesia with intubation not only eliminated the horror of operating using only local anesthesia, but it also guaranteed that the patient would be getting the appropriate amount of oxygen to the blood during the whole surgical procedure. Urea (an organic chemical) turned out to be a blessing, because it decreased cerebral swelling and allowed to perform the procedure under markedly safer conditions. The death rate from surgery fell drastically. The first anesthesiologist who started intubating patients at the Diakoniski hospital was Dr. Fibak, father of the later famous tennis player had been a year ahead of me at the Medical Academy. We learned the basic technique from him, and each one of us could then administer this anesthesia. While I remained much more interested in surgery, Jas Solawa switched to anesthesia and became our main anesthesiologist.

The working conditions on the top floor of the Diakoniski hospital were not easy, in fact, almost unimaginable. After great efforts made by Dr. Powiertowski and Dr. Dowzenko, we were given money to construct a new building next to the Diakoniski hospital (the hospital was located in a big park full of old trees). Construction began and moved along rather quickly. We all desperately tried to get together the necessary technical equipment. We fought for two apparatuses for general intratracheal anesthesia, as the new building would have two operating rooms. We needed shadow-less operating lamps and of course the appropriate tools. With much difficulty, we completed all this, though Dr. Powiertowski put in the most energy and effort, and it was really to his merit that the Neurosurgery Clinic in Poznan was created.

I remember that one of the biggest problems was getting operating lamps. Despite sending off the appropriate order to the warehouse of the Ministry of Health in Warsaw, we didn't get the lamps. On the phone, we were told that there were no lamps. At his wit's end, Powiertwoski sent me to Warsaw so that I could get inside the warehouse and see what was there. After getting through a lot of bureaucratic red tape, I got inside that sanctuary. The worker responsible for the lamps was angry that the matter had gotten this far and claimed stubbornly that there were no operating lamps. When I finally went inside, I saw not one or two but maybe twenty or thirty such lamps.

"Why are you lying? I mean, you have so many lamps here!"

With anger he replied, "These are not operating lamps but shadow-less lamps!"

Well then, this was one well-connected warehouse manager.

Incidentally, I also found a bipolar coagulation apparatus, which was essential in brain surgery.

⧚

My father got very sick. He had a very high fever, and you could hear wheezing in his lungs. He had a dry, sharp cough. His condition quickly worsened. He was taken to the first Internal Medicine Clinic at the Diakoniski hospital, in which I also worked. Professor Roguski, my teacher and the director of the clinic, examined my father, looked at the X-rays, and concluded that it was pneumonia with a bad prognosis and practically untreatable. In those days, we had two antibiotics, penicillin and streptomyacin. My father's pneumonia didn't respond at all to this treatment. At that time, I had Orlowski's recently published textbook of internal medicine at home. My mother pored over these volumes the whole time, looking for diagnoses and eventual treatments of diseases. I went home at night depressed, and she was waiting for me in the doorway.

"Listen, Janusz, I found what Stach is sick with in the Orlowski book. Read this, on this page; it is interstitial pneumonia. The treatment that Orlowski describes is to give high doses of aureomyacin. Mortality is almost one hundred percent."

I grabbed the text. Indeed, both the clinical manifestation and the X-ray findings were exactly like those that Professor Orlowski described. I didn't have any doubts. But where would I get aureomyacin? Thanks to I don't even know what contact, I found out that you could get it on the black market. One ampoule cost five hundred zloty—I was then earning eight hundred a month. I found it, and the transaction took place in some private, obscure apartment. I only had one ampoule. I told the head of the ward, a kind lady who knew me well, what the diagnosis had been and what I wanted to do. She didn't have any objections, because she was sure that my father would die in a few days or at most a week. Indeed, he looked terrible, though he was conscious. I explained the situation to him and that we were actually going to experiment on him. He agreed, knowing there was nothing else to be done. After the first intravenously administered dose, he had a strong allergic reaction, with a high fever, chills, and sweats. Aureomyacin at that time wasn't very pure. The hemoglobin count in the blood was falling very quickly; the next day we gave him a transfusion and another dose of antibiotics. My grandmother's brother, Father Klimm, loaned me some money; he was my best friend and caretaker. The second and third doses were very hard for my father to take. We had to do another transfusion just to keep him alive. After the fourth, his fever broke, and he felt better but was incredibly weak. A week later, I was allowed to take him home. He stayed in bed most of the time and walked with difficulty.

In that time, apart from working in the hospital and the neurosurgery outpatient clinic, I also took work in a general outpatient clinic, working late into the night. I was eager to earn as much money as I could.

Summer came, and it got warm. My father needed rehabilitation, but it just wasn't a possibility, because we didn't have the money to pay for it.

Somewhere not far from Poznan, there was huge, pine forests. Among them, one could find small hamlets and settlements. My mother and I decided that in those conditions, in the fresh air in a pine forest, my father would have the best chance for recovery.

I rented a big room in a hut located behind the village in the forest. I brought a lounge chair and a samovar in which you could boil water well by heating it over burning pinecones. I put my parents there together with our dachshund Baj (he was still a puppy then). There were three beds in the room, along with a table and a couple of chairs. Every Sunday, I brought food, such as milk, eggs, and cheese, and sometimes my mother bought a chicken in the nearby village. My father would spend most of the day on the lounge chair in the shade of the billowing pine trees. Even now, after many years, I can still see him sitting under a pine tree, petting our dachshund, Baj, with a very thin hand.

In the afternoon, when the sun would shine through the thick pine branches and light up the reddish trunks, the clear, clean air was drenched in the terrific smell of resin.

After a few weeks, my father started going for short and then longer walks. By the end of August, he felt pretty good and wanted to go back to work.

At the end of August, I was walking through the city center of Poznan with my father when we came face to face with Professor Roguski. He recognized my father immediately, he also knew me quite well. He was dumbfounded and speechless, as he had been sure that my father had died long ago.

In the United States my father's illness is well-known as Legionnaire's disease. Even now, death from it is quite common. In those days, it had simply been a miracle thanks to my mother's diagnosis, Orlowski's textbook, and black market antibiotics.

Dr. Lebkowski was hired for the senior assistant position in our neurosurgery ward. He was a banner-waving party member with graying temples. He was not very pleasant, acting as though he were above us, even though we had created this ward with Dr. Powiertowski out of nothing. Dr. Powiertowski had to be accommodating to him for obvious reasons, and so Lebkowski took the position next in line after the chief, pushing me and Feliks Tokarz down. We didn't like him because of his arrogance, but we had to take it.

It happened that, while I was on call, I admitted a patient to the ward with an acute subdural hematoma that required immediate surgery. Dr. Powiertowski was in Warsaw, again fighting for equipment, so my responsibility was to call Dr. Lebkowski and inform him of the surgery for which we were preparing. He told me to prepare everything, which included shaving the head, and to let him know when the patient was already on the operating table, and then he would come and be so kind as to operate. With our surgical nurse, Madzia (the best creature who ever walked the earth), we quickly prepared for the surgery. The patient was on the table, and his head had been shaved. I had already performed a lot of these procedures at that time, and I didn't have any doubt that I could do it well. Lebkowski just wanted to show off his higher rank. I was never known for my patience—or sound judgment—and, without calling him, I just operated on the patient.

The surgery went very well; the patient was saved. He went back to the ward in a terrific state, and I went to the call room, where I had a bed, to take a nap. After a couple of hours, I got a phone call from Lebkowski, "What's going on? Why didn't you call? What's taking so long?"

"The patient has already had surgery, and he's doing fine on the ward," I responded.

Silence fell on the other end of the line. There was only the sound of quickened breathing and then, "I'll show you!"

Dr. Powiertowski came back the next day, praised me for the good job I had done, and the matter ended there. From the time of that surgery, there was no kindness shared between my older colleague and me. When I was already in the United States, I heard that he had become a professor of neurosurgery in Bialystok.

Professor Spett, who was the director of neuroradiology in the neurosurgery clinic in Krakow, came to our neurosurgery ward on the top floor of the Diakoniski hospital. The sophisticated older woman with gray hair greatly impressed me with her knowledge, diagnostic capabilities that were then limited, and her wealth of clinical material. I asked Dr. Powiertowski to send me to Krakow for a month-long course in neuroradiology. While there, I could also familiarize myself with the functioning of that clinic and have the chance to see Professor Kunicki, nationally recognized neurosurgeon. The matter was settled, and I was to go at the beginning of the year, in the winter. Before leaving, my good friend Bronek

Stachowski and I went to Zakopane for a few days to do some skiing. The weather was beautiful. We hit the slopes almost directly from the overnight train. Zakopane was covered in a coat of snow snuggled against the massive mountains; it was breathtaking. I was completely out of shape, so I could hardly walk at the end of the day. Bronek, however, was full of energy and firm in his decision to go out dancing. Despite my protests, we went to the closest club. I did dance, though I tried to hold tightly to my partner, as I didn't feel very sure-footed.

Bronek and I often wagered as to which one of us would be the first to get a pretty girl. Not far from us, some young people were sitting at a table, and, amongst them, there was a very pretty young woman. I asked her to dance; she didn't refuse. She was very nice, sat with us for a while, and danced with me again. Her partner wasn't thrilled about this and came over to me almost in a rage. The girl laughed and joked, making fun of her companion. The girl finally returned to her date and we went back to the hotel and fell into a well-deserved sleep.

After a few days, I reported to the neurosurgery clinic in Krakow, located near Botaniczna Street and stood right in front of Professor Kunicki. He was a thin man with somewhat squinting eyes that shone with intelligence and a sense of humor. He looked at me when I introduced myself. "Oh, so you're the guy who tried to steal my son's girl!"

I went numb! I saw, though, that Dr. Kunicki was quite pleased with the attempted stealing; he must have been happy that his son met the challenge.

Kunicki was a wonderful, really world-class, surgeon. In those days, he was already operating with great success on the pineal gland, which is located exactly in the center of the brain. His team was disciplined and well educated. His right-hand man was Dr. Liszka, who I suspect didn't have a personal life, because he was always present in the clinic. Kunicki and Liszka performed all the most difficult surgeries together, though truthfully, the two of them working together looked rather strange.

In the midst of surgery Kunicki in a calm and hushed voice

asked Liszka, "How many years have you been working in the operating room?"

"Five, Professor."

"That's funny; I got the impression that you started working yesterday."

Poor Liszka, who was incidentally Kunicki's favorite, took the taunting in silence; it actually didn't affect their working together at all.

During the morning, I stayed in the operating room and in the afternoon and evening went to the neuroradiology department. I went through hundreds of X-rays that the professor got for me. She also often helped me read them. I really learned a lot then.

The Carnival period before Lent was ending, so I decided to buy some doughnuts for Mardi Gras. I was living in a tiny old hotel with massive, medieval walls. From my window, I could see the snow-covered roofs of old apartment buildings and church spires shooting up into the sky. It was hot as anything in my room; a tiled furnace lit early in the morning radiated heat into my small kingdom, so it became warm and cozy. I got dressed and went outside. The air was crystalline and, despite the early hour, the sun lit up the sky and gave a silver glow to the statues of saints that decorated the church wall. I took a deep breath, and it was somewhat hard for me to breathe. It turned out that the temperature was about thirty-five degrees below zero!

I went to the market, while the snow crunched underfoot. It was a windless day, the air was still, and only the hurried pace of bundled-up people indicated that winter here was not a joke. Old Krakow looked beautiful. On the right side of the market, just next to Hawelka restaurant, there was a pastry shop where you could buy good doughnuts, and that's where I went. It was already around ten a.m., and some Krakow ladies were sitting at tables with espresso and pastries. The café area was almost full, despite the rather early hour. To the right of the entrance, there was a long counter, and behind it there were all different kinds of delights on the shelves. Of course, because it was Mardi Gras, there was a huge stack of fragrant, freshly baked "paczki" (traditional Fat

Tuesday pastry). I ordered a big box of them; it was going to be a gift from me to the neuroradiology department. During the ceremonious filling of that box of doughnuts, an older individual walked in wearing a worn-out thin coat. His neck was wrapped in a scarf, and he had a rather red nose, suggesting an inclination to drinks that were stronger than orange soda. He came inside, and tears were trickling down his cheeks.

"I can't find . . . oh it's awful . . . I can't find . . . what am I to do? I can't find . . ." he repeated.

One of the ladies, taking the role of a Good Samaritan, took pity on the unfortunate individual.

"My good man, what can't you find?"

He responded without hesitation, "I cannot find my prick." Obviously everything shrank in the freezing cold.

The juxtaposition of this drunkard in the urban prudish atmosphere of the coffee house was really incredible!

The morning was sunny. Through a slightly opened window, you could hear the screeching of streetcar wheels making a sharp turn just next to the apartment building where I was then living. This screeching could be heard more and more often, then you could hear footsteps and people's voices—the city was waking from a night's sleep and starting to pulse with life. I quickly shaved and washed, swallowed some hot coffee and bread, and ran out of the apartment. At the turn where the streetcar had to slow down, I jumped on and, got to Grunwaldzki, and then transferred to the streetcar going toward the Diakoniski Clinical Hospital. I wanted to get there as quickly as possible, and I had good reasons. We had finally moved into the new pavilion, which after long arguments and periods of waiting, had been built especially for the neurosurgery and neurology on the terrain of the hospital park. There were new, clean patient rooms, a lot of space, new beds and sheets, and most importantly, two large operating rooms that seemed like an incredible luxury after four years of being just under the roof of the Diakoniski Hospital.

The ward wasn't yet set up, and the nurses were organizing the call room and putting medications away into the medicine cabinets. Only one operating room had a shadow-less lamp; one had not yet been installed in the other room. We had two operating tables, two new Czech coagulation apparatuses, and two machines for anesthesia. We were also lacking surgical instruments. That which we had gotten before was used to equip the first room; the second set was still being completed. Sister Madzia, the head of the operating room, tried to do what she could so that we would have all the necessary instruments. Unfortunately, the bureaucracy in the People's Republic of Poland was terrible in those days. My chief, Dr. Hieronim Powiertowski, often spent long hours in various institutions of the Ministry of Health in Warsaw, practically begging for one kind of equipment or another.

That day was particularly important for the neurosurgery clinic team, because Professor Adam Kunicki, the national consultant on neurosurgical affairs, was visiting. We greatly honored him and liked him for his knowledge, his fatherly attitude toward us, and his particular, somewhat biting, sense of humor. That honor and admiration was linked to respect and even anxiety over not appearing foolish and showing only our best sides. He came especially to help and to use his authority to get us all the equipment we needed.

But there was no time to discuss this matter. We had just begun to make our rounds of the ward, discussing our current needs and possible solutions, when one of the nurses, agitated and upset, informed us that workers from the Cegielski factory had left work and walked into the street, protesting against the arrest of a delegation that had been sent out to negotiate raising their slaves' wages. This delegation was detained in the UB bunkers on Kochanowski Street. Shortly thereafter, we got word that another crowd had joined the ten thousand protesting workers, and that the human wave had covered Wilda (one of the districts of Poznan) and was heading toward the city center to the party building. Later, I found out from my mother, who at the first mention of the strike went in the direction of the Cegielski factory, that a crowd of people, taking up the entire street and both sidewalks, from apartment building to apartment building, was marching toward the city center. No one bothered them; the militia was simply afraid of the ominous, silent mass.

We were all anxious, upset, and worried, waiting for more news. We didn't have to wait long before more happened.

At ten o'clock—I remember this clearly—Dr. Powiertowski received formal notification from the "authorities" as the head of the neurosurgery clinic that we needed to prepare an emergency surgical ward, because there would be wounded. We understood that the "people's government" had decided to deal with the Polish workers with violence.

Meanwhile, the protestors had already reached the party building, and they also broke into the prison and set the prisoners free. They somehow got hold of the rifles and ammunition of prison guards who didn't defend themselves. The whole crowd then went to the UB building on Kochanowski Street, protesting against the clear violation that had been carried out on their delegation. A teenage boy, Romek Strzalkowski, and two young women whose names I don't remember, stood against the background of the banner-waving demonstration. They were the first to be hit by machine-gun fire from the UB bunkers. Romek Strzalkowski fell, and the crowd got frantic under fire. There were many wounded and dead.

At eleven o'clock, the first wounded were brought in who had been shot in the head. Chaos erupted, because we weren't ready. Dr. Powiertowski immediately took the first one into the operating room, and Dr. Tadzio Wenzel, who was a year behind me, assisted him.

Feliks Tokarz, who was at the same level as I was in neurosurgery, immediately began taking care of first aid for the wounded that were pouring into our ward—starting IV's, recommending transfusions, and determining who qualified for surgery. In the first few minutes, it became obvious that one operating room would certainly not be sufficient and that people who managed to get out of the hell on Kochanowski Street might then die from blood loss and a lack of immediate surgical attention.

"You have to get the other operating room together immedi-

ately; we don't have a second to lose," Tokarz barked at me, spattered with blood. He was trying to do a lot of things at once—to
diagnose every problem, to ensure proper first aid, to identify the
wounded (which wasn't always possible and there wasn't always
time), and also to eliminate those who were hopeless cases for
whom help would really be futile.

There were three of us who were well trained—Bronek
Stachowski, Solawa, and me. We could thus create a surgical team,
though we didn't have a surgical nurse. The tools would just about
suffice, but the biggest problem was that we didn't have a surgical
lamp in the second operating room.

I ran down the blood-spattered corridor to the ENT clinic. I
knew Professor Zakrzewski well, and I asked him to please give
me a forehead operating lamp and to send along a surgical nurse.
He understood the situation very well and came up with both in
just a few minutes. The young woman delegated by the ENT ward
was horrified, "I've never scrubbed in for brain surgery. What will
happen? How will I manage?"

I cheered her up and comforted her as best I could, all the
while rushing toward our ward.

In less than an hour, we had the second operating room up and
running; Dr. Tokarz's calls for patients needing surgery were getting more and more urgent. I turned to Professor Kunicki to begin
operating in this room.

"You know the local conditions, so you operate; I'll watch over
everything and help Tokarz select patients," he responded.

Jas Solawa intubated the first patient. Bronek and I scrubbed
in and began the first surgery. I don't remember all the details
of what we did. I only know that we operated from eleven a.m.
until five o'clock the next morning, without a moment's rest and
without even changing surgical coats, only changing our surgical
gloves. Even today, I feel overwhelmed with helplessness thinking
about that day, when after opening up a head that had been shattered by machine-gun fire, it was obvious that we couldn't do anything to help. I remember those patients for whom all we could

do was properly clean the wound, stop the bleeding, and prevent cerebral edema.

Still, after all these years, I can see the dark operating room lit up by the beam of light from the forehead lamp, the large, attentive eyes of the surgical nurse looking out above her white mask, the silhouette of Jas Solawa's head leaning over the anesthesia apparatus, and Bronek's hands, suctioning the blood that was pouring over the operative field, revealing bleeding vessels and seemingly understanding every one of my needs. From time to time, I heard Professor Kunicki's voice behind me, "That's enough here; you still have to clean that up, closer to the ventricle. Be careful not to cause bleeding from the venous plexus (a conglomerate of venous blood vessels)."

I needed those words to keep calm and not make bigger mistakes. I was very young and inexperienced—truthfully, I had four years of neurosurgery behind me, but it wasn't a lot of training. From time to time, the silence of the operating room would be broken by orders from Feliks Tokarz to operate faster, because he already had the next candidate, who really couldn't wait much longer.

Dr. Powiertowski and I operated without stopping and without even changing our surgical coats, as I mentioned. My legs swelled up from standing, but I didn't feel tired. It was as though I was in a trance, some kind of euphoria. When the last patient was taken off the table, the surgical nurse started sobbing spasmodically and pressed her head against my chest for comfort. I didn't mind at all. As she continued to press her body against me I was tempted to respond in kind. I could tell that she was sexually aroused in the release from the tension of surgery. I also remember a young woman, a student, who brought blood and lab results to the operating room and her glance that was full of horror and wonder. Luckily, four of the people on whom I had operated survived, and two died. Dr. Powiertowski had similar results.

When we were still busy operating, in the early morning hours, we got word that we wouldn't be getting any more wounded, because a field hospital had just been opened. Indeed, the inflow of wounded stopped as though it had been cut off by a knife. From people who reached us later, I learned that a tank regiment had joined the crowd. Then, Russian divisions were sent in, and a massacre began. We were informed that the wounded were going to be sent to the field hospital, and in fact, they didn't need much more medical help as everyone had simply been murdered. I can't give an exact number of the people killed in those hours by Soviet agents, but I do know that, in our new ward, an entire large room was filled with corpses, and that's what was happening in every surgical ward in Poznan. Rumors circulated that five hundred people died in that massacre locally, though as far as I know, this figure was never validated. I do know that a mass of dead people were transported from the UB building on Kochanowski Street.

I learned more accurate information about the first phase of the massacre on Kochanowski Street from a patient on whom I operated. He lived in an apartment building across from the UB building, and he saw the crowd gathering and the children waving banners. All of a sudden, when shots were fired, he felt something warm flowing down his face; he touched his forehead and, horrified, figured out that he was touching a soft bloody mass—his own brain. The machine-gun bullet had cut off part of the bone and damaged the frontal lobes. This patient recovered in good condition, but others were not so lucky. The damage was often very severe, crippling them for the rest of their lives.

When there was peace again in Poznan and the famous trial took place, the "people's government" decided that the doctors operating on those wounded people should be awarded with crosses or service medals. In the neurosurgery clinic, only one doctor, Dr. Lebkowski, was given an award! I don't remember having seen him during the rescue attempts of those who had been shot, and I don't remember having seen him in the morning when we finished operating. He just disappeared. But of course he was not only a member of the PZPR but a quite active participant in that regime monster.

A lot of years have passed since those events in Poznan, and often over the years, Polish blood was shed at the hands of Bolshevik agents. Was it shed in vain?

I really don't know. Only the younger Polish generations can answer such a question, but for now, they remain silent.

Around eleven o'clock the next day, I walked out of the clinic and headed home. The streetcars were running less frequently, and there were only a few people on the street. From time to time, shots were fired, and a bullet whistled here and there. UB jeeps full of people who had been arrested sped by on the street. They were all taken to the UB building on Kochanowski Street or to the prison on Mlynski Street. Shortly after, the trials began. The prelude to them was a radio introduction by Comrade Premier Cyrankiewicz, the same man who, as an informer, chose women from the concentration camp in Auschwitz for brothels for the SS. His words rumbled to all of Poland: "The hand of the reactionary movement was raised against the people's government, and we will cut off that hand!"

We wondered about the Polish lawyers who defended the accused. After the first regime furor, things relaxed a bit. Some of those imprisoned were released, and their sentences were lowered. It was clear that for the price of several hundred Poles' lives, a change was coming about, and though not a big one, it was still apparent. A pamphlet called "Po Prostu" came out that gave a "human face" to communism. Stalin had already been murdered by Beria, who was in turn killed by Malenkow. Khrushchev was in charge and disavowed the "cult of one leader." It was well known that Bierut went to Moscow in a fur and came back in a coffer, and people found satisfaction in talking about it. Truthfully, the structure of the government stayed the same, and the prisons were still full, but you could feel something relaxing, and the source of it was changes in Moscow.

In December 1955, I received orders to report on January 2 to the military camp in Przemysl for six weeks of army training. I couldn't do anything about it. My mother got a turkey somewhere, and with it, I went on my way. From the railroad yard, I finally reached the old military camp. Behind the wall, there was a row of barracks built before the first world war out of red, already quite blackened bricks. The square between the buildings was vast. On the other end there stood a similar building, from which the smell of rotten potatoes wafted. It was cold, the beginning of January. The snow whitewashed the dismal poverty in a thick layer on the roofs and by the buildings and was carelessly shoveled into piles. The diagonally falling rays of the winter sun shone in the cold.

I reported to the commanding officers along with many others. We were told to go in groups of twelve to twenty to the appropriate barracks. The floor was cement, and the latrines were to the right of the entrance, where there was also a long basin with faucets, on which frozen droplets of water hung. Metal beds with straw-filled mattresses were set up in the barracks. The temperature inside was seventeen degrees Celsius below zero. A soldier stood by the entrance who gave out uniforms, "cover-ups," coats, shoes, and bed sheets, with a thin blanket and a hard pillow. We were told to get undressed and put on the uniforms. I had on a warm undershirt and a thick flannel shirt. I didn't listen to the orders and quickly put my uniform on over everything. Because I was the first one in uniform, I was made the head of the room. Our first task, so as to survive somehow, was to find a way to heat the room. There was a huge, old tile furnace, though of course it wasn't lit and was quite cold.

Walking into the camp, I noticed that the back of the vast square wasn't fenced in with a wall but with crumbling fence posts, on which rusted wires hung.

I sent out some of the group for those fence posts. I found a prism of coal somewhere in the corner. We brought our treasures together and lit them in the furnace. Before it started heating, a suffocating smoke came out through the cracks in between the tiles. So we had two options: either to freeze or to choke from the smoke. We chose the latter. After a while, when the furnace had heated up and the cracks between the tiles became smaller, the smog also decreased to the point at which we could breathe. We never managed to get a decent temperature, but the water in the room no longer froze.

The on-duty officer gave us a schedule of tasks. Everyone stood outside the barracks in a group of about three hundred. The colonel and other officers came, among them a young lieutenant with a reddish, inconsiderate face. We stood in the snow. Our shoes were made of buckskin leather and absorbed water like a sponge. We stood through the morning report with wet and cold legs. The whole regiment was made up of doctors from various parts of Poland. I don't remember a single one who approached this training with enthusiasm or who was happy with the people's government.

Early in the morning, we were taken to the barracks that stank of rotten potatoes. Breakfast consisted of runny, water-based kasha in which you could occasionally find a microscopic crackling, big chunks of black, terrible bread that didn't even resemble bread, and tasteless black water without sugar that was called coffee.

The first day, I couldn't eat any of it, but when hunger kicked in, I ate that luxurious meal, trying not to think about what I was putting in my mouth. Others reacted similarly. For dinner, we got the same kasha, only thicker with more cracklings, the same soup, and freezer-burned potatoes. The feast was topped off with the same black water without sugar. It's easy to guess that supper was exactly like breakfast.

Each one of us had brought some kind of provisions, whether cold cuts or cake. As the head of the room—my authority was accepted without question, because, like one, we exhibited hatred for the people's army and government—I ordered that the food be assembled in a pile and then appropriately divided into portions. My turkey disappeared with the first feast.

We were allowed to go outside with a pass rather often. There was an obscure restaurant where you could get some pork chops with bigos (a meat and cabbage stew) and potatoes. Because we were all chronically freezing, they served us alcohol with our meal. One of the surgeons got so drunk that he passed out. We carried him back to the camp and laid him in bed. He slept through the night, the day, the next night, and woke up not even feeling too bad.

We couldn't fall asleep at night because of the cold. So we bought vodka, and one of us was put on duty. We all went to bed on command, and then the one on duty would walk from bed to bed with the bottle and a glass in his hand and give each of us a third of a glass of vodka. The warmth of the alcohol soon spread through our bodies, and that's how we fell asleep.

Our training took place in a well-heated room. We unbuttoned the cover-ups, and everyone dreamed of sitting down on the furthest bench so as to peacefully snooze in the warmth. I decided to put it upon myself not to learn how to assemble and disassemble a rifle, but my idea didn't work out. The act was repeated so many times that despite my will, I became familiar with its function.

One day, I wandered outside with a pass to that ugly restaurant. On the way, I met the red-faced lieutenant. I didn't even think of saluting him; I just forgot that I was in a lowest-ranking soldier's uniform. He was furious beyond belief, filed a complaint against me to the colonel, and ordered that I be locked up in the detention center. The colonel was a decent man, so he just reprimanded me and ordered me to return to the barracks. That lieutenant was also our political instructor.

A few days after that event, we were again positioned outside in the snow in a long line, and the lieutenant with the red face and slight Belorussian accent stood before us and began teaching ideology. We endured the awful presentation in silence, though no one had any warm feelings about the speaker. He finally finished and yelled, "If you have any questions, then report to me!"

A thin and tall doctor stood at the end of our row. He raised his hand.

"What do you want?" asked the happy lieutenant, seeing that someone wanted to ask at least one question.

"Excuse me sir, I humbly request permission to go on the side, I feel like shitting" he responded.

I thought that our leader would be consumed with fury, and that tall, stick of a doctor with his very still face became our hero.

We went through a sharp-shooting course, sometimes using a TT caliber .45. The gun had six bullets. We would shoot five and the sixth stayed in the chamber. This training was led by the same "ideological" officer. We reminded him when he was waving the gun around that there was still another bullet in there.

"You morons!" he snapped. "There's nothing in there, look!" He pulled the trigger and fired a bullet just next to my foot. He backed down, and you could hear someone say, "you idiot!" in the back row.

One night, we were torn from our beds, gathered on the square, and given rifles with sharp ammunition. I found out that a division of the UPA (*Ukrainska Powstancza Armia*, the Ukrainian Uprising Army) had appeared near Przemysl. The rumor ended up being false, and after a few hours of waiting, we were allowed to go back to the barracks.

After six weeks, I went back to Poznan. When my mother opened the door, she wrung her hands at the sight of me. "You stink terribly; go to the bathroom immediately!"

We had a small bathroom with an even smaller bath, but it was equipped with a gas stove. I threw off the stinking rags that hadn't been washed in six weeks and sank into the warm water. It was one of the greater delights of my life! I came back with purulent bronchitis and a fever, but I was young and felt better in about a week.

I was finishing the fifth year of my specialty in neurosurgery. I was able to get my work about a rare brain tumor in a newborn published in the American professional magazine, *Journal of Neurosurgery*. My God, that took me a lot of time and energy! I had to send out the text in English without any mistakes! To my astonishment, the article was accepted, and I was soon sent several author copies on shiny, good-quality paper. I was proud of myself. I had already published several articles then in Poland, but finding myself in world literature was something extraordinary for me and for my colleagues. We didn't have any contact with the Western world, nor did we have the means to get appropriate literature, not to mention individual contacts. Those copies of my article became like a tiny window opening out into a huge, wonderful world.

Once a month, I went to Warsaw for the training in Pavlov theory that I already mentioned. But for the authorities even that was not enough. A Pavlov course was organized for us in the asylum in Tworki. We lived there, ate there, and were trained there. We could meet with patients who were allowed to go outside in a vast park. The park was beautiful, and the early fall sunlight made the huge trees seem golden. Sitting under one of them, I turned my face to the sun to enjoy the last moments of warmth. I suddenly heard a voice next to me—it was an older man in glasses. He seemed kind, sat down, and started talking. The endless stream of words that flowed from his mouth was a targeted, flaring attack against the regime. I was shocked by his intelligence and his ability to create brief, precise associations, jumping from one subject to another. The motivation behind his words was always the same—hatred and aversion toward the "authorities." I already had decent training in psychiatry and figured out that this man, a well-known writer, was in a manic state of the manic depressive psychosis. Almost against my will, I found myself under his influence and got the impression that he was actually healthy and that the surrounding live reality was in a state of paranoia. He was obviously sick, but communist paranoia was the only thing being formally taught in Tworki at that time, by comparison he was the one who looked healthy. Our teachers were Dr. Wald, who was Jewish—Professor Konorski's enemy—and a banner-waving regime supporter; "Frania" (I don't remember her last name), who was also Jewish; and also Professors Jus (also Jewish), who were psychiatrists.

They tried to twist and turn Pavlov's ideas to their own purposes, based on some experiments that had been performed on dogs. That pseudoscience about cortical and subcortical stimulation didn't have anything to do with real knowledge and didn't take into account either brain anatomy, structure, or even its most basic function. It was just more party mumbling, another method of making people brainwashed, another form of paranoiac indoctrination.

Our teachers were dangerous people. They placed political adversaries in the psychiatric ward in Tworki and destroyed them with the help of psychotropic poisons like LSD or electric shock therapy. I heard that the Jusow couple, Wald and "Frania," participated in this criminal, awful form of activism, as they were supposed to carry out the orders of the Office of State Security.

Much later, the Jusows decided to immigrate to Canada—the matter of criminal activism was becoming more and more public, and perhaps they concluded that it was better to remove themselves from it. Wald stayed in his position.

After finishing my fifth year of specialization, I took an exam, after which I was recognized as a specialist in neurosurgery. At about the same time, I defended my doctoral thesis. My topic was radiological changes of the skull in children with brain tumors. I gathered the material that I had worked up at the Warsaw clinic. The work was accepted, and I got my doctorate in medicine.

New possibilities opened up before me. I got an offer to open a neurosurgery ward in Szczecin at the neurology clinic—with the condition of transforming it into a neurosurgery clinic and having the possibility for doing a professorship.

I remember my trip to Szczecin. The university staff welcomed me very warmly. They were counting on the development of such a ward, and they also trusted me. I looked at Szczecin. It seemed somewhat foreign, remote, and gloomy, sunk in the clouds of a cold, autumn day. I also understood that if I were to take on this not-so-easy task, I would never leave Szczecin, that it would become my home and place of work. I returned from there feeling undecided, because it wasn't what I really wanted. I wanted to leave, to see the whole big world, and to learn something new and move forward. I couldn't do that in Szczecin.

At about the same time, Professor Lucjan Stepien was organizing a neurosurgery ward at the Polish Academy of Science in Warsaw; it was tightly linked to the Neurophysiology Institute that was headed up by Professor Konorski. The ward was supposed to fulfill a dual role—to treat patients needing neurosurgery, and also to run clinical investigations, coordinated with experimental work on animals at the Nencki Institute. A unique unit was being developed, in which clinical work was to go hand in hand with scientific research. Without any hesitation, I put together an application and was hired as a senior assistant in this facility.

Moving to Warsaw was not an easy undertaking. I had been living with my parents, and getting even the smallest apartment was just about impossible—we didn't have the necessary funds and lived rather modestly. For my benefit, my father resigned from his position in the Department of Agriculture in Poznan and got work as an inspector at the Ministry of Agriculture in Warsaw. We sold the apartment in Poznan and, for that money, bought a partially finished little one-family house in Wola Grzybowska. The house stood in a large field, one in a row of identical houses. There were two rooms downstairs and a kitchenette, and two more rooms could be made upstairs in the attic.

I took an electric train to get to Warsaw. An icy wind blew across the platform that penetrated deep into your bones. I often had to go twice a day and return late at night on the days when we had scientific meetings.

The neurosurgery ward at the Polish Academy of Science, whose head was Professor Lucjan Stepien, didn't have its own building. It was located next to the neurosurgery clinic at the Medical Academy that was headed up by Professor Jerzy Choróbski. When I started working, I was *de facto* working for Professor Choróbski, who supervised all of the work of the clinic.

He was my teacher and a person of above-average intelligence, as I already mentioned; he had been educated at the McGill Institute in Montreal under the direction of Professor Penfield and at Northwestern University in Chicago, where Paul Bucy was the head.

He had obtained his training in neurosurgery before the outbreak of the Second World War. He survived the war in Warsaw working as an industrial doctor in a factory that designed and produced airplane parts. He never spoke about his wartime past, but I know that he had meaningful memories from that period. The following event stuck in my mind. When the Germans occupied Warsaw, they immediately became interested in that factory. The Fokkewulf Company took it over to make molds there—molds that were essential for mass production of airplane parts. The factory really meant something to the war machine of the Third Reich. There was frequent sabotage there, the conspirators were killed, and often the molds that were produced under German supervision were faulty, which significantly delayed the production of Fokkewulf planes.

An older man worked there, a metallurgy chemist—I don't know his name—who started acting like the Germans' lackey from the very first day, coming to them with increasingly new projects to improve production. The Poles treated him with contempt and indignation. His laboratory was just next to the place where the appropriate machine stamped out the molds one after another. His cooperation with the German occupier led to the AK's (*Armia Krajowa*, Home Army) decision to execute him, but they got orders from London to leave him alone. Only after the war did others find out that, while living with contempt and danger, he had been creating a diversion, by modifying the alloys used in production and changing the parameters of the machines that made these molds. You can just imagine the degree to which he damaged Luftwaffe production!

Professor Choróbski ignored the party and the dirty games that took place in the Medical Academy in Warsaw.

Almost emaciated, with thin somewhat monkey-like ears and a sharp, penetrating stare, he inspired both fear and respect—and an attachment and likeability that are hard to understand and rationally justify. I never saw him praise anyone, but he could always manage to convey that he recognized the effort and achievement of one of the doctors beneath him.

Formally, we didn't work for him and were somewhat second-degree workers, but he treated us just like the others. He could rebuke me just like he could rebuke Dr. Rudnicki, who was his favorite. He had to function in an ocean of party hypocrisy. Szapiro, Selecki, Kozniewska—they were ardent Stalinists. The rest of the party members, like Toczek, Haftek, Bidzinski, and Wislawski, belonged to the party for purely opportunistic reasons and tried not to participate. Kepski was in the army, so his position was somewhat different. Dabrowski was the youngest, and I don't know if he belonged to the party, though if he did, he certainly wasn't active. Professor Witold Sierpinski had a totally unique position; he was a very strange person with great intelligence, absent-minded, uncoordinated, and at the same time quite fiery; he had been a member of the Communist Party of Poland before the war. Most of those Stalinist bozos were his colleagues from either pre-war political activism or a shared Jewish heritage. He could have really made a career for himself in those days and put himself up on a pedestal, but—strangely enough—he didn't do that. He worked in neurosurgery and joked and made fun of everything, including the "authorities." No one was afraid of him. He was also very useful when some kind of equipment had to be acquired for the clinic. He would go to the Minister of Health, who he treated informally, and usually managed to get something. I figured out, rather quickly, that he had been an idealist totally disillusioned. It was easy to guess by what.

The physicians' lounge was on one end of the ground floor of the neurosurgery pavilion. It was furnished with a long table, a rack, a wash basin, and lots of chairs. That was where people had conversations, drank coffee, and discussed surgery and call schedules. And that was also where there were conversations not related to work—so as to have a moment's rest. One day, I asked Sierpinski, who had a rich past from the period of the Occupation, what he thought to be the greatest achievement of his life.

Without hesitation, he responded that when he was still a small boy, he would go to the meadows near the Vistula River to play. The stronger and bigger boys would regularly beat him up and ordered him not to say a word about it at home. For weeks, he endured this torment, choking on his tears but not admitting what awaited him there. Finally, he couldn't take anymore and told his grandmother everything. She said to him, "If he beats you up and sits on you, then look for a rock with your hand and hit him on the head with it."

The next day, such an opportunity presented itself. That stronger boy was sitting on him, Sierpinski had been laid on his back, and the boy was beating him all over. Witek Sierpinski remembered his grandmother's advice. Desperately, he felt around for a rock; he didn't find one but did find a pile of human excrement. Without hesitating, he scooped up the whole pile and threw it in the rogue's face. The effect was instantaneous. The other one got off him, and he happily escaped. That event was, in his mind, the greatest achievement of his life.

He later played a very important role in my life.

One day, we were all sitting together—neurosurgery assistants together with a group of neurologists and psychiatrists—at a joint meeting. One of the psychiatric assistants presented a case of psychological disorder in a middle-aged man with a strong build. The patient had difficulty concentrating, made stupid and nonsensical jokes, didn't work, and managed to spend all the money he had on nonsense.

During the in-depth analysis of these problems, Professor Choróbski sat with his back turned to the speaker, behaving rather rudely, and whispering the entire time in Dr. Rudnicki's ear. We were all a little shocked at this behavior. When the presentation was finally over, Professor Choróbski stood up and, incidentally without stopping, turned to Rudnicki, "Well, uh, friend, schedule surgery for that meningoma this week."

That remark dumbfounded us. But it turned out that he was right and that the patient did have a benign brain tumor in the frontal lobes in the front part of the skull.

I was on-call one night. A patient came to the emergency room with severe pain on one side of his larynx that radiated down into his neck. These symptoms were characteristic of the rather rare neuralgia of the glossopharyngial nerve.

Thrilled with my shrewd diagnosis, I admitted the patient to the ward. The next morning, Professor Choróbski was making rounds. He walked into the four-person patient room, listened to the results of one of the patient's tests, and not even turning toward the bed where the neuralgia delinquent lay, asked, "What idiot admitted this schizophrenic?"

I was shattered—he was right of course. To this day, I don't know how he recognized it.

Professor Choróbski belonged to the Harvey Cushing Society, an American organization of neurosurgeons created by Louise Eisenhart—the former secretary of Dr. Cushing who later finished medical school and became a well-known neuropathologist. He received the *Journal of Neurosurgery* every month, which was the only source of new information in our specialty for us. Routinely each week, articles were given to certain assistants to translate. Then, the material was presented to everyone at a special conference. Professor Choróbski didn't concern himself with his trainees' degrees of fluency in English.

He quickly figured out that I understood the assigned text much better than the others. I had been learning English all the time I was in Poznan, going for lessons to the very kind Scottish lady, Mrs. Guzy, the wife of an RAF (Royal Air Force) pilot, and I was also learning in Warsaw—besides which I had already pored over the volumes written by Bailey, Buchanan, and Bucy. As a result, I was always given the longest and most difficult text to translate. The professor, of course, didn't bother expressing even one word of recognition, but I knew that he saw, knew, and appreciated it.

There were a lot of interesting individuals among the assistants at the Warsaw clinic, such as Dr. Zbigniew Szlaminski, who was Jewish thin, with a worn-out face and the thick glasses of one who is near-sighted; he always had a cigarette stuck to his bottom lip. He lived his own life; he didn't care about any authority, whether of the party or at work. At this moment, I see Dr. Stepien, who was small, almost crotchety, with his near-sighted lenses over his eyes, in the physicians' lounge beginning the morning discussion. Of course, Szlaminski wasn't there. After fifteen minutes, he calmly walked in, not saying "good morning" to anyone, with a bored expression on his face and went to his locker. Not in any hurry, he took off his hat, a thick nondescript colored scarf, and similarly colored coat.

Stepien, who rather prided himself on his dignity, moved restlessly in his chair. The meeting was interrupted, and everyone waited, curious to see what would happen.

"My colleague, Szlaminski, you're late; we started the meeting fifteen minutes ago!"

Szlaminski calmly lit a cigarette, turned to the irritated and already red Stepien, whose eyes flashed with anger.

"Sure, so what of it?" And without blinking an eye, he looked at the agitated professor who couldn't do anything to him, for Szlaminski was Jewish and also a party member. Incidentally, he was quite a decent person and never caused anyone even the slightest harm. He had a pleasant demeanor when someone approached him kindly, but he wouldn't let anyone put the squeeze on him.

After a few years of work, I found out that he had very interesting past from the period of the Occupation. False Ausweiss—the documents required by the German administration, the General Government—had been produced in Warsaw. They were distributed to Lwow, among other places, to save the Jewish people there. Szlaminski was one of the people who transported the false documents. There were always two who went together, one carrying the dangerous goods, the other to stand by him—usually it was someone who spoke German without any foreign accent and who wore a leather coat that was popular among secret agents of the Gestapo. The railroad yard in Lwow was guarded by Schupo—the German armed guards. They stopped Szlaminski, opened the suitcase, and with two fingers, on the top and bottom, checked the thickness of the base. Of course, it was too thick, because that's where the transported documents were hidden. Szlaminski was lost. His partner, however, performed an act of insane courage. He ran up to the armed guards, insulting them with the most vulgar words and yelling that this was his prisoner and that they had nothing to do with it. He flashed some piece of metal that he had stuck under the lapel of the leather coat, then kicked Szlaminski and pushed him in front of him. The dumbfounded armed guards didn't even react. Szlaminski and his friend rounded the first corner, broke into a run, and were saved.

Another very interesting figure was Juliusz Wocjan, fat and quiet, with beautiful Semitic eyes and a full face. He had a tattoo of a camp number on his forearm—he had survived Auschwitz. He was mainly interested in pediatric surgery. He had a kind demeanor and was easy to deal with. I never saw him angry or saying anything sarcastic about his colleagues. His weakness was cuisine. Another neurosurgeon of the clinic, Mietek Geldner, who was also Jewish, shared this fancy. Two doctors were on-call at the same time at the neurosurgery clinic, there was often a lot of work, so one had to operate while the other would take care of on-call consultations. Those two took call together, so that in the moments of quiet, they could cook their own dinners in the call-room kitchen.

That custom, established by a long tradition, was changed by the malice of those left behind, under the leadership of Jaz Haftek. They were carefully watched so that they would finish their culinary ritual and prepare their favorite meals, then, in the last moment, someone finagled a phone call from the admitting room—one was called for an emergency, the other for an immediate consultation. They couldn't do anything about it, so they left their dinner and went where they were supposed to go. The culprits immediately ate the meal that had been prepared. When the unfortunate gourmands came back from their unnecessary trips, the only things left were a few empty pots.

I liked Wocjan. His weakness, perhaps something he took from the camp with him, was fear of any kind of disturbance of the rhythm of life. Some of the wicked people took advantage of this weakness of his in another joke that was even poorer in taste. During that period, doctors were called in for army training from time to time. Poor Julek got a phone call at home.

"This is the on-duty officer at the West Warsaw railroad train station. You must report at two a.m. with a food supply that will last you for twenty-four hours. You are going for training."

You can imagine his panic. His wife, who was also plump and sweet, prepared his provisions and, precisely at two a.m., he ended up at the empty train station. No one could tell him where the on-duty officer could be found. It turned out there was some kind of railroad guard there. Julek sat there until four in the morning, and to top it off, the guard scolded him that he was disturbing his sleep. These are the kind of pranks that took place at the Warsaw neurosurgery ward.

Jas Haftek, who was small, thin, pugnacious, ready for a fight, and who was also "red," was the initiator of such jokes. But then, even he experienced a rather dangerous incident. At three in the morning, he was walking home after a late surgery. It was empty and silent on the streets. He heard a cry and saw two bandits robbing some person right in front of him. Jas was wearing a coat along with a German motorcycle cape that looked quite military. He carried a pipe in the pocket of that coat, and he would pose while trying to smoke it. Not really thinking, he pointed the pipe through the lining of the coat and yelled, "Get your hands up!" The bandits got scared, the victim of the attack disappeared around the first corner, and Jas Haftek was left alone with the two bandits. But he didn't lose his wits. In a flash, he figured out where the nearest militia post was and threateningly ordered the bandits to walk in front of him. He led them to the post. The militia jumped on him at first, because carrying a weapon in those days was pretty much unthinkable, but they only found a pipe. When the bandits saw it, they wailed in anger. Jas Haftek praised himself on his victory for a long time.

Stefan Banach, the son of the famous mathematics professor, was a rather interesting character. His mother was Jewish. Stefan had a hefty build after his father and black, curly hair and dark eyes after his mother—eyes that were hidden behind thick, horn-rimmed glasses. He dressed all in black, both his overcoat and his suit. He carried an umbrella and overall looked very distinguished.

A schedule of surgeries hung in the physicians' lounge along with the designated assistant doctors. Stefan Banach would walk in a very dignified way and approach the schedule of surgical duties—he almost touched his nose to it, because he was so near-sighted. When he didn't see his last name there, which meant he pretty much had a free day, he would start dancing wildly, to the wonder of the young interns. That sudden outburst of joy was just as suddenly over. And then, again distinguished, he calmly got undressed.

I haven't talked about Stas Toczek or Mieczyslaw Geldner yet. They were both older than me; they both had good surgeon's hands. Stas Toczek's fate strangely would cross with my own in the future. During that time, he was happy to get Choróbski's approval, and rightly so, because he was a devoted and intelligent doctor. He belonged to the party; like many of them, he had succumbed to pressure and then really regretted it. He was a big guy with a low forehead, graying bushy hair, and slanted eyes—really not your typical Pole. He spoke slowly and calmly and operated in much the same way.

Miecio Geldner was much older than me. He was Jewish and a gentleman. He also operated well and was well-read. He steered clear of party agitators, though he probably also belonged to the party. Our fates also crossed after many years.

I forgot to mention Gruszkiewicz. He was Jewish with bright straw-like red hair, the same color eyelashes, and a fair, freckled face. He made fun of everyone and made all kinds of faces behind Choróbski's back.

On Saturdays, we made grand rounds—everyone was dressed in clean, white coats. After rounding on patients, we went to the small laboratory, and then Professor Choróbski sat down at the microscope and read out histological samples of those who had surgery that week. In moments of generosity, he would let one or another of us look through the microscope to point out the characteristic features of the tumor. The rest—and there were a lot of us, because apart from the assistants of the neurosurgery clinic, there was also a team from the PAN Department of Neurosurgery—didn't really know what to do and stood in silent respect. Wislawski was doing neuropathology then, and he was the only one who knew at what the professor was looking. Gruszkiewicz, who with his restless temperament could never stand still for even a moment, whispered, made various faces, and eventually leaned his elbow on a glass panel that held reagents essential to the preparations of histological samples—not to mention that they were all different colors. The pressure on the glass panel was strong enough that all the little bottles flew into the air, and in seconds, the whole team of doctors of the Warsaw clinic looked like painted Easter eggs! Professor Choróbski was actually speechless; Gruszkiewicz disappeared without a trace for a few days.

During those sessions, we also dissected brains preserved in formaldehyde of patients who had died after surgery. There were always a lot of these brains. In those days, the primary death rate from brain surgery, which had been about seventy percent, was greatly reduced, but the primitive conditions, as well as the lack of disinfecting solution and antibiotics, meant that many patients died not from their original illness but from developed infections. With disgust, I remember how surgical nurses would gather bloody gauze off the floor to wash it so that it could be used again. With disgust, I also see them trying to repair surgical gloves, that had been used many times, using glue intended for patching bicycle tires!

It's no surprise that infections were then a daily occurrence.

In those years, human life wasn't the most valuable commodity. The pharmaceutical industry was beginning to develop, but there was never enough medication. At one point, that meager supply of self-made medicines was cut off suddenly. After many years, I found out that the Soviet Union was using the renewed Polish pharmaceutical industry for the production of deadly chemical weapons!

Our salaries were unspeakably low. My salary then was a little over fifteen hundred zloty a month. I earned an additional five hundred for high-risk neurosurgery work. In addition I earned 500 as a consultant at the pediatric clinic. Also with the work at the Psychiatric Institution in Tworki and with extra call nights I was making about four thousand a month. Fabric for a men's suit then cost seven hundred zloty per meter!

My father's and my salaries were enough to live on, but when it came to a serious investment, like buying clothes or a coat, we really had to rack our brains.

I had two, or rather three, chiefs. The first was Professor Choróbski. The second—because I was a worker at the PAN Neurosurgery Clinic—Professor Stepien. And finally the third chief was Professor Konorski, who was responsible for the scientific aspect of that department.

Stepien came to Warsaw from Lodz, and then the Lodz clinic was taken over by Szapiro. He came with "his people"—Mempel, who was a good three or four years older than me, and Jadza Srebrzynska, who was about my age. All of them were Jewish. Stepien didn't admit to being Jewish, but he had a typical Semitic appearance. He wasn't a party member, but he worked as a neurosurgeon in the hospital attending to State Security officials in Warsaw.

The next in line after Stepien was Professor Sierpinski, then Adjunct Slowik who, though he wasn't Jewish, had a powerful position, because he was a devoted communist. Stefan Zarski and I were at the bleak bottom. Zarski was a neurologist, and I don't really know why he went into neurosurgery. The bloody work in the operating room didn't appeal to him at all, and he soon left to continue working as a neurologist.

Professor Stepien wasn't known for his pleasant disposition; he supported and showed off his favorites whenever he could, but he only had harsh, unpleasant, and really undeserved criticism toward me. To him, I was a stranger who needed to be broken. But I had a tough back and wouldn't let it be broken. Even so, I—a grown man and neurosurgeon—secretly cried several times because of him. I was treated decently by Sierpinski and Professor

Konorski, who saw the discrimination. Konorski rather liked me, because I had a lot of initiative and did real work. You couldn't say the same about "Colleague" Mempel—one of Stepien's favorites—who Jadza Srebrzynska called a "free thinker" behind his back, which was an implication that he was rather a slow thinker.

Apart from clinical work, we were also required to do so-called scientific work. Konorski was interested in speech impairments, and we had worked out a rather precise method of ascertaining not only the types but also the degrees of speech defects caused by damage to the brain cortex. Because I had worked on aphasia in Poznan and had written my master's thesis in psychology based on that work, I didn't have much trouble working with Professor Konorski.

It happened that we had a patient who was an engineer who had a well-defined tumor located in parietal operculum bordering the lateral fissure on the left side, thus in that half of the brain where the speech area is located. The tumor was removed, and the patient came out of surgery in excellent shape. He didn't have any obvious speech impairments. He was a fan of classical music. One day, he discovered to his horror that he couldn't hear the music despite his preserved hearing.

This intrigued me, so I started digging through neurophysiological literature and finally musicological, and I discovered that in order to hear music, you not only had to have a sense of rhythm, but also had to actively symphonize with the rhythm by active use of the muscles of the oral cavity and the throat. Some people also include the extremities. Thus, this patient had an impairment of the proprioception (or so-called "deep-feeling"), exactly in the area of the oral muscles—his motor activity was not coordinated with the perceived melody and rhythm—and this interference was making it impossible for him to hear the music properly.

Konorski became very interested in this and told me to keep working on it. After that, I tested many, very many, patients for a sense of rhythm. The result of this work was a published paper. I also wrote an essay about the function of the frontal lobes on the basis of clinical material, and finally a paper about the specific nature of certain states of aphasia. And so I had three written papers. "Colleague" Mempel didn't have any. Professor Stepien called me into his office and declared sternly, "Colleague Subczynski, you have three papers ready, and Colleague Mempel doesn't have any. It can't be like this. The article about speech impairments will be printed in his name!"

Well, then—case closed. I didn't have any means of defending myself then. I only knew that my dislike of that little venomous man had only increased.

Soon, however, I got sweet revenge for my suffering. During that time, I already had several written papers, a doctorate in medicine, a master's in psychology, as well as specialty training in neurosurgery. I was only a senior assistant like Mempel who, besides his specialty, didn't have anything else. Professor Stepien often emphasized the necessity of promoting Mempel to an adjunct position, but it was impossible, because it collided with the demands of the Polish Academy of Science. I, however, fulfilled all the necessary requirements. The Academy bureaucrats immediately made me an adjunct. When Professor Stepien found out about this, he frothed at the mouth and screamed that Colleague Mempel was being harmed and that I didn't deserve that position, but there was nothing he could do. And Professor Choróbski was secretly pleased, because he didn't like Stepien; later on his aversion was fully justified.

And so I moved from the physicians' lounge to the adjunct room, where Rudnicki reigned and where Slowik hung up his coat.

Despite his strange opinions, I liked Slowik. He was an honest person, did his job well, and didn't get in anyone's way. He couldn't stand our "scientific work," but he felt right at home in the operating room. I haven't seen many surgeons as talented as he was. He moved slowly, and every movement was well thought out.

The operative field looked like an image from the anatomy atlas, with minimal bleeding. That slow surgeon finished operating much faster than others did, and the patients came out of surgery in good condition.

When I became an adjunct, we very often operated together, assisting each other. To this day, I get a warm feeling in my heart when I think of him. My God! How many years have passed since those days!

⌁

There were two operating rooms in the neurosurgery clinic pavilion—the first was on the ground floor, and the second, the main one, was on the first floor. Professor Choróbski operated in this larger one. I assisted him in brain surgery more than once. He walked into the operating room full of energy, wiped his thin hands on a sterile towel, and put on a surgical apron. The patient was already not only under anesthesia and covered with surgical drapes, but he also had an opened skull and exposed brain. Choróbski was a good surgeon and a good diagnostician in a surgical situation. The assistant had to understand each movement he made and be familiar with his surgical reasoning and method. He didn't say anything to the surgical nurse, who was incidentally his second wife, other than some mumbling; she had to know what to hand him at any given moment. After a few hours of work, droplets of sweat appeared on his white, bony forehead, and his hands started shaking. He got up from the operating stool, leaving an open wound and unfinished surgery.

"Well then do what needs to be done, and close up."

He walked away from the table hunched over and weak. More than once, he left Dr. Rudnicki—with whom he liked to operate—Stas Toczek, or me, practically speaking, in the middle of surgery. Together with the younger assistant, we calmly finished the procedure, usually with success. Thanks to intratracheal anesthesia and huge improvements in surgical technique, the surgical death rate was already much lower.

I couldn't understand what was happening. After such an exit, Professor Choróbski often came back into the operating room, stood behind us, and interrupted with his usually rather sarcastic and apt remarks. He looked terrific and was again full of energy and vigor.

From the doctors who were closest to him, I finally found out that he was a drug addict thriving on morphine. This was very shocking. Years before, he had had tuberculosis and was treated with thoracoplasty, after which he had severe pains due to nerve damage. He started taking morphine because of the pain and became addicted to it.

Despite his dependence on continuous doses of morphine, he undoubtedly surpassed everyone in knowledge and intellect. The addiction did, however, ruin him physically—he was really thin, sometimes irritable for no reason, and sometimes apathetic.

One day, he called me into his office, where the walls were covered with photographs of him together with the most prominent neurosurgeons of that time—Olivecrona from Sweden, Penfield from Montreal, Bucy from Chicago. He sat behind the desk and whispered to me confidentially, "Well, my colleague, uh ..." and somewhat hesitated here, "write a prescription for morphine; here's a blank one."

It hurt me to write that prescription, but on the other hand, it was also nice to have his trust.

A few weeks later, a sad event happened. As a result of lacking the drug, he had an attack from morphine withdrawal on the clinic's premises.

Each one of us was shocked and felt compassion for our teacher, who had virtually created the field of neurosurgery in Poland. He was weak and sick, and completely dependent on the satanic drug. The professor was taken home, and the appropriate consultant was brought in. Professor Stepien, who suddenly showed up during Choróbski's attack, made sure that everyone around saw him in such a state. After Professor Choróbski was taken home, Stepien immediately assumed full authority and announced that Professor Choróbski was and would be incompetent and that he would be directing everything, not only as the head of the PAN Neurosurgery Ward, but also as the head of the neurosurgery clinic of the Medical Academy of Warsaw.

We were disgusted by such a declaration at the time a tragedy was unfolding before our eyes.

Stepien did everything he could to pretty much destroy Choróbski, the father of Polish neurosurgery, and a good doctor and person. He immediately reported the incident to the authorities at the Medical Academy and tried to intervene in the party structure through Sierpinski. But, Sierpinski washed his hands of the matter and refused to participate in the destruction of the professor.

Dr. Rudnicki, who was not a party member and was civil minded, told Stepien what he thought of him right to his face. Dr. Kempski, who had been hired from the army, also didn't mince words and clearly described the baseness of Stepien's behavior. I didn't have anything to say; I had to keep quiet, because if I had opened my mouth, it could have ruined my life. Still, I was on Professor Choróbski's side like all the others. Behind the dictator's back, we tried to figure out what to do.

Stepien called for a meeting in which the entire team was supposed to declare that Professor Choróbski was incapable of working. The meeting ended up a fiasco; no one even opened his mouth. The atmosphere was awful, and Stepien fell into a terrible rage.

Still, he did everything he could to become the formal head of the neurosurgery clinic and to ensure that Professor Choróbski would be seen as incapable of continuing to run it.

Then the day came when Dr. Rudnicki, who was closest to the professor, told me that I was to go to Professor Choróbski's home at a specified time along with the clinic's other doctors. Mempel wasn't asked—he was too close to Stepien. We got there around five p.m. The professor himself opened the door. Physically he looked better, though he was somewhat depressed and—for the first time—humble. He knew us all quite well. He started talking in a quiet voice, said that he was recovering from the drug addiction and had already made good progress, and that he could function rather well. He lifted his thin arm and showed us that his hands no longer shook, even though he was no longer taking morphine. He asked us to help him return to work. We were all his students, and he was now turning to us for help! This meeting almost brought tears to my eyes. After all these years, I see him exactly as he was in that moment, so close to our hearts.

I was convinced and still am convinced, to this day, that he really could have performed the role of the head of the clinic. He just needed some help, which we were all glad to give. Still, Stepien's conniving work began to have some effect. Professor Choróbski was fired, and Stepien was made the temporary director of the Warsaw Neurosurgery. He was very happy because of it, rubbing his small hands together, his eyes shining beneath his thick, near-sighted lenses.

Professor Choróbski didn't come back. I know that he thought well of me. He died after some years. I don't even know when, because the train of my fate rolled along different and rather distant tracks. When I was struggling for my specialty privileges in the States, I was never embarrassed to mention my teacher's name—the honorable, late Professor Jerzy Choróbski.

During the period when Professor Choróbski was still head of the neurosurgery clinic in Warsaw, Professor Penfield visited us; he was the head of neurosurgery at the McGill Institute in Montreal. His visit was a great event. For the first time in my life, I met a Nobel Prize winning laureate in my specialty. Penfield wrote a monumental work together with Professor Jasper about temporal epilepsy, which was a huge step forward in understanding brain function and surgical treatment of epilepsy.

He was a tall, older man with gray hair and blue eyes that looked at us good-naturedly; he had a modest manner and quiet voice. His wife was a kind, sophisticated woman with gray hair that she wore tied back in a thick knot.

Professor Choróbski arranged a meeting, during which those of us who could manage well enough in English presented clinical cases. With great fear and worry, I demonstrated a case of temporal epilepsy—Professor Penfield's specialty. At the end of it, I asked shyly what his opinion was and how he would proceed in this case.

"You know, man," he responded, "I would really like to know more about this subject, because I don't understand much."

This wasn't sarcasm. He said what he thought and felt. I understood then why he was made a Nobel laureate and why the whole world honored him.

About six months after Penfield's visit, Professor Jasper came; he was a specialist in electroencephalographic changes, mainly in temporal epilepsy.

It happened that a few months before that, I had been called to the private home of the Israeli consul, asking for discretion. The consul's daughter, a beautiful and kind sixteen-year-old girl, had some strange attacks, in which she had involuntary muscle movements but didn't lose consciousness.

Our specialist in electroencephalography was Tadzio Bacia; he was intelligent and took initiative, a real man of science. We discussed this case. Tadzio, like me, wasn't sure if we were dealing with some kind of hysterical attacks or if it was something organic, a real disease of the brain. We did several EEG tests, usually with normal results. In one of them, however, we discovered abnormal potentials in the temporal lobe. We came to the conclusion that my young patient had temporal epilepsy.

I discussed the entire matter with her father and prescribed anti-epileptic medication. The muscle cramps stopped, and she felt better.

During a working meeting with Professor Jasper, I presented that case together with Tadzio Bacia. Our guest looked at the EEG tests and definitively determined that what we thought were abnormal potentials were artifacts, and that on the basis of this data, we shouldn't, really mustn't, begin anti-epileptic medication. We were shattered. The next day, I called the consul and told him Professor Jasper's opinion. The medication was stopped. Three days later I got a phone call from the consulate. My patient had a full epileptic attack—this time with a loss of consciousness. I put her back on anti-epileptic medication immediately. Even Professor Jasper could be mistaken.

In addition to my responsibilities in clinical work, I had to participate in conferences at the Neurophysiology Institute that was run by Professor Konorski. During those conferences, the results of experimental investigations were presented by workers of the institute. Then they were discussed, and the results they got were compared to the data in world literature. Konorski maintained international contacts and was one of only a few people who made trips to America and who worked with American institutions. His field was behaviorism—he described it in Pavlov terminology as the higher functions of the brain—though his subject matter didn't have anything to do with the physiology of the brain in the way that it is understood today. The field involved a lot of information about the localization of particular mechanisms, such as engrams of speech elements, representations of memory mechanisms, and the possibilities of performing more than one thing at the same time.

His wife, who we were supposed to call by what I think was her maiden name, Mrs. Lubinska, also worked with American institutions, but in the field of pure neurophysiology— functional mechanism of the peripheral nerve.

After one of Konorski's trips to America, a young neurophysiologist came from the United States. I don't remember his name now, but he was of Jewish descent, had a pleasant manner, and was intelligent. He could only communicate in English. For the first time, I came in contact with this language in a situation in which scientific work was being discussed.

I understood almost everything, and because I never lacked the ambition to be the best, I started voicing my opinions in the discussion in a more or less reasonable manner. It was, however, rather limited, as not many workers of the institute could spit out even a few sensible phrases in English.

At about the same time, I don't know in what way, I came face to face with a rather strange guy—a young Irish painter who had decided to live in Warsaw for a while. He wandered around and didn't have anything to live on. For supper and a small fee, he talked with me in English, as he didn't know any other language. He could only say a few words in Polish. These conversations helped me a lot and made communicating much easier during the conferences with our American visitor.

Our work on speech impairments caused by regional damage to the brain intrigued Dr. Milner, who was working on the same problem in the McGill Institute in Montreal. The head of the institute was Dr. Penfield, and his right-hand man, the electroneurophysiologist and specialist in EEG, was Dr. Jasper. As a result of these contacts, Professor Stepien was invited to the Canadian Institute for a yearlong fellowship.

I was then operating rather often. One day, I was removing a large parasaggital meningoma (a neoplasm located right in the vertex of the head). It was a benign tumor, but it was difficult to operate on because of the significant blood supply. Professor Stepien walked into the room and stood behind me. I was struggling with a venous hemorrhage, trying to coagulate one vessel after another. Slowik was helping me. Professor Stepien began directing me, bothering me during difficult work. At my wit's end, I turned to him and suggested that he leave the operating room. In silence, he did as I had asked and distanced himself. I finished up the surgery, which ended up being a complete success. I was already thinking about what I had done and what the consequences might be. Right after writing my post-operative notes and making sure that the patient was in good condition, I went to Stepien's office, apologizing for my behavior. To my wonder, he didn't hold a grudge against me. Being a good surgeon, he understood my reasons. He said only, "The next time, you better not throw a professor out of the operating room."

The neurophysiology entourage from countries under Soviet domain organized a conference in Poland. I don't remember the date now, but in any case it was in the middle of the summer.

The organizer and host of the conference was Professor Konorski. A little palace near Warsaw was chosen for the conference location where the foreign delegation would stay, and we would travel there. There were Hungarians, Romanians, Czechs, and Slovakians, and there was also a Soviet delegation, quite numerous, as some of the neurophysiologists had "guardians" from the KGB.

My participation in this conference, which was boring and full of "the achievements of Soviet science," wasn't very eager. I soon found something in common with one of the Slovakians who liked music as much as I did. We differed in that I could barely play a little sonata on the piano, while he was a skilled liturgical musician on the organ. We left the conference room discretely and went to all the nearby churches. After speaking with the pastor, we were allowed to go into the choir so that my visitor could play. He really played very well, and he hoped to try out all different kinds of organs. That's how we spent the whole day—without causing any harm to Soviet science.

The Soviet delegation didn't say a word, looking fearfully at their "guardians." I couldn't stand it, and it wasn't just me. We came to the mutual conclusion that we should figure out a way to get them to talk. We bought a pile of timber wood from peasants, who lived nearby, and we placed it in an old beautiful park, then we supplied ourselves with the appropriate amount of alcohol. We spread the word that we had organized a bonfire in the name of "friendship of Socialist countries." No one could oppose such an initiative. I remember that evening. Night fell, and it was warm. The smell of timber and smoke rose from the big bonfire. Alcohol disappeared quickly. First the "protectors" of our Russian guests got drunk, and then they, too, got quite tipsy. It's not even worth mentioning the others. We managed to get them to begin speaking freely and to say that which was not supposed to be said. The next day, the Russian delegation looked pretty bad, while the "guardians" looked at us dismally. They couldn't do anything, however, because they broke the KGB rules on their own by getting drunk in a hostile country. I count that bonfire as one of the important achievements of my life.

In the year 1959, there was a similar conference in Bucharest. I was part of the Polish delegation, along with Jadzaa Srebrzynska, Mempel, Professor Stepien, and of course Professor Konorski. I don't remember why now, but I was flying there the following day, after the rest of the delegation had already departed. I landed in Bucharest and walked out of the airport. I had the address where I was supposed to go. I couldn't communicate at all with local people. I tried in Russian, badly in German, in Polish—nothing was working. In the end, I wrote the address on a piece of paper, and the taxi driver understood and took me to the proper hotel.

It was an old, once elegant hotel designated only for the foreign delegates. Time had already worn it down quite a bit. For years, it hadn't been renovated. The rooms were large with bathrooms in which the baths and decor were from another era.

We woke up early in the morning and gathered in the hotel lobby. A young Romanian woman was waiting there who had been assigned to the Polish delegation as a chaperone. She was kind, polite, and intimidated. She loaded us together with the other delegates onto a bus standing outside the hotel, and we drove through the streets of Bucharest. We stopped in front of some building. The door opened and we went inside. It was a restaurant only for the privileged. The food was delicious—supposedly the kitchen was run by the king's head chef.

From there, we were taken to the conference room. The meeting was boring—full of the same talk of "Soviet science achievements." I was intrigued by Professor Tkaczow; he was a big, fat guy with a red face and similarly red nose. Rumors were going around that he was the tool in Beria's hands who was used to eliminate Stalin. To this day, I don't know if that was true.

After the session we were taken back to the same restaurant for a very good dinner. I developed a particular liking for the Romanian-style soup called *czorba*.

Two days of such a conference were all that my system could take. Even the trip to the neurosurgery clinic didn't help much. While there, however, I saw something that I had never before seen nor would ever see again—two patients sharing one bed!

The third day, I decided to go "out into the world" on my own. When our chaperone was loading us onto the bus, I moved in the bustle to the other side. The bus drove off, leaving me on the street to my own devices. Before leaving, we got pocket money in Romanian lei. It was quite a bit more than a scientist's monthly salary in Romania. With cash in my pocket, I went for a trip through the city. Bucharest, despite the poverty visible on every corner, was a beautiful city. The sun lit up the white walls and turned this different world golden. I went to the market, which reminded me somewhat of the prewar market in Polesie. There were wagons that were harnessed to horses, men in fur hats, and a crowd of women buying and selling vegetables. It was already well into the afternoon when I made my way back to the hotel. I saw our chaperone, who was horrified and trembling, in the hall. She was nearly hysterical with fear! Professor Konorski stood next to her along with some Romanians in civilian dress. It turned out that my little excursion resulted in the mobilization of the Bucharest militia, including the secret one, and that our chaperone was in danger of being imprisoned. They also threatened me, but Professor Konorski defended me. Despite all the deceit and terror in the People's Republic of Poland, it seemed like a paradise when compared to Romania.

After we returned, the problem arose as to how to prepare for publishing a volume of research papers related to the higher function of the brain. This volume was to be, in a sense, the crowning achievement of years of Professor Konorski's work. It was to be composed of experimental work done at the Nencki Institute, as well as clinical work from the neurosurgery ward of the Polish Academy of Science.

Konorski needed someone from our group to help put together this volume as a logical whole, to make up proofs and eliminate any discrepancies. It was not an easy task; it was burdensome, demanding a great deal of sacrifice. It also meant that, for at least a month, that person would be disconnected from clinical work and would instead be poring over papers at the Nencki Institute under Konorski's supervision. Professor Stepien didn't have any doubts as to who to assign—of course, me. The rest of our team took the decision with relief; no one really wanted to do it.

The next morning, I reported to Professor Konorski. He gave me a desk, brought a pile of materials for publication, and told me to start making up proofs. If I had any problems, I was to come directly to him.

Unlike my colleagues in neurosurgery, I didn't mind doing this work at all. It required concentration and tact, as you had to verify changes with authors over the phone, and it was also interesting and enriching. I sat in the Institute for long hours, often into the night. Konorski would come to me, evaluate the progress of the work, advise, and sometimes change or add something. I saw that he was pleased with me. Thanks to our closely working together, a thread of understanding and cooperation developed. My task required familiarity with the subject and a concept of the volume. Konorski saw that I had seized upon his original idea and that I could further develop it.

When the essential part of the work on the manuscript was finally finished, I had to go to Krakowskie Przedmiescie Street to a publisher specializing in scientific works. I spent about a week there with a Polish linguist who made language corrections. I always thought that I could write in Polish rather well, so I was amazed at the number of mistakes she found, mainly in punctuation.

After six weeks, I returned to clinical work. Things were bad in the neurosurgery clinic. Post-operative infections were becoming a regular occurrence! A decision was made to close the hospital, sterilize it, and begin anew, but there were a lot of patients lying in the hospital with infected post-laminectomy (spinal surgery) wounds on their backs, and I also saw a patient with a "mushroom" on the brain that was infected and coming out of ruptured sutures in the skin. Someone had to take care of these patients; a lot of them needed surgical cleaning of their wounds. This work was awful and thankless—most of those patients were going to die.

Professor Stepien told me to perform this task. So I had to "repair" patients and try to heal awfully infected wounds. I managed to save a few of them, but some did die. I dismally remember that period of my life—feeling despair, suffering, and hopelessness as a powerless doctor.

In the year 1960, Stepien finally left for his yearlong fellowship at the McGill Institute in Montreal. During that time, he had already been performing surgery on the focus of epilepsy, mainly in the temporal lobe. The patient was woken up from anesthesia after the brain had been exposed, an electroencephalography was done, looking for the focus of the epilepsy, then the cerebral cortex was electrically stimulated in various places, so as to map the functions of the brain. Stepien performed these surgeries well. The McGill Institute was then leading the world in that field, so his yearlong fellowship was very significant.

After the professor's departure, my life got easier. Thereafter, my direct chief was Professor Sierpinski; he didn't meddle at all—just wanted some peace and quiet and had complete faith in us, knowing that we could perform all the clinical work well. Tadzio Slowik looked after this last part, ensuring orderliness and good organization, and Rudnicki directed the Medical Academy team—Professor Choróbski had already been completely removed.

A few other doctors left our neurosurgical center. Geldner and Gruszkiewicz had gone to Israel. Geldner became the chief of neurosurgery in Tel Aviv, and Gruszkiewicz worked under his direction. Shortly after, Stefan Banach went there, too. Selecki had gone to Israel much earlier, but he ended up in Australia eventually.

9

Communist Tyranny

I THINK IT WAS during my first year of medicine that the authorities held the infamous "three times yes" voting. This vote, which was heralded as a sign of full support for the Soviet occupation, was of course fixed. The results of the voting were simply reversed—and so the votes that supported the regime, of which there were very few, were changed to "no" while the almost ninety percent of negative votes were changed to "yes."

In the propaganda tabloids, you could read that the nation supported the ruthless battle against the reactionary forces, against the degenerate gangs of the WiN (*Wolnosc i Niepodleglosc,* Freedom and Independence Organization) and other independence organizations that were still fighting. The triumph of General Swierczewski (who changed his name and was originally Jewish) was heralded in the fights against the groups of the UPA (*Ukrainska Powstancza Armia,* the Ukrainian Uprising Army). We had no idea then of the extent of ruthlessness with which the Ukrainian people in Bieszczady were being treated.

In those days, the *Zwiazek Walki Mlodych* (Fighting Youth Organization) was weakly represented in the medical field— though it was gaining more and more members. My high school friend, Mieczyslaw Wender, was one of those who understood the force behind the tides and joined the party rather early on.

There was a joining of the PPR (*Polska Partia Robotnicza*, Polish Workers Party—continuation of the anti-Polish Communist Party of Poland) and the PPS (*Polska Partia Socjalistyczna*, Socialist Party of Poland). After the former illusion of a multi-party system, this allowed for the clear dictatorship of one communist party that was directly controlled by the Soviets. The Democratic Party and the PSL (*Polskie Stronnictwo Ludowe*, Populist Party) still existed, but they were puppets of the PZPR (*Polska Ziednocona Partia Robotnicza*, Polish United Workers Party).

The food supply was meager; it was livable and no one went hungry, but the standard of living was poor. I remember that for a long time you could only get calf's hooves, because there was nothing else at the butcher shops. After many, many years, when I was already in the United States, I found some information that, during that time, the regime was selling mass amounts of calves to Italy; the money from this financed Bierut's palaces and the fancy life of "the people on top." Boleslaw Bierut, a colonel in the KGB, had been imposed by the Soviets as the President of "Polish People's Republic."

In those days, we knew that Hilary Minc, one of the main bosses in the PRL, was Jewish, though we had no idea that nearly the entire government except Bierut, was made up of Jews brought in from Russia. They had Polish last names like Rozanski and Swiatlo. Stalin purposely used communist Jewish mafia to eliminate the Polish intelligentsia, to destroy national identity, and to enslave the nation completely.

I remember placards with an image of a soldier, wearing a four-corned cap with an eagle without a crown, who was poking at a poor creature with a bayonet—the phrase above this scene read: "The spit-on dwarf of the reactionary movement."

We came to see the awful truth that our hope for freedom, which we dreamed about during the dismal days of German occupation, had not been fulfilled and would not be fulfilled anytime in the near future. We found ourselves under a different occupation, differing from Hitler's in method but not in aims.

This ugly truth wasn't fully obvious yet during the Christmas of 1947. The clutches of the regime had not yet completely squeezed us then, and an illusion of normalcy existed, an illusion that, of course, things would have to get better, that something would change. I remember those holidays clearly. We had a decorated Christmas tree, and Christmas Eve was as it was supposed to be according to the Vilno tradition of my grandmother and mother. My uncle Wladek and his wife Nata came over with Andrzej, who was already a teenager, and Stas, who was still small. We had traditional poppy seed cake and other seasonal dishes. My grandmother reigned at the table, happy to have her loved ones close to her and thankful that everyone had, by the grace of God, survived the nightmare of German occupation and a new better life was beginning.

When I think of her, I always see her the way she was during that last Christmas Eve—smiling, joyful that none of her loved ones were going hungry, that the children were learning normally in school, and that I—her quiet source of pride—was finishing my second, most difficult year of medical school. When she was dying, she knew that I would definitely become a doctor—I had already passed all the necessary exams. It was something unspeakably important to her.

During the time I worked on the top floor of the Diakoniski Clinical Hospital, something happened that left a permanent mark on my life.

It was already dark. Lights shone in the long corridor, and in the nurses station at one end of it. The patients' rooms were dim, somewhat lit up by the light that fell in from the hallway. It was silent. This silence was only occasionally broken by the sound of the young on-call nurse's quick footsteps that echoed in the empty corridor. From the patients' rooms, you could hear the deep, slow breathing of sleep, the difficult breathing of people whose lives still hung in the balance.

After the last rounds, which I made with the night nurse, I went back to the physicians' lounge to study Bailey's classic work about brain tumors with the help of a dictionary.

I was then an assistant in the newly opened neurosurgery ward in Poznan; our ward was located on the top floor of the Diakoniski hospital, right under the roof. You entered the ward through large glass doors. Just next to them was the only elevator, and ahead there was a short corridor that ended at the small and only operating room. To the left of the operating room was the physicians' lounge, where I resided. A long perpendicular corridor linked all the patients' rooms.

Half lying on the bed, drinking the remains of some cold coffee, I arduously waded through the jungle of symptomatology and anatomical changes associated with cerebral gliomas.

Suddenly, the familiar silence of nighttime at the hospital was broken by the sudden noise of a door being thrown open, the clamor of many boots, the metallic clang of weapons, and sharp cries of orders being given out. I flew out of the call room, not knowing what was going on. In the dim light, I saw uniformed people with automatic weapons in their hands that were pointed in all directions. In the middle of them, there was a stretcher with an inhumanly emaciated unconscious man. I was struck by the difference in the uniforms of those who had come. Some had regular uniforms, while others' were greener. On the rude faces that were red from vodka, you could see fear and uncertainty.

The officer leading the group stepped forward and asked, "Are you the on-call doctor? If you are, then you have to bring this guy back to consciousness! He must speak; he absolutely must speak! It's an order, you hear?"

Dumbfounded, I went over to the stretcher and leaned over the man who was struggling to breathe, clearly near death. It was hard to estimate his age, he was probably over forty, because the stubble of a beard that had not been shaved for many days was a little white from gray hairs. His hollowed temples and black sunken eyes indicated that he was malnourished and dehydrated. He was covered with a gray blanket, at the end of which two awfully emaciated feet stuck out. I looked at them, and my heart stopped. The soles of those feet were charred black!

The officer's voice interrupted my moment of horror. "Listen, you, we don't have time. You have to do something so that he can speak; we need his information immediately. Instead of staring at him, get to work!"

I understood what was going on; this man was a prisoner who had been tortured terribly and was already dying, and from whom the bandits of the UB hoped to get some information that was necessary and crucial to them. They were also undoubtedly scared of what their superiors would do to them if they failed. Their great anxiety was obvious in their quick and sudden movements and the weapons pointed at the one entrance to the ward, those glass doors and elevator. It was clear that they were after something or someone.

The horrified on-call nurse ran over from the nurse's station at the first sound of their arrival and now desperately looked at me, deeply scared, understanding the danger of the situation.

I got myself together. I also understood that I was in danger, and I knew what I should do.

"Please prepare a bed in the last room, the one next to the call room, so that we have easy access to the patient. We have to start an IV immediately—Ringer's lactate with five percent glucose solution. Please also prepare an injection of strychnine."

My ordering tone and calmness had a certain effect on the UB agents and prison guards. They stepped aside when, with the nurse and the orderly, we grabbed the stretcher and carried it to the room. Once there, we closed the door a little, took off some of the unfortunate person's dirty rags, and laid him on the bed. It wasn't until then that we could get a good look at him. He was inhumanly emaciated, had bruises all over his body, his nails had been partly ripped off and were covered in dried-up, black blood, and his breathing was shallow and fast. He was unconscious and was barely sensitive to pain.

"Doctor, doctor, for God's sake, don't save him!" the nurse pleaded in despair.

I didn't have any doubts that the victim of the UB agents was near death, mainly from dehydration and electrolyte imbalance. I was also convinced that saving this person would be an unforgivable crime. Of course, I couldn't say this. In response to the desperate pleas of the nurse, I said loudly and emphatically, so that I could be heard in the hallway, "We will do everything we can. The IV should go slowly, not faster than ten drops a minute; we have to wait and see how he reacts to it."

The nurse threw me a quick glance that was full of understanding. She knew that such treatment would not prevent death. Her glance revealed not only understanding but also gratitude. After a moment, I went out into the corridor, put on my most professional posture, turned to the lieutenant, and said, "Well, then, the situation is very serious; your prisoner is near death. We will do everything in our power to save him, but his chances of regaining consciousness are almost zero."

The officer swore rudely and scratched his somewhat dirty head. "Too bad, we have to wait. You and you," he said, selecting people, "stand guard at the room and don't let anyone in other than the doctor and the nurse; you will be at the main entrance so no one can sneak in here. The rest follow me."

The doors banged again. The heavy steps of metal-embossed boots could be heard on the stairs. The two UB agents and prison guards didn't really know what to do with themselves. Quickly, I told the orderly to give them chairs so they had some place to sit. The nurse looked at me and started talking to one of the UB agents to get information out of him. I went back to the physicians' lounge and fell onto the bed. Thousands of thoughts raced through my mind, dominated by a feeling of horror and fear. After about fifteen minutes, a quiet knocking announced the nurse's arrival. It turned out that the prisoner was a member of an anticommunist organization that everyone knew about and whose remaining members were still fighting in the Poznan region. He was a member of the WiN (*Wolnosc i Niepodleglosc*, Freedom and Independence Organization).

While transporting him from one prison to another, his friends, who had to have received the proper information, attacked the convoy. We never found out what happened, but judging by the fear of the UB agents, we could assume that it got heated. They wanted to find out who the attackers had been, as well as where they lived, from the tortured person.

In the morning, the prisoner's breathing got shallower, then at a certain moment stopped completely. The muscles relaxed, and the jaw dropped. The peace of death was with him. Those who had committed this crime were never punished.

That night's call seemed to lift some kind of curtain, behind which I saw the collective truth of Polish reality at that time. There wasn't the time or conditions normally to think about the terror that was then so widespread. We got used to the fact that the press lied, that you had to stand in long lines to buy anything, and that you could get better merchandise if you had connections. We also got used to the fact that there were stores for the chosen few "behind yellow curtains" to which we had no access.

Deceit, terror, and pauperization became something "normal," something that was part of daily life. Slowly, a person would get accustomed to it, lose the ability to imagine living differently in freedom, independence and dignity. We accepted as normal not being able to buy quality goods but rather only what the authorities discarded at the market. Slowly, the abnormality of the whole situation—in which base people, the worst dregs of society, governed and "sought revenge," sitting in the party committees or as "personnel" clerks—was accepted as normal.

In the Medical Academy of Poznan, it wasn't any better. Career-seekers, who sold their souls to the Russian occupant, ruled, advanced, and got professorships without doing any of the work normally involved; they decided who would be admitted into medicine and who wouldn't be. Everyone was afraid of them, from the youngest assistant to the professor, and they rightly feared them, because these people determined their fates.

Mietek Wender, who I already wrote about, who was an active member of the PZPR (*Polska Ziednocona Partia Robotnica*—the Polish United Workers Party), was making such a career for himself while still in the university. He became an adjunct, and by a strange coincidence, Dr. Zwodziak, who had previously held the position, was drafted into the army. Shortly thereafter, "Comrade" Wender became a professor and then he, not Professor Dowzenko, decided what shape the Neurology Clinic would take.

In that period, I had nothing to do with him; I only heard things about ruining the professor's reputation in order to destroy him. Much later, I found out that Mieczyslaw Wender took over as head of neurology after removing Professor Dowzenko. I don't know what happened to the latter one. Such things were happening everywhere, not only in neurology. Slowly, the regime supporters were taking over all the higher positions in the university departments.

Now, years later, most of them are on the retirements they earned, but the sea of evil that they created over the years exists to this day, and it won't be easy to get rid of it. That moral destruction, in which the rule was that evil was good and good was evil, that Marxist-Leninist paranoia, that making the population less than human was—and is—a state that is just as awful as killing the best sons of the fatherland.

⁂

Still, you had to live daily life and be happy with the little things, because no one can live without some moments of joy. I remember the rattle of the streetcar wheels that woke me up, the sun's rays looking through the window, and the smell of spring after a long winter of gray weather. I remember going with my mother to the Grojecki cemetery where my grandmother was buried. The grave was well cared for. The tomb was made of granite, and there was a plate of marble surrounded by a little wall with flowers inside. The cemetery was old and huge, hidden in the shade of trees; it was peaceful and quiet with that overwhelming peace that would sneak into the soul and lessen all wounds regardless of will. I remember the walkway covered with yellow leaves in the fall, the quiet rustle of falling leaves, and graves bundled up in snow, white and peaceful in the chilly air.

I remember the time of Lent and going from church to church on Good Friday to visit the ceremonial tombs of crucified Jesus. I remember the piercing cold that came from the church walls and the shining tomb of the suffering figure of Christ. Often, the ceremonial tombs were decorated symbolically, showing the suffering of Poland through His suffering.

During the last week of Lent, I always went to the basilica for the performance of the Stuligrosz boys' choir. At this very moment when I close my eyes, I can hear that choir performing the song, "Stabat Mater Dolorosa." The Stuligrosz choir was like a ray of light that the Russian occupier was trying to extinguish with the help of those who had sold out the nation. They failed.

10

A Ray of Hope

ONE WINTER DAY, when I was throwing off my snowy and muddy boots in the adjunct room, I glimpsed a piece of paper on the floor that had already been quite dirtied.

"What's this?" I asked Tadzio Slowik, who was changing for surgery.

"Nothing important, just some circular concerning international scholarships from the Polish Academy of Science," he responded.

I picked up that circular and started reading. It included a list of requirements that you had to fulfill in order to be eligible for an international scholarship through the Rockefeller Foundation. The main conditions were: appropriate age, a doctorate in medicine, a specified number of published works, and knowledge of the English language. I met all these requirements. The candidates were then to be evaluated by one of the directors of that foundation.

I was then very interested in stereotactic surgery of the brain—surgeries performed through a small opening in the head with an apparatus that allowed to reach a particular point in the brain with the precision of a few millimeters. Irving Cooper in New York was one of the best in this field. These types of surgeries helped in Parkinson's disease and athetotic movements. I really wanted to go to Cooper and gain this knowledge, and then establish it in Poland.

Immediately after reading that circular, I ran to Professor Sierpinski and, unspeakably excited, showed him the piece of paper.

"I would like to go to Cooper for training in stereotactic surgery. Would you agree to let me do this, and help me?" I asked.

"If you want to try it," he said, "I'll sign all the necessary papers."

I got the forms, filled them out, and with Sierpinski's signature as the director with full responsibility for the neurosurgery ward put in an application at the Academy chancellery. Soon after, I got a piece of paper saying that I was to report to Professor Infeld on such and such a day for an exam in the English language. I had no idea then who he was. Only after I was already in the States did I find out that he was a physicist closely linked to the production of the hydrogen bomb and a Soviet agent, who literally at the last minute before being arrested managed to get on the deck of the *Batory* ship that was docked in the port! The Russians didn't want him in their country; the matter was incredibly delicate, so he was placed in the Polish Academy of Science.

In revenge, American authorities prohibited the docking of the ship *Batory* in any American port.

I reported to Professor Infeld at the specified time. He was a thin, older Jewish man with graying hair. He welcomed me politely, then switched to English and asked if I understood him, asking why I wanted to leave and where I wanted to go. I understood him and responded relatively properly. He said that my knowledge of English was sufficient and that he didn't see any obstacles to my going. About a month later, I received another statement that I was to report to one of the most luxurious hotels to have a conversation with Director Miller, an American who was evaluating candidates for the Rockefeller Foundation scholarships.

I went to that meeting feeling agitated and nervous. The kind older man smiled at me, held out his hand, and asked me to sit. He started asking me what I did, what kind of scientific research I hoped to do in America, how old I was, and what my qualifications were. Hesitating and speaking brokenly, I responded to all of the questions. In the end, he told me that I qualified for a Rockefeller Foundation scholarship and that he would recommend me to the foundation authorities. I was in seventh heaven as I returned to Oczki Street where our clinic was located.

I had already written a letter to Dr. Cooper asking if he would accept me if I were to get the scholarship. He said that yes, of course, he would. It seemed that the matter was settled and the trip was just a matter of time. It's worth adding that I was the only candidate going to Dr. Cooper—if there had been a party candidate, he would have had preference.

During that time, Professor Stepien returned from Montreal. When he found out about my plans to leave, already close to being realized, he fell into a rage.

"Colleague Mempel should go first. He deserves a trip, and you don't. This has all been dirty work behind my back."

This row ended in nothing; the matter had already progressed too far.

A month went by, then two and three, and there was still no response from the Rockefeller Foundation. Finally, after four months, I received a letter in which I was recognized as a candidate for the scholarship but was not given any funding for the trip, because the scholarship was designed only for scientific research, not for professional development such as my work in New York would have been.

I was shattered. I showed the letter to Stepien, and he was unspeakably happy.

"I told you nothing would come of it. Very well, it was a good little lesson; write a letter immediately to Cooper telling him that you can't go."

Well then, I wrote such a letter, and two weeks later I got the following response: "Please, come anyway; we will finance your stay and work here."

The invitation from Dr. Cooper decided the matter. Because I had already qualified for an international scholarship by the Polish Academy of Science, there were no other formal obstacles. Professor Stepien had to face reality. My stay there was to last a year.

Because the trip wasn't financed by either the Polish Academy of Science or the Rockefeller Foundation, I was just going with a contract of making $250 a month. I had to pay for the trip there and get some pocket money. It wasn't easy considering my and my father's salaries.

I had one nice suit and a tuxedo that I got when I went once to a ball at the Warsaw Philharmonic. Besides that I had a few old pairs of pants and some sweaters. I had another pair of pants sewn from lightweight wool in an aquamarine color, and a nice wind-breaker—and that was it. Oh, and I also had to buy a suitcase; it was light and rather large, made of plastic. This preparation completely wiped us out of money. And it turned out that a ticket on the ship *Batory* cost eleven thousand zloty; it was so expensive because there was only one luxury cabin available. And a train ticket from Montreal to New York had to be added to this price, because the only port *Batory* could sail into was Montreal.

I got a passport at the Mostowski Palace rather easily. The UB agents working there already had my papers from the Polish Academy of Science, together with the confirmation from the party committee that evaluated every departure. Sierpinski took care of this approval of the PZPR for me through his old communist connections there.

I went to the American embassy with the invitation from Cooper to get a visa. I had to wait some time in the waiting room before I was called. I sat in the company of peasants from Podhale who were being sponsored by their Chicago families. These types of people could leave "the people's fatherland;" the intelligentsia could not. I sat in a hard metal chair that was "made in the USA" feeling quite bored. Then, a group of tall black men in thin polyester jackets that were a colorful Scottish plaid, and awfully wrinkled in the back, came into the waiting room. They spoke loudly and quickly. It was a basketball team. I didn't understand a word. That throaty sound horrified me, as all my knowledge of English seemed worthless! Feeling slightly broken, I went to the vice consul's office and explained the matter. I understood him much better. I got the visa right away.

I don't remember now how my father got the money for *Batory* and the train to Montreal. In those days, I was allowed to exchange zloty for five dollars—this was to be the capital with which I would travel. When I made the exchange, the head of the bank walking by became interested in me. He asked what I was doing and where I was going. He told me that because I had a contract, he would personally lend me an additional twenty dollars from the bank with the condition that I would promise to return it within two weeks of getting to New York. This was a valuable and kind help.

In the final days before my departure I had to invite the whole clinical team for a farewell party. I then had a small, thirty-six-meter apartment near Miodowa Street. From the balcony, I could easily see into the park by the archbishop's palace. Almost everyone came. All the alcohol was consumed and because there hadn't been enough of it, even the cherries were eaten from the bottle from which the liqueur had been made. I remember that at one moment Tadzio Bacia went pale and said goodbye to me. Sierpinski, who had an unusual sense of humor, said, "Well then, if Tadzio is a good communist, he'll puke in front of the bishop's palace, and if not, then in front of the Ministry of Health."

It turned out, though, that it was neither here nor there. After a while, through the commotion of drunken conversations, I heard a monotonous knocking on the door that went on for a long time. When I opened the door, Tadzio Bacia stood in the doorway with tears in his eyes.

"Listen, Janusz, it's something awful. There's no way out of your building."

He had gone down to the basement and was wandering in circles lost for at least half and hour!

The time came to leave. I already had my suitcase packed. We were eating supper—my father, mother, and Andrzej, my cousin who was going to take me to port Gdynia. We ate in silence; it was the evening before I would leave for a whole year, for an unknown adventure, far across the one thousand kilometers and deep Atlantic. My heart felt tight, and my enthusiasm waned completely. Looking at my mother, I thought, "My God, why am I doing this to them, why couldn't I just keep living like I had been, what force is pushing me to hurry off that I can no longer control?"

11

The Road to a New Life

THE MOMENT CAME to say goodbye; it was so strange. I couldn't find the words or even tears. I took one last look at my mother standing in the doorway and my father leaning out behind her, and then heard the sound of our footsteps on the stairs before we stepped into the dusk of night. I looked around again. I looked at the lit dining room window. I was overcome with horror that I might never come back here, might never again see my parents, and that I was leaving the life I grew up in for another that was foreign and unfathomable.

We arrived in Gdynia early in the morning on a crowded overnight train tired and hungry. We reached the port. From a distance, I saw the ship *Batory* docked by the port building. I said goodbye to Andrzej, we hugged, and I asked him to say goodbye to my parents for me once again. I went inside the port building. Someone checked my passport and ticket, and I was allowed to pass through the narrow entrance and then up the moveable walkway up to the deck. I stood there with my suitcase in my hand not knowing what to do. A steward came up to me, looked at my ticket, and took me to the cabin. It was on the uppermost deck and wood-paneled with a large window and a luxurious bathroom. I looked at all of this dumbfounded not knowing what to do or what to think. Images of my farewell and the crazy past few days swam in my head. I was hungry and awfully tired.

I heard a knock at the door. After that I said, "Please, come in," the same steward appeared in the doorway. He asked me if I was hungry and if I'd like something to eat before dinner. I responded that I would gladly have something to eat. He came back after a moment with a tray holding a carafe of aromatic coffee, along with a pitcher of cream and a large, fresh roll with a thick layer of ham. There were also some butter cookies.

We ate well at home, but that snack was such a luxury for me. I inhaled the crusty bread and gulped down some coffee. I felt better; in the darkness of pessimism and near despair, there was now a faint light of hope. I threw myself on the comfortable bed and immediately fell asleep.

The slow wail of the horn woke me up. *Batory* was getting under way. The moveable walkway had been removed. A small tugboat with rubber tires all around it whose deck stuck out just above the water was pulling the massive hull of the *Batory* out of the port. It was four o'clock. A piercing wind blew in from the ocean. A rainbow-colored trail of petroleum flickered on the dark water. The shore and the port started getting further and further away. The little tugboat left us, the ship's engines came on, and we started moving on our own power. I went to the luxurious restaurant. When I was given a menu, I was pretty much shocked by the incredibly diverse offerings. An unspoiled victim of the People's Republic of Poland, I "read" that menu from top to bottom, ordering everything in turn. The waiter wasn't surprised, smiled at me understandingly, and brought one course after another, hors d'oeuvres, excellent soup, then a delicious entrée, dessert, and coffee and cookies. This dinner really lifted my spirits. I came to the conclusion that things might not be so bad after all.

I went out to the deck again. It was already dark, and you could see the shining silver path reaching to the horizon on the smooth ocean, floating behind the ship. It surprised me that this disturbance of the water by the ocean liner's wake lasted so long, for a few kilometers.

A young woman was leaning on the bar of the handrail. I started talking to her. She was going to America to marry some Polish guy that she didn't know much about. He had visited Poland, and after a few days, she agreed to marry him; now, she was sailing to her wedding. That's how young Polish women at that time left the communist paradise, often shattering their lives with random partners.

The number of voyagers on the deck was getting smaller minute by minute. It turned out that the short and sharp waves of the stormy Baltic caused a lot of people to get seasick. That also happened to the woman I was talking to, who went pale and quickly disappeared. I didn't see her again until the port in Copenhagen. I couldn't understand how you could get sick from the swaying of the ship. It was rather pleasant for me. Then again, during my childhood, I spent an entire zloty riding around on the carousel, when one ride cost only five grosz!

The next morning, we sailed through Skagerrak and Kattegat. I could see the green coast of Sweden in the distance. Shortly after we arrived in Copenhagen, we were let out onto the mainland, and for a dollar, I went on a tour through the city with the rest of the group. Everything astonished me—the old apartment buildings, the crowded stores, the traffic in the streets. We sailed away in the afternoon making our way in the direction of England. The dark, almost black water of the North Sea suddenly turned light green. We sailed into a gulf stream. The air was also somewhat different, warmer and gentler. I inhaled the clean air that was permeated with the scent of the sea with pleasure. There were now a lot more people out on deck. They spoke many different languages, such as Swedish, German, and English. Again, I felt somewhat lost and uncertain. After supper I went to the movie theater. An American Western was being shown. With shock, I concluded that I hardly understood anything the actors were saying. That night, I sat in my cabin going over English grammar and trying to soak up as many idioms as possible.

We sailed into Southampton. This port, which was huge, dirty, and blackened from coal dust, made a depressing impression. Again, a lot of passengers came aboard. You could hear less German being spoken now and more and more English. At dinner, the dining room was full.

After sailing out of Southampton, we were supposed to sail out into the Atlantic. This plan yet had to be changed. It turned out, though. One of the Polish Americans, an older man who had come to Poland after years to visit family, suddenly fell ill. He lay in his cabin with peritonitis, afraid to say he was sick. A steward finally discovered him there. The ship changed course and before evening docked in the Irish port of Cork so that the sick man could be taken to a hospital as quickly as possible. I remember the red hair of the Irish pilot who brought the ship into the port. We didn't stay there long. Then we sailed out into the Atlantic. After going over a short wave on the La Manche Canal, the North Sea was behind us. *Batory* slowly climbed up and flowed down on a long and much bigger wave of the Atlantic. The sun was just setting, reaching to the end of the ocean. We were sailing in the direction of that sun. When I looked back, I saw Ireland getting further and further away, with green hills and white, steep cliffs that were red in the setting sun. I couldn't take my eyes off that view.

My neighbor in the next luxury cabin was a Russian. He was sailing to New York and made my acquaintance. He must have taken me for some prominent communist individual from Poland, as I was traveling in such luxurious conditions. He was a trade attaché going to the Soviet embassy. I didn't clear up the matter for him. When he delicately tried to find out who I was, I answered in silence, and he didn't ask again. Still, he concluded that he could speak rather freely with such an individual, who was perhaps a high-ranking official of the SB, KGB, or GRU. I didn't ask him anything, but he began speaking, mainly from boredom. Among other topics, he began discussing the Soviet system.

With disarming and shocking sincerity, he said, "Well then, the communist system in our country cannot be maintained if the people get more than eighteen percent of the GNP! You have to maintain an incredibly low standard of living so as to govern. And the majority of the GNP has to be designated for defense, the military, and spreading revolutionary propaganda throughout the whole world."

It's important to remember that this was a period of military and propagandist Soviet offensive; communism was spreading like wildfire in South America, Africa, and the Arab countries. It seemed that nothing and no one could stop the invasion of this inhumane system and Soviet dictatorship. The person I was speaking with saw reality this way and, with this perspective, was sailing to New York to participate in breaking the back of "rotten capitalism," whose most glaring manifestation was the United States.

The words of this man, speaking about the planned distraction of the free world and turning it into a life of misery—words stated without the slightest consideration of the danger of their meaning—stuck in my memory forever. It was a lesson that has stayed with me all my life. Though I experienced a lot in the bonds of communism, this calculated crime against humanity showed me the totality of Satanism that was the Soviet system and communist ideology.

〜

I had strange, unpleasant dreams. I woke up groggy, feeling weighted down with a headache. Finally, I opened my eyes.

And I saw my legs sticking straight up into the air. This state didn't last long, however. After a moment, my legs went down, and I found myself in a hunched-over position, seeing myself clearly in the bathroom mirrow, whose doors were rhythmically opening and closing. After another moment, my legs were again up in the air. I looked up at the ceiling that seemed also to be moving rhythmically. Dumbfounded, I got up from the bed. The weight of my whole body was thrown forward, and I fell into the bathroom and hit the sink. I gathered my wits and understood that the Atlantic was showing off what it could do. I felt a little sick. I did shave, though, and I got dressed and left the cabin. I reached the door leading out onto the deck on which a red sign hung: "Entry forbidden." But this didn't stop me, and I decided to see what was going on. I opened the door.

It was cloudy, and the deck was slippery. I let go of the door handle—and then slid down the deck toward the ocean at full speed. Horrified, I grabbed onto a line, knowing that I could easily find myself in a tin precipice, from which no one would be able to rescue me. I didn't fall off the deck and just held tightly to each available handle and railing. The windows of the ship were for the most part covered by metal plates. Apparently, the crewmembers had done this during the night. I slowly climbed up onto the highest deck, just next to the captain's bridge. The view was really incredible. Huge mountains of gray water slowly rose above the ship—we found ourselves in a valley from which you couldn't see the horizon, only two walls of water; soon after, we would be on the top of the mountain of water with valleys on either side. These were not waves like those that beat on the shore. Mass amounts of water moved up and down. The ship suddenly became as small as a shell. The mountains of water were so high that I was splashed with water even on the highest deck.

Despite my not feeling so great, I decided I should go eat breakfast. I went to the restaurant hall. There was no one there but a very bored waiter. I ate a substantial meal and immediately felt revived in body and spirit.

On the *Batory*—the old, original one—there was a large swimming pool where I often swam. Usually, I only saw a few people there; the rest of the passengers didn't take advantage of this facility. I got the idea that that's exactly where you could truly appreciate the waves of the Atlantic. Essentially, I held onto one edge of the pool and waited for the wave to reach its peak and let go. The force of the wave threw me over to the other edge of the pool. And there I would go through the same procedure again. Refreshed, I was already in pretty good shape. Almost all the passengers stayed in their cabins suffering from seasickness.

At dinner that day there were only two people—me and the captain of the ship. He invited me to sit together with him. He ordered two Cognacs, claiming there was no better medicine for such seesawing, and that afterwards, we should eat a lavish dinner. Indeed, I felt completely fine. The next morning we were sailing on a calm ocean.

In the evenings, by the light of the moon and stars, I would sometimes stand for hours on the back platform thinking that the endless water was taking me further and further away from my loved ones. I looked at the keel made silver in the moonlight and thought, "This is the path on which I am drifting away into the unknown."

We had already sailed the majority of our journey. *Batory* was moving on the northern route approaching Labrador. The air became crisper and so clean that each breath was a pleasure. Dolphins were jumping around the ship, and you could see fountains of water spurted up by whales. Here and there on the horizon, I could see mountains of ice.

One night, I woke up feeling hot and stuffy with a headache. I uncovered myself, but it didn't help. I noticed with surprise that the ship was no longer swaying and that it was moving smoothly, as if there were no waves. I went out onto the deck. The air was somewhat foggy, and you could feel humidity like that in the hottest pavilion of the Poznan palm court. The sun broke through that humidity. On both sides, I saw a shore covered in green meadows and trees, from which flashed the red roofs of settlements and the tall steeples of churches. We were on the St. Lawrence River. The banks, initially far away, were getting closer and closer. On the river, you could see colorful sails on white yachts, fishing motorboats, the whole rush of a different new world. I was struck by the fact that the colors seemed more vivid than in Poland. I said this often to my friends, but they didn't believe me. I got an objective proof many years later. I took a photograph in New York, then a few days later in Paris. The New York photos were in more vivid colors, while the Parisian photos were in pastels.

Batory entered the port in Quebec. It was the end of August, and it was hot and humid. I didn't go onto the shore—just saw the pretty city from the deck. The next day, we were already in

Montreal. After the passport formalities and a brief discussion with a customs officer, I found myself in the early hours of the afternoon with my suitcase and winter coat on my arm in front of the port building. I reached the train station, ate something, and got on the train going to New York. Again, the passport officials and customs officers came by. My first impression of the American terrain was its vastness. The train passed by forests and meadows, and sometimes houses appeared amidst the tree branches, while other times we would pass through the center of a pretty town. Night fell. My traveling companion asked me where I was heading. I said that my destination was St. Barnabas Hospital in the Bronx. I had no idea what the map of New York looked like, only knew that Manhattan was an island surrounded on the west side by the Hudson River and on the east side by the East River. I also knew that the Bronx was an area located on the mainland. The person I was talking to suggested that I not ride until the last station, which was Grand Central Station located in the center of Manhattan, but that it would be closer for me to get to the Bronx if I got out at 125th Street. And that's what I did.

I stepped outside around midnight and found myself on a street where I didn't see a single white face. My traveling companion failed to mention that getting out at 125th Street put me in the center of Harlem! Terrified, I looked around—I saw a taxi and waved at it, then it drove up. A heavy-set black guy with a fat, meaty back sat behind the steering wheel. I asked him to take me to St. Barnabas Hospital. He knew what I was talking about, and we went on our way. We drove into some dreary corners on the western branch of the Hudson; merchant ships and trailers stood above the black water. There were huge halls and barracks on the banks. The trip seemed to take a very long time. We were driving into increasingly desolate neighborhoods. Two thoughts circled in my head—whether my driver happened to be planning to take me to some deserted area, rob me, and leave me, or maybe even kill me, and whether I had enough money to pay for the cab ride. I watched with horror as the meter clicked to an increasingly higher fare.

Finally, we ended up in a much better neighborhood. Through an iron gate, next to which a guard stood, we drove into a park over which the walls of St. Barnabas Hospital loomed. Luckily, I had enough to pay; with the money I had left over, I bought stamps to send a letter to my parents letting them know that I had arrived and was still alive.

I went into the hospital hallway. The man on-call at reception called someplace, and after a moment, another individual showed up, introduced himself, and confirmed who he was. "We've been waiting; I'll take you to your room."

We walked through a large square into another, smaller building, then down a corridor and up the stairs to the first floor. The corridor was somewhat dark, and the doors on either side were painted a dark brown color that you often see in the bathrooms of small train stations in Poland.

He opened one of the doors and turned on the light. I found myself in a rather small rectangular room. The door was on one end, the window on the other. On the left was a bed with sheets, under the window a table and chair. There was a closet to the right of the entrance door. Also to the right was a second door that led to the bathroom, which I was to share with the person in the neighboring room. It was incredibly stuffy, and the window was closed. My guide told me that I was to come to breakfast in the morning in the hospital cafeteria. Then he said goodbye and left. I threw down my suitcase and coat, tore off my jacket and sweaty shirt, and opened the window. This didn't do very much. The humidity and heat outside was almost just as unbearable as inside the room. I was awfully tired and disconcerted. I looked at the dirty walls, the narrow window, and the metal bed. Not used to the climate, I felt like I was choking on the exhaust-filled New York air. I sat down on the bed and cried. Yes, cried! *wimp*

But I had to make do somehow. I put my things in the closet, got undressed, took a hot shower and not wiping myself off, threw myself on the bed. I slept through the rest of the night.

12

Dr. Irving Cooper

THE LIGHT OF the sun's rays woke me up. I was momentarily disoriented, but memories of the last few days quickly came back to me. I got dressed and went to the hospital cafeteria. It was large, and there was a huge buffet at one end where you could choose a dish. The room was full of small, square tables where doctors sat in white coats.

It hit me that they represented all different nations, colors, and races. At one table, there were four individuals with black hair and olive skin. I found out later that they were Turks. They spoke loudly in a throaty incomprehensible language and gestured a lot. Their dark hair and similarly dark eyes distinguished them from others. I filled up my tray with food and sat down alone at a table. A doctor with fat, somewhat bluish lips, a long, full brown face, black eyes, and deeply wrinkled cheekbones sat down next to me. He asked me who I was. It was easy for me to understand him; we spoke without much difficulty. That ease of understanding came from the fact that he was Peruvian, from Cusco, who didn't speak English too well, so we were pretty much at the same level. He was doing a six-month rotation with Dr. Cooper. He was a neurosurgeon and was to perform stereotactic surgeries in Lima.

Soon after, a tall doctor with a military posture and thick lenses sat down with us. He spoke with a different accent, and it was harder for me to understand him, as he was speaking in full sentences. I figured out from the accent that his native language was German. He was an Austrian—and later my friend—Ferdynand Rossman, who was also a neurosurgeon doing a fellowship with Cooper. They took care of me, took me to the neurosurgery ward full of patients, and introduced me to a Chinese doctor, Dr. Lin, who was then Cooper's right-hand man. He welcomed me rather kindly, and then started asking questions. I had a lot of trouble understanding what he was saying; he was from Taipei in Taiwan. He had an accent typical of people whose native language is Chinese. After a moment, another doctor joined us, somewhat older, shorter, with gray, smoothly combed hair, black eyes, and the distended rib cage of a swimmer. He was Greek, and his name was Dr. Angelos Caracalos. He was then learning how to perform stereotactic surgery under the direction of Dr. Cooper.

We waited for Cooper in the corridor by the nurse's station. Suddenly, I saw a tall man with reddish hair, a long face, and light blue eyes. He had the same reddish hair on his hands. His face expressed not only self-confidence but almost arrogance. He had the characteristic walk of a flat-footed person and was trim and proportional.

This was the person for whom I had crossed an ocean—Dr. Irving Cooper. It hit me that he was very young, full of energy, a typical organizer and leader.

"Do you understand me? Do you understand what I'm saying to you?" he asked.

"Of course," I responded.

"Ah, that's good, you have two weeks off so as to become familiar with the work environment, and then you have to get to work."

And so our conversation ended. I was formally accepted onto his team.

Another doctor came with Cooper who was small and thin, with a tousled black mane of hair and slanted eyes. He was a Japanese doctor whose name was Keizo Matsumoto.

I had traveled to train with Cooper with the conviction that I would end up in a university clinic like those in Poland or other European countries. How different reality looked! The St. Barnabas Hospital was a hospital for the chronically ill. Cooper set up his practice there, as the working conditions were good. His practice brought in a lot of profit for the hospital, and the hospital, in turn, supplied him with two terrific operating rooms that were equipped with X-ray machines and designated an entire ward for his patients. Later, I found out that there was another ward of patients on the higher floor whose surgeries had been unsuccessful or who had complications. These people were not shown to hospital visitors.

I struggled terribly the first day. I heard only English, and in addition, it was spoken with an accent that I wasn't used to hearing. I desperately tried to understand what was being said. I had the most trouble in situations when a few people were speaking at once.

That day, Cooper made rounds with the entire group and with his personal secretary, to whom he was giving a lot of statements. Most of the patients suffered from Parkinson's disease that was advancing rather slowly, causing muscle rigidity and tremors, often on one side of the body but sometimes on both. These patients had a slow gait, and their face appeared like still masks. These were the patients who were treated with stereotactic surgery that caused small and appropriately localized damage to the brain—in the optical eminence. Such damage stopped the tremor on the opposite side of the body and decreased muscle rigidity. With interest, I watched the patients after surgery, paying attention to everything—doctors orders, bandages, and postoperative rehabilitation. We all went into the operating room; Cooper had a few patients designated for surgery. The operating complex was made up of a large room with metal lockers in which you hung your clothes and then changed into green linen pants and a similar surgical shirt, the room for surgical nurses, and the preparation room where you could find surgical instruments and materials, as well as two large rooms permanently equipped with X-ray machines that hung from the ceiling.

As much as it had been hard for me and frighteningly foreign that morning, that entrance into the operating room took a weight off my shoulders. The greenish tiles and the rush of surgery—all of it was familiar and close to me. I felt somewhat at home.

I was assigned a metal locker that was to be mine permanently. While changing, I looked with curiosity at the other surgeons, who weren't associated with Cooper. One of them declared at the top of his voice, "Well then, Kennedy acted like a complete idiot; it would have been hard to act any worse."

Another agreed and added, "This whole administration is terrible; nothing good will come of it."

In astonishment, I listened to this conversation lasting another moment until they went to operate. "Apparently," I thought, "this country was very different from the one I had left; apparently, there was freedom of speech here and the freedom to criticize the highest dignitaries in the country."

This first glimpse of functioning American democracy was almost shocking and also cheering for me. I thought to myself, "So you could live like this, you could not pretend to approve of what you hate and detest and not be threatened by persecution, discrimination, or the ruining of the soul?"

I watched the surgery that Cooper was performing with interest. The patient first had a pneumoencephalography—injection of air to the cerebral ventricles through a lumbar puncture. This way, you could radiologically visualize the third cerebral ventricle, the strategic structure in stereotactic treatment that was located exactly in the center of the head.

Then, with local anesthesia—of course after sterilizing the operative field and putting on the surgical drapes—Cooper placed a tripodic apparatus, which had micrometric screws allowing for directed placement of the cannulae into the appropriate target. On the lateral X-ray of the skull, you could identify two essential operating points, which were commissura anterior and posterior, and from the frontal X-rays you could determine the width of the third ventricle. This data was incredibly important because, on their basis, the site of therapeutic lesion in the appropriate center of the optical eminence has been determined. The localization error could not be greater than two millimeters. Then, a hole was drilled in the skull dura matter was incised, incision was made with the cautery on the brain and then cannula was inserted no more than one centimeter into the brain tissue. The successive X-rays were supposed to show whether the cannula was placed in the right site, which had been previously marked on the X-ray's point. Finally, the cannula was placed deep in the brain where it belonged. The cannula was connected to a complicated apparatus that allowed for gradual spherical freezing of the brain tissue at the tip of the cannula. By controlling this apparatus, it was possible to perform smaller or larger controlled tissue damage. The patient, who was an older man, suffered from Parkinson's that was manifesting in muscle rigidity, disturbances of gait, and a unilateral tremor with a frequency of six per second.

During the freezing period, the patient was told to hold his hand out before him. It trembled. The lesion was made on the other side of the brain because of the crossover of motor pathways. I watched, fascinated, as the trembling stopped, disappeared, and the patient could completely and freely move his hand.

This was my first lesson in stereotactic surgery.

Even though Cooper had promised me that for two weeks I was only going to be familiarizing myself with the work without any obligations, after a few days I was told to work up new patients, to gather personal information, the whole medical history, how their problems started and when, what the first symptoms were, and how things had progressed. I had to fill out a huge form with information that would give a basis from which to evaluate the patient.

Considerable language difficulties didn't cause me too many problems at work. Each patient, caring about his own well-being, did everything he could to ensure that I understood and that the information documented in the medical history was accurate. These patients were my first teachers. Slowly, I got to understand them better, and I got used to the accent that had been unfamiliar to me. I expressed myself properly but with some difficulty. I had brought the detective novel written by Agatha Christie, *The Murder of Roger Ackroyd*, over from Poland, and with a dictionary in my hand, I read it at night to become familiar with popular idiomatic expressions. Then, I tried them out on patients and colleagues. I remember when one of them said in astonishment, "Where did you get that old English saying? No one says that anymore!"

I read that crime story several hundred times, and it helped me greatly.

After a few days, I worked up the courage to go outside the hospital's iron gate and walk around the streets. I passed by a few empty side streets and then found myself in a busy Italian neighborhood. With curiosity, I looked at the stands full of fruit that took up half the sidewalk, a huge fish store that was wide open, a street stand on which, apart from fish, there were crabs, lobsters, shrimp, and octopus. The smell that wafted from this stand didn't exactly whet the appetite. The doors and windows of the apartment buildings were open—the humidity of early fall in New York affected everyone. There was a lot of traffic on the street, mainly pedestrian—women buying produce, men with shiny, often curly, black hair, usually dressed in dark colors, trucks full of merchandise. All of this made up a picture that was quite different from what I was used to; it was interesting and exotic.

I smelled the pleasant scent of good cookies and bread—there was a bakery and pastry shop on the corner and behind it a small textile shop. On the right, there was a pizzeria that smelled of spices.

I went further. The busy Italian street ended at a perpendicular avenue—Fordham Road. There was a movie theater on the left side, and if you went to the right, you could go to the zoo—one of the most beautiful in the world—the botanical gardens, and Fordham University. Venturing to the left on this avenue led to a shady and dangerous Puerto Rican neighborhood.

I went back to the hospital for dinner. Ferdynand Rossman,

Keizo Matsumoto, Walz, a Jewish American man, and I sat together at a table. I looked at my mealtime companions, my colleagues, and I was struck by a strange thought. This little table represented all the sides that had been fighting during the Second World War; Ferdynand, a Wehrmacht soldier who had been torn up by shrapnel; a Japanese man, the deadly enemy of America with a samurai background; an American Jew, for whom the two previous men should have been enemies; and I, a Pole, who survived the German occupation with difficulty. Now, we were sitting together, talking, eating and working together; we didn't hold any grudges against each other, as if we didn't even remember anything of that nightmare!

I understood at that moment why the United States was such a power; it was because of the possible co-existence of such different nationalities and different religions as one, without fighting and without trying to destroy each other, and agreeably aspiring toward realizing their own personal dreams in accordance with the law. This possibility is the value that gives the States a unique place in the history of the world; it was a huge experiment yielding unexpected results.

⫼

After a few weeks, I was comfortable enough with the work that I could be on-call, even give the nurses orders over the phone. I became friends with Dr. Levin, a small, thin Jewish man, who was Cooper's anesthesiologist. He was a philosopher of sorts with a good sense of humor and the ability to see himself without any illusions. One Friday, he invited me to his house for the weekend. His house was a nice mansion, well furnished and lighting in a pleasant neighborhood of Long Island. The day was particularly tough; there had been a ton of work in both the ward and the operating room. The heat hit like a sledgehammer the moment you stepped out of the air-conditioned operating room and hospital door.

We got into Levin's car, which had heated up like an oven,

because he didn't have air conditioning. We opened all the windows and headed to Long Island. The ride took over an hour. There was no air conditioning in the house, and it was hot and humid. Mrs. Levin was a kind Jewish woman of Hungarian descent. Their young daughter behaved strangely; she was silent and wouldn't look at me. Dr. Levin told me that it was their greatest hardship—the daughter was a schizophrenic.

Mrs. Levin wasn't strictly kosher, because for dinner she served a deliciously prepared ham. During dinner, as the only guest, I didn't have a moment's peace. I had to pay attention to everything that was being said and had to respond sensibly. My head ached, and I was extremely tired. Finally, I was taken upstairs to my room. With horror, I noticed that it was even hotter and more humid. The room had heated up like an oven from the sun beating down through the thin roof. I tried to at least open the window, but to no avail, as it had been nailed shut for unknown reasons. Resigned, I took a hot shower so my skin could let off some steam and threw myself on the bed naked. I hardly slept the entire night. In the morning, I didn't care about anything. I shaved and got dressed. I met Dr. Levin and his wife in the kitchen. He asked me if I wanted to drink some coffee. I accepted this offer. He poured me a mug of good, aromatic coffee, and said something else, to which I rather mechanically responded. Mrs. Levin started asking me how life and work were in Poland. I responded without really thinking and suddenly noticed that I wasn't having much trouble with English. All my hesitations were gone, and I could speak freely. From that day on, I didn't have problems with the language.

I found out from Dr. Ferrarelli, one of the Italians, that if you made a right on Fordham Road, you could get to a Catholic church—an Italian cathedral. The next Sunday, I went there for Holy Mass. The church was massive, with a nondescript style, with two towers. Inside, it was quite dim, especially when you had just come in from a brightly sun-lit street. The windows were huge, colorful stained glass that were lit up in all the colors of the rainbow, a rich, gold main altar over which stood an eternal light in a red lantern. There were two naves and two equally rich altars on either side.

The church was full. Soon, the priest and his ministers came out, went up to the altar, and began Mass. The first words of the Latin Mass tugged at my heartstrings; they were so well known and familiar to me. *Laudatur, Jesus Christus, Ora pro nobis, Oremus.* The pieces of the prayer sounded like words from across the ocean—from home. When I closed my eyes, I was again in the Capuchin Church in Warsaw, and I could see two angels with long, hanging legs high up on both sides of the dark altar, the dark plaques of the Stations of the Cross on the white walls, and large blackish confessionals.

I opened my eyes. Around me were people with olive-skinned faces, women with either scarves wrapped around their heads or hats. But the words of the prayer remained the same. I really regret that the Catholic Church started using local languages and that its universality in the presence of one language—Latin—was ruined. Then, right then, I understood how essential an element that language was. The thousands of kilometers that separated me from home, from my traditions, ceased to exist when I heard the same words, the same prayers.

During the first days of my stay at St. Barnabas Hospital, I had to go to the payroll department. I received "Social Security," a document with an identification number that served as the registration of every legally working individual in the United States. I found out that I would be receiving my salary downstairs every two weeks. Because payment was always two weeks behind, I didn't make any money for the first three weeks. I remember that my first paycheck was roughly forty dollars, and the next about $180, after taxes were taken out. I thus spent the first month practically a prisoner in the hospital, moving around only in the nearest proximity, because I didn't have any money. My supply was enough to buy postage stamps that I needed so as to send a letter to my parents. At the end of the month, I got the first response from my mother, who was full of worry and also happiness that

I had arrived safely and that I was managing, and realizing my American goal.

It was early fall in 1961. In Washington there was to be a conference of the American Association of Neurosurgeons with the participation of all the international elite. I really wanted to go there, but I didn't have the means. Ferdynand Rossman loaned me forty dollars and paid for our trip together to Washington in his old car. We were to stay at the YMCA, where you could sleep for a few dollars a night. In Washington, Ferdynand mistakenly turned left at one moment. He almost caused an accident. The other person, who at the last minute had slammed on the brakes and stopped in time, opened the window and started screaming at us. But our knowledge of the English language was not good enough to understand these vulgarities. Our opponent soon figured out that we didn't understand him, got embarrassed, and started apologizing. And he had been right!

At this very conference of neurosurgeons, we were able to talk to the operating surgeon on-screen for the first time while he was performing a surgery. It was very exciting. The surgeon, who was the first to be doing this, was performing a Frazier surgery that involved getting to the middle of the skull to reach the trigeminal nerve under the dura and the transecting of the sensory branch of the nerve so as to eliminate the awful facial pain of *tic doloreux*. Between the bone of the skull and the dura matter, there are multiple venous plexus that have a tendency to bleed a lot. And that's what happened. You could see that the operative field was covered in blood despite the suction; the surgeon tried to stop the bleeding using gauze and tried to find the source and coagulate it. Someone in the room asked what he was doing. He responded angrily, "Can't you see that there's a bleed, you idiot? Leave me alone and go to hell."

After that pleasant exchange, the transmission was cut off for a while. When it was turned on again, the operative field looked like one straight out of the anatomy atlas—there was no bleeding, and the surgery was finished.

That trip to Washington and participation in the neurosurgery conference was a big deal for me.

After returning to work, I was usually busy for an average of ten to twelve hours a day. I made rounds in the mornings, then participated in surgery, and then I admitted and worked up new patients in the evenings. Dr. Cooper's practice was a private practice; in his office, after evaluating patients and deciding to operate, they were admitted to St. Barnabas Hospital. The American hospital has a completely different structure from a hospital in Poland or even in Western Europe. It can most accurately be compared to a hotel, in which patients pay for a bed, operating room and nursing care, etc. The surgeon has an arrangement with the patient that is separate from the hospital.

Cooper had a huge practice. Thanks to its great reputation, patients came not only from the United States but also from South America. They were usually very wealthy people, who could afford the luxury of this surgery. At that time, Cooper charged two thousand dollars per surgery, a sum that was huge in those days. You could get a burger and large coke for twenty-five cents! And such surgeries were performed from six to twelve times a week! He was a multimillionaire, and we, foreigners, were poorly paid for hard work. We got knowledge in return that we could then, after returning to our countries, use for the good of others.

This is one of the incidents that happened in the operating room. We had a patient, a very wealthy woman with Parkinson's disease who had come from one of the countries in Latin America. I was performing the surgery; Cooper just walked around, supervised, and politely spoke to the conscious patient. Our anesthesiologist and my rather strange friend, Dr. Levin, sat next to her. He knew a few dozen words in Spanish that he would use routinely in surgeries on people who spoke that language. To calm down the nervous woman, at one moment instead of saying, "*no tiene miedo*" (don't be afraid), he would say, "*no tiene mierda*" (don't hold shit)! You can just imagine what happened then!

After getting my first paycheck, I sent the twenty dollars that I had borrowed to the bank in Warsaw, gave Rossman back his forty dollars, and had enough left so that I could buy an éclair or cream puff in the Italian bakery or go to the movies on Sunday. I found out that in American movie theaters, at least in those days, when you paid for a ticket, you could sit there all day. There were always two movies being shown, and you could buy hot dogs, orange soda, or cola in the concession stand. The movies had another great advantage—they were air-conditioned.

After church, I went to the movies, bought a ticket for somewhat more than fifty cents, and I sat there all day watching two movies twice in a row. My dinner was hot dogs and orange soda. I didn't sit there for no reason. When I watched a movie for the first time, I didn't understand the dialogue, but I became familiar with the action. When I saw the same movie a second time, I understood a lot more. The movie theater was a place where I could learn to understand the spoken language, and it helped me a lot in this way.

One time, I went to the movies later than usual in the afternoon. I sat through four showings, and when I went out on the street, it was almost midnight. There wasn't a soul on Fordham Road; I heard only my own footsteps in the penetrating silence. After a while, the sound of footsteps reached my ears. I looked around. I saw a group of a dozen black teenagers who were busy vandalizing everything in sight, turning over garbage cans and ruining everything that was in their way. I quickened my pace, but it didn't do much good. They saw me and with a yell started running toward me. I didn't wait around, and with all the strength I had in my legs, ran away toward the hospital. I turned into the Italian neighborhood, but they were getting closer and closer. Finally, I saw the desired hospital gate. The guard at the gate understood what was happening and yelled, "Run, I'll stop them!"

I ran through the gate, and my tormentors were just behind me. The guard stood in the gate with his revolver out and yelled that he would shoot. It helped. They stopped and, swearing and shaking their fists at me, they turned back. He saved my life.

I didn't know that there were people among the lower category of workers in the hospital who, if not exactly communist, were extremely left wing. Because I had come from a communist country, they assumed I must also be communist. I didn't know about any of this. One day, one of them invited me for a meeting led by Martin Luther King, an already well-known leader of the black movement in those years. I was curious what the meeting would be like and had no idea what company I would be in. It wasn't a meeting as much as a mass demonstration in a huge hall full of black people, though there were a few white people. King spoke. He repeated his famous words, "I have a dream." He repeated that phrase after every statement, excited the crowd more and more, moving into a more and more hysterical tone. He was a professional manipulator propelling and stimulating the atmosphere of the crowd! I looked around the room. His words were full of hatred. Almost everyone was hypnotized. I may have been the only one in the room who didn't fall into the mass hysteria! I thought that if he ordered that crowd to go out on the street and slaughter white people, they would do it without hesitation!

I lived in an old but presentable building in which only a small portion of the apartments was designated for "residents," doctors in training; the rest were occupied by older, rich ordinary people, who were either no longer capable of living independently, lonely, or just trying to escape from the obligations of daily life. St. Barnabas Hospital, like that building, was surrounded by a beautiful, vast park full of old trees, walkways, and benches. On the bottom floor of our building, there was a large room with a television where older men and women would sit in chairs and couches in the evenings, reading or watching television. They always looked pleased to see me and invited me to join them. I was an exotic attraction for them. I became friends shortly after with a sophisticated lady who was over ninety years old. She told me about her youth. She was born in New York. In those days, both the Bronx and Brooklyn had been green with meadows on which cows and horses grazed. Her father was a doctor. He woke up early in the morning, his wife made him breakfast, usually a thick steak with a lot of vegetables. He ate it all, then loaded leather bags on his horse full of instruments and rode on horseback to round on his patients. Surgeries were most often performed in the kitchen on the kitchen table. These were the years right after the Civil War between the North and the South.

Walking through the park, I often ran into a certain couple from that building. She was a petite, thin, older woman; he was also older, tall, and somewhat hunched over. He carried her shawl and leaned over her; her face would light up with a warm smile. From my ninety-year-old friend, I found out about their past and what had linked them and divided them.

Years ago, when she was seventeen or eighteen years old, she met a young man with whom she fell madly in love. The feeling was mutual. But the family stood on the road to their happiness. She was a woman from a good and wealthy home, while he was poor, only just then getting educated and from a different social sphere. Their love was brutally ripped apart. The door was shut in the face of the young man, and the young woman was given away quickly in marriage to an appropriate partner. Many years went by, during which a lot happened. She was married for years, had children and grandchildren. He also got married and had children who grew up and went on their way. Her husband died, and she was left alone. He was also widowed and decided to live in this building where you could share your loneliness with others.

To their astonishment, after almost fifty years, they met again. He was no longer a young man, nor was she a young woman. But the long ago feelings lasted through all those years of separation. At this moment, when I close my eyes, I see them walking slowly through the walkway of the park that was covered with the gold leaves of fall. I see how they sit together on the bench, how he wraps her in the shawl to protect her from the cold, damp wind, snuggling together on the couch in the living room, exchanging glances and smiles.

They created a beautiful anomaly in that materialistic world devoid of romanticism. Romeo and Juliet—only in a different situation, in a different era—and perhaps bestowed with a much deeper feeling that the tragic pair in Shakespeare's play.

Soon after I started working for Dr. Cooper, I got a notice from the hospital that I had to take an exam in the English language. I wasn't thrilled about this, because my English was far from perfect. It turned out, though, that the exam was quite easy, at least for me. I got two printed columns of "hard" words that I had to match up. Of course all the "hard" words came from Latin, and I knew them well.

In October of 1961, I got another notice that I couldn't work unless I took the ECFMG (Educational Commission for Foreign Medical Graduates) exam. I had no idea what exam this was, so I went to Cooper with the document and asked him what to do.

"This doesn't concern you," he said. "It's an exam for residents who want to do a specialty."

I thought to myself that this exam must have some significance and offer some privileges. I went to my Turkish friends, who were doing residencies in internal medicine, and started asking them questions.

"Oh, that's a terribly difficult exam of all of medicine; it's almost impossible to pass. We tried a few times already and nothing came of it."

"What's the purpose of this exam?" I asked.

"Certification of the diploma," they said.

I understood that this was the first and essential step toward getting physician's privileges in the United States. At the same time, I met Dr. Laszewska, the head of the rehabilitation ward at St. Barnabas Hospital. She was the only person with whom I could speak in Polish. As a young woman, she and her mother had been taken from the Eastern regions of Poland to Siberia, and then reached England together with Anders's army, which is where she finished medical school. She confirmed from the outset that the first step to getting physician's privileges in the United States was passing that ECFMG exam. She also said that the exam was hard and that you only had forty-five seconds for each multiple-choice question. The Turks showed me the textbook from which they had prepared for the exam, and a small booklet with questions. I took that booklet. The questions were difficult, and in most cases,

I couldn't answer them. They touched on all areas of medicine, both theoretical and practical. But I knew I should take the exam. I sent a fifty-dollar fee in with the application—which was a sky-high cost for me then. I started studying in the evenings after work. Soon, I became convinced that in the booklets of questions, the answer to question 123 was often in question 245, and so on!

Apart from medical knowledge it was important to know how to take the exam. There was no place for nervousness and panic. You first quickly had to answer all the questions you knew for certain. Then you had to go through the unanswered questions again. After answering the first round of questions correctly, at least twenty more became obvious. There remained some for which there was no answer. You still answered them, going only on instinct. There was a chance that twenty to thirty percent of the time, the answer would be correct.

The exam was scheduled for April, so for all of late autumn and winter I pored over that really difficult material. My advantage was that, during my work in Poland, I always had to study intensively, so I fell into a routine of soaking up the knowledge.

Finally, the time for the exam came. It was to be on a Monday in April. Before the exam, I got the weekend off. I wondered what else I could do to increase my knowledge. And I got a unique idea. I went to the hospital library, which was well stocked with textbooks and monographs, and chose the thickest volumes of general pathology, surgery, obstetrics and gynecology, and other disciplines of clinical medicine. I lugged them all to my little room and started flipping through them, not reading the text but only looking at the illustrations. When I understood them, I went further; when I didn't, I read the appropriate text. Thanks to this method, I answered at least sixty more questions correctly.

I reported to the awful place early in the morning. It was a large room, with individual desks with metal chairs, in between which people walked who were supervising to make sure the exam was taken properly. In front of us, there was a thick notebook that we weren't allowed to open. At the given command, we could open that notebook. I saw printed columns of questions and answers with variously formulated structures. Of course, I got nervous, but advice from one of the doctors at St. Barnabas helped—"Janusz, before you start, look around the room well, and notice that there are lot of people there dumber than you."

And so I did that. I went through all the material once, then again. I still had some time left (the exam was timed), and I looked at a few other questions and answered them. Of 360 questions, there were only about twenty left that I couldn't answer at all. I filled in a circle anyway, hoping that at least some of them would be correct. Overall, I was disgusted and convinced that I hadn't passed. The minimum for passing was seventy-five percent. I returned to the hospital in a sad state. After two weeks, I got a notice that I had passed the exam with an eight-one percent, and then soon after that, I received the appropriate document for the certification of my diploma.

Not long after starting work with Dr. Cooper, Dr. Ling, a fully qualified neurosurgeon, left because he had done his professional training in Taiwan, and it wasn't recognized by the American Board of Neurosurgery—the highest branch that decided who could or couldn't become a specialist in that field. So he had to start from scratch.

Dr. Caracalos didn't have enough training in neurosurgery, and neither did Keizo Matsumoto. Only Rossman and I had more experience, and Cooper quickly figured this out. Soon, we were performing surgeries in the following way: Cooper operated in one room, and I or Rossman in the other. During the critical moments of the surgery, Cooper came in for a few minutes, and that was the end of his participation. Still, the surgery was performed in his name.

I became valuable to him. I soon figured out that the localization of the damage to the postero-lateral nucleus of the optical eminence did not produce as good a result as similar damage about one or two millimeters to the back and one millimeter deeper. This damage not only alleviated the tremor but also significantly improved the performance of the extremities on the contralateral side.

I looked for evidence of this fact and came to the conclusion that it had something to do with inervation from the cerebellum to the nuclei at the base of the skull. Cooper noticed this change and wanted me to operate even more.

One day, new visitors arrived—we had a lot of visitors, from almost all over the world—who wanted to learn more about stereotactic surgery and Cooper's surgical technique. These new visitors were rather out of the ordinary—it was a Soviet delegation from the Lomonosow Institute in Russia. One of them was the head of neurosurgery, another his proxy, the third and youngest, Kendel (I may be messing up the name), who was to perform stereotactic procedures in Moscow. Their interest wasn't limited only to stereotactic work. They were also interested in little poor me! They were astonished that a Pole had been contracted to work with Cooper and asked how much I made and how much of the money I earned I had to pay to the Polish government. When they found out that I didn't pay anything, their astonishment was even greater. Well then, they came and went, leaving behind them the dismal stench of Soviet system.

Together with Keizo Matsumoto, we began clinical research on the electric potentials in muscles in Parkinson's disease. We worked well together until the moment when I found the data confirming our assumptions in some international literature. Happy, I ran to Matsumoto with this work.

"Look, we're on the right track!"

He didn't say a word, just shrugged his shoulders and left. I couldn't understand this. It turned out later, when he had calmed down, that his samurai pride couldn't cope with the fact that he hadn't been the one to discover this data.

After a warm autumn, winter came. A chilly, piercing wind that got into your bones blew through the straight streets of Manhattan. When I had a free weekend or Sunday, I sometimes took the subway to Manhattan. In comparison to the Bronx, it really looked impressive—beautiful Fifth Avenue extending far, far away, Central Park, Rockefeller Center. Sometimes, I would spend hours walking the streets and side streets, amazed at this world—

Times Square, with its glaring neon, always crowded with people, pizzerias open wide onto the street. Inside, a young baker would show off throwing dough in the air and turning it quickly, which he would then bake into a pizza before gaping eyes. For twenty-five cents, you could buy a piece of hot, freshly baked pizza with pepperoni, mushrooms, and peppers along with a large glass of cola. Sometimes, I would eat this right on the street. There were also quiet, peaceful streets where wealthy people lived in many-storied, old buildings. Apart from Central Park, there were no trees to be seen. Manhattan is divided into a grid of straight streets, and only in the lower, oldest part can you find a lot of variety in the architecture.

Sometimes, I would take these long walks well into the evening. I noticed that on Lexington Avenue, on the eastern side of Manhattan, you could see young, handsome men with makeup on their faces in seductive clothing. I couldn't understand who they were and what they were doing. Only later was it cleared up for me—they were male prostitutes waiting for homosexuals.

I got to know Dr. Ferrarelli, who was a pathologist in St. Barnabas. He was a strange person, Italian, who wasn't easy to understand, because he spoke quickly with a strong, Italian accent. Fate had made him a pathologist, though he should have been born in the period of the Renaissance or at least the Enlightenment, as he was much more taken with beautiful music and architecture than medical literature. We soon discovered many common interests and opinions and, despite the language barrier, could understand each other very well. One Sunday, he suggested that we go visit his dear friend, a prelate at the Italian cathedral. After Mass, we went into the rectory. He was a very kind older man with gray hair and dark, kind eyes and a gentle smile on his full face. Dr. Ferrarelli introduced me. The prelate was very intrigued by me—in those days seeing someone who came from behind the Iron Curtain was a rare occurrence. He spoke warmly and wished me all the best in my life. After returning to the hospital, Ferrarelli told me his life story.

In the beginning of the twentieth century, before the First

World War, two boys were orphaned in a small Sicilian village. One of them was eight years old, the other five or six. They didn't have any other close blood relatives; the village was poor and no one could adopt them. They had an uncle in the United States. He was contacted, and offered to take care of them.

With difficulty, they were provided with the money for the trip. The two little kids ended up in Manhattan. The uncle, however, didn't show up, as he had died in the meantime from a heart attack. They found themselves alone on American soil, without knowing the language, without money, and without anyone to take care of them. The older boy was quite capable, though. He reached the Italian neighborhood of Brooklyn with his brother. He stole fruit from stands and bread that had fallen so as to survive. They slept under bridges. Soon, they got in touch with some older boys who also lived on their own and kept busy stealing and making mischief. Through them, the older boy became soon involved in the Sicilian mafia. He was short, small, very thin—no one would notice him. He was very well suited for dealing drugs and delivering messages. He started earning money. His first step was to protect his younger brother. He gave him to a boarding house run by nuns that was linked to a Catholic school. He himself became a "Mafioso." His duties and earnings from the mafia slowly grew. After he grew up, he became a "soldier," one who was armed and carried out the mafia's crimes. His younger brother finished grammar school, then high school and joined the seminary. His older brother supported him and did everything so as to help him and not expose him to any contact with the Sicilian mafia.

When the younger brother was ordained and became a vicar in one of the parishes, the older brother was arrested along with other members of the mafia. After a long trial, the verdict was given—the death sentence. He died in the electric chair.

This little boy, for whom the older brother had sacrificed his life, was the prelate. How tragic human fate can be, and how boundless love can be, when tragedy and crime can sometimes weave together in one inextricable knot.

Christmas was drawing near. Manhattan was full of lights and decorations, there was a huge Christmas tree in Rockefeller Center, the melodies of Christmas carols flowed out of every speaker, and stores overflowed with merchandise, crowds of shoppers, and smiling children. I was very sad as it was the first time I had ever been away from home for the holidays. I got letters that were two weeks behind, and I wrote often, pouring my loneliness and sadness onto paper. I wanted to spend the holidays alone, but I was invited to the home of the Laszewski couple in Forest Hill. They had three daughters—one about thirteen years old, another much younger, and the third was only three years old. Christmas Eve, lights, Christmas trees. The children got tons of presents. The youngest girl tore open one colorful package after another, discovering newer and newer treasures. Finally, surrounded by them, she started crying, because she didn't know what to do with it all! Excess is sometimes just as difficult as lack.

Dr. Rossman lived on the hospital grounds in a small apartment above the garages. There were two large rooms, a kitchen, and a bathroom. Mrs. Rossman often invited me over for what she called "a real dinner"—she didn't have the greatest opinion of the hospital kitchen. Sometimes, we had wiener schnitzel and talked about the superiority of European culture over American. The Rossmans didn't have much on which to live. Truthfully, he made somewhat more than me, but he had a lot more expenses. One of the patients offered him two tickets to the Metropolitan Opera in thanks for his care. It was a rare event in their lives. He solved the problem of who would care for their children during their evening escapade to Manhattan rather easily—by giving it to me. The children spoke German and English. Because they knew me well, it wasn't a problem. Mrs. Rossman gave me specific instructions—when I should give them dinner, how to watch them so that the youngest one would eat everything, how to get them all to go to bed.

We were left alone. The girls were at first somewhat shy, but this didn't last very long. They sat around me in a circle, and the oldest brought over the tales of the brothers Grimm—of course in German—and told me to read. German was never the brightest spot of my education, but I was forced by the young person and started speaking with difficulty.

"You can't read," she said and left to play with dolls with the others.

In that degraded state, I put dinner on the table. It went off without any greater hitch. Soon, however, the little one started pitter-pattering about and yelling something.

"She has to go to the bathroom," the oldest one said, "and you have to help her."

We went to the bathroom together, I helped her get undressed, and sat her on the "throne." The awaited result soon came. I had to clean her up, and then I let the happy young person go free.

The hour came when the children were supposed to go to bed, and here, a problem arose. I managed to keep at most two in bed at once, but the third was able to leave. Not knowing what to do, I looked around the room and saw a leather belt on the door. I went up to the door, and the whole group of young people disappeared from view. Soon, their peaceful breathing was a sign that my task had been done.

Winter passed by. The sun beat down more and more strongly; the light green of young leaves appeared on the trees in the park. Dr. Inohosa left us, returned to Lima, where he was a military doctor with the rank of colonel. Matsumoto also finished his year-long stay and returned to Japan. He was a candidate to take over the future pulpit of neurosurgery in one of the largest Japanese cities. He had two worries—the first, that the university would buy the equipment for stereotactic surgeries together with a machine that controlled cooling of the cannula, and the second—that he was too thin. He explained to me that in Japan, advancement in a professional career was linked to fat. A professor without a well-rounded belly simply wouldn't inspire confidence! Later, I looked at many Japanese professors, and indeed, all of them with the exception of one were well fed.

One warm Sunday, Rossman suggested that we go together on a trip to West Point—the very prestigious old military academy in the United States that had been established by Tadeusz

Kosciuszko, a Polish citizen who had been a hero in the American revolution. The day was beautiful and sunny. Without much trouble we reached the huge parking lot located just on the Hudson River, whose mighty, wide waves beat against the steep black granite cliffs. The road from New York to West Point ran parallel to this river. I then witnessed something unbelievable. Warships stood many kilometers away, counter-torpedo ships, cruisers, and frigates. They were gray steel and immobile, with empty, open hatches. The cannons were aiming into far-away space. With no protection, empty and discarded, they had been sentenced for destruction.

Hundreds of cars were in the parking lot. A cheerful crowd of colorful women's dresses and light men's clothing was dotted here and there by the ceremonial uniforms of cadets—all of this was against the background of fresh greenery and white buildings. The smell of freshly-mowed grass completed the celebratory folkloric view. We got out of the car and started looking around. After a moment, Mrs. Rossman noticed that her youngest three-year-old daughter wasn't with us. We started looking for her fervently. She disappeared, as if she fell right into the earth. And just next to the parking lot were the black granite cliffs that created an abyss in which the river was swirling! We ran between the cars, started asking people, notified the military police and the civil police, and even the cadets joined our search. At least half an hour went by, but there was no sign of the child. I collected myself after the initial shock and thought that she couldn't have gotten very far on those little legs of hers, so we should look for her in the parking lot, somewhere near the car. I went back to where the Rossmans' car was parked and started looking under other cars. I saw her sitting curled up underneath Rossman's car. Mrs. Rossman's gratitude was limitless, while the rescued person sitting in the back of the car and kept kicking me in the head. Despite this hindrance, I was rather proud of myself.

Soon, even Rossman left to continue his residency in neurosurgery and to get American privileges in his specialty.

Cooper increased my salary and assured somewhat better conditions.

Among other things, there were tennis courts on the hospital property. Even though I tried to save as much as I could—I wanted to bring as many dollars back to Poland with me as possible—I bought a tennis racket and started participating in the matches with other hospital residents. Soon, I was playing pretty well and, despite the eighty degree weather, could play for fours hours without a break. We played singles and doubles. It happened that I was playing singles against one of the Turks, who was a rather good tennis player. The rest watched.

At one moment, someone noticed, "Well, then, we are watching an international match, Turkey against Poland."

This excited us a lot, and our ambitions were heightened. We played with all our energy so as to defeat the opponent. It wasn't easy, because our ability was at a similar level. I had a bit more endurance than my opponent, however, and won the match.

The summer was slowly coming to an end, and September was approaching and so was the time of my departure. I didn't want to go back, because I was really getting sucked into this different way of life. Besides that, I could also move forward in my specialty field, continuing to gather the newest knowledge. Additionally, Cooper didn't want to lose me. We made arrangements so that he would double my salary, and I would write a letter to Professor Stepien asking to let me stay another year. The Polish Academy of Science would receive a machine for cryosurgery in exchange for this that would be used in the operating room. The cost of such a machine was roughly five and a half thousand dollars.

Such a gift was essential, for without that machine, I couldn't begin stereotactic surgery in Poland. After a few weeks, I got formal permission to continue my work at St. Barnabas Hospital for the entire following year.

Despite the difficult conditions and despite the endless work and loneliness, I did find rest living in a world where no one cared for me, but also one in which no one wanted to harm me. During all those post-war years, I trembled wondering if I would get into university, if they would destroy me, if I would be able to do a specialty, if I could protect myself from the party pressure, so as to preserve my independence and human dignity, and if I could endure the discrimination and persecution that culminated in Professor Stepien. I also lived in a deceitful world in which I couldn't say what I thought, in which I had to accept idiotic communist paranoia as truth in silence, and had to pretend that I agreed with it.

Here, in St. Barnabas Hospital, there was none of that. For Cooper, I was simply a valuable asset that he had purchased for a laughably low price. He treated me without any special favor. When he didn't like something, he said so without reservation, just treated me normally. The dimness of the regime circumstances in Soviet-occupied Poland began to fade from my memory. I discovered a different world that was, truthfully, indifferent and even cruel for the weak, but at least it wasn't riddled with lies. The United States appealed to me more and more, while the memory of the circumstances in Poland horrified me and the scheduled return looked ominous.

Human memory is a strange thing. I missed my parents terribly, as well as the Polish nature, the Tatra Mountains on whose peaks I once took a trip in my younger years, the pine forests and sandy hills, where mushroom caps reddened under the white birches. Looking at the walls of the Bronx and the treeless streets, my thoughts often returned to Poland. Her image became clearer in my mind, veiled only with the bluish fog of nostalgia. Only the splinter of Soviet occupation, the splinter of well-organized tyranny and deception, stayed in my heart.

Cooper often talked to me, asking about the circumstances in Poland and how it was to live and work there. I told him the truth, and also told him that I missed my parents.

"No problem," he said. "I'll give you the apartment the Rossmans lived in, and you can invite them here. It'll be a nice surprise for them."

Not really thinking, I wrote a formal invitation to my parents, as I already had the apartment guaranteed for me by the hospital with Cooper's intervention. I didn't have to wait long. The regime authorities refused to give my parents passports.

The situation became very clear. My parents were not allowed out of Poland because of, I believe it was, paragraph 401, though I could be mistaken, that stated that their departure would threaten national security. If I didn't go back, I would never see them again. In that stage of my life, I still had illusions. I wanted to use my knowledge and enthusiasm for the good of Poland. That refusal showed me to a great degree that I was wrong, that I was dealing with an indifferent cruel regime not concerned about anyone or anything. My mother wrote to me in her letters that I shouldn't go back. She agreed to this separation for my own good. My father, however, didn't understand why, when I had a possible professorship on the horizon, I didn't want to live in the "people's" fatherland.

My stay with Cooper was reaching its end, and September was again approaching, as was the time for my departure. It happened that sometime in the middle of August, Cooper invited me to his house. I met a lot of interesting people there, and I got into a discussion with Walter Cronkite, the famous commentator from television. He was a typical representative of liberal thought—almost Marxist—and thought that nothing really bad was happening in the countries dominated by the Soviet Union. This upset me greatly.

Cronkite noted me because I was a curiosity from behind the Iron Curtain. He made the assumption that I was a loyal, happy participant in the Polish workers' paradise. This was very revealing to me of his mind set. When I explained to him the real nature of communistic tyranny, namely that the ideology suffocates out all personal thought and initiative, he was so enamored with the communist ideology he could not comprehend the truth. It was very revealing and shocking to me of the leftist elements in America.

I also met another man, who was older and kind. His name was Professor Malamut. He was responsible for the funding that

John Kennedy's government had designated for scientific tests in the field of medicine. He became quite interested in me and asked about the conditions in the Medical Academy and in the Polish Academy of Science.

"I have a ton of money in my hands for scientific tests in medicine, really millions. Here, in the States, we don't have enough of a work force to use this money appropriately. What would you say if we were to make a deal with the Polish Academy of Science or the Medical Academy in Poland to do this work together? We would finance the costs and determine the specific topics. The research would be published under the names of Polish authors, and I would have only one condition, that they would be coordinated with the whole of the program."

I was amazed that he had made such a proposition. I was pretty much enchanted. Polish medicine, which was so poor in those days, would have plenty of willing workers, and there was no lack of rats and mice, so most of the funding could be spent on bettering the standards of patient care. I told him that I didn't know enough to be able to give him a concrete response, but I would go to the Polish Embassy in Washington very soon and put forth this proposal to the ambassador. I couldn't imagine that there would be any kind of difficulties.

Incredibly excited by all the possibilities that were opening up before me, I took the Amtrak to Washington the very next day. I ate a bowl of spaghetti and meatballs with tomato sauce in a small outdoor Italian restaurant. Strengthened in body and spirit, I walked toward the Polish embassy.

The first worker I met there was a bit puzzled that I wanted to speak directly with the ambassador, but when I explained that I had really important information, she returned after a while and told me that the dignitary would see me. I found myself in a spacious, elegantly furnished office. A person who was about fifty years old, with a fat, red face and hunched back sat behind the desk.

I introduced myself, and he got up from his chair. He asked, "What do you want?" I responded that I didn't want anything for myself, and then I repeated the conversation I had with Professor Malamut. I also presented the financial possibilities that would be available to Polish medicine.

He listened, commenting, "Well yes ... this, because more, oh, really? The other ... we'll see ... no ... good ... that you said ... yes, of course ..."

I listened to this rambling not understanding at all what was going on. I found myself on the street still not knowing what to think about all of this.

In two days, I got a telegram from the Polish Academy of Science.

"Come back immediately, you have overstepped your bounds!"

"The people's government" had lost the means to finance Polish medicine and its scientific collaboration with the National Institute of Health in the United States. And I was treated as the individual who stood in the way of realizing the real goals of this administration—in essence, crushing, pauperizing, and completely enslaving the Polish nation.

I had bought a ticket on the German SS *Bremen*. My things were loaded aboard. A Volkswagen car—which looked so great with its new design—that I had purchased was supposed to be waiting for me in Cuxhaven. My work with Cooper ended, and my place was taken by Dr. Waltz, a Jewish man from New York who had gotten a specialty in neurosurgery.

Literally, in the last few weeks of my stay, Professor Isydor Tarlov called me; he was a neurosurgeon at Flower and Fifth Avenue Hospital, located in the very center of Manhattan. He had bought the equipment necessary for stereotactic surgery and offered me work. I thus had the possibility to stay, and with better conditions. I informed my parents of the new situation. My mother definitively told me not to come back; my father was silent. I decided to go back.

13

Return to Purgatory

I NSTEAD OF TAKING the sea route, as I had planned, I decided
to return my ticket for the ship and bought a ticket on Air
France so as to stay in New York another week—only my
belongings sailed away. Despite Tarlov's and my mother's persua-
sion, I didn't change my decision to return to Poland. If I didn't go
back, I would never see my parents again. Tarlov, for whom this
situation really wasn't working out, did understand my reasons
and respected them. We made a deal that when I would give him
the word from Poland, he would send me an invitation to continue my scientific work. It was the only guarantee that I might
have a chance to return to the United States.

In the old hotel where I was then living—it was full of cock-
roaches but inexpensive—I didn't sleep for days thinking about
what else I could do and how I could resolve this situation. I didn't
have any doubts that they weren't waiting for me to return to
Warsaw, especially after that telegram. They would really be astonished if I suddenly showed up. I would be in a way uncomfortable
for them, as I would be demonstrating loyalty to the government
by coming back, and I would have qualifications that others didn't
have, so I would be a potential candidate for professorship, some-

thing over which everyone was fighting. I would go back, bringing with me all that I had earned in America, money and a car. I had a small, warm apartment in the old town neighborhood near Miodowa Street. The work that I had written in the States could certainly be accepted as a thesis for professorship. My parents would no longer have that paragraph hanging over them that their departure to a foreign country threatened national security. And what of me? Maybe I could escape from this climate of internal games, and maybe no one would particularly bother me, because, as I mentioned, I would be a fierce competitor.

I spent hours thinking about the mental state of people living with the baseness and violence of the regime and thought that using appropriate psychology and understanding of the mentality of people in high echelons of the system somehow I could get through. Of course, it was like a game of poker, and the stakes were high.

Tired and upset, I finally fell asleep. I dreamed that I was standing on the edge of an endless ocean full of sharks whose ominous fins were shining in the sunlight; the dream was in vivid colors that I had never before experienced. I know that I had to step into this ocean, and I was awfully afraid, knowing I didn't have a choice. I slowly started stepping into the water. I woke up drenched in sweat.

The day before my flight, I noticed that my pants were dirty and wrinkled. I changed them and took the dirty pair to the cleaners. They took them, and I walked away some seven or eight blocks when I realized in horror that all my cash—seventeen hundred dollars—was in those pants! I had taken the money out of the bank the day before. I rushed down the street like a maniac and ran inside the store. The owner stood at the counter, looked at my horrified eyes, and said, "You're lucky that I'm an honest man."

He gave me back everything and didn't expect any reward for it.

I flew in to the Orly airport in Paris. The passport control and customs officials were especially nasty that day. I finally went outside. I had no reservations at a hotel, so I took a taxi and explained to the driver in poor French that I wanted to find some cheap hotel. He wasn't the most honest person, and I could see that he was beginning to drive me in circles. I barked at him—this helped—and we drove into a poor neighborhood near the Gare de Lyon and stopped in front of a small hotel. It was completely full. The same thing happened at the second and third. Finally, my driver brought me to a particularly lousy place. Yes, they had a room for me, and they asked if I wanted to rent it by the hour. I said I only needed to stay one night. The hotel came to life in the night hours. You could hear laughter, noise, and slamming doors. I closed the door to my room and fell asleep with difficulty. This hotel didn't exactly serve as a place to relax and rest.

The next day, I flew to Hamburg and reached Cuxhaven at night. The SS *Bremen* was supposed to arrive the next day. I had made arrangements with the Volkswagen Company to bring the car to me at the port where the ship would be docked. A cold, piercing wind blew from the ocean.

I stepped into an old tavern. Downstairs, which was full of hefty, rough tables, you could smell beer and fresh bread. I ate a simple but satisfying supper and then was taken to a room upstairs. It was a tiny room with a big bed and two down quilts. For the first time in a week, I slept deeply and well. In the morning, I ate a few eggs and a fresh Kaiser roll, then drank some coffee and went to the port. The SS *Bremen* had already docked. I found my things, went to the walkway by the ship, and started looking around to see if my car was there. I saw it—pretty, white, so different from the original bug. A young person stood next to it and started waving his hand at me. He was a student who was making extra money by delivering cars. He gave me the keys, helped me load my bags, said goodbye, and left. I was left with a car that I had never before driven in a country I didn't know with a really limited knowledge of the language. And I was supposed to drive this car all the way through Berlin so as to get to Warsaw!

I went on my way. I reached Hamburg and got gas and ate some bread in its suburbs, then went in the direction of Hanover, then Berlin. I got onto the Autobahn. About halfway between

Hamburg and Hanover, I saw a group of military vehicles; the line of them was long and seemingly endless. I saw tanks and soldiers in very familiar gray uniforms. The regiment was moving to the east, in the same direction I was going. The sight of it hit me like a brick. I could see the days of 1939 all over again. I had seen that same kind of regiment in Lublin after the city's occupation; I had seen those same soldiers, wearing the same symbols and hats. Horrified, I thought that the Third World War was beginning, and that I could be driving into a battlefield. But that's not what was happening. These were just autumn training exercises of the Bundeswehr. After many years had passed, when I was talking with a German friend in America, we figured out that he had participated in those very exercises.

I drove through Hanover and, near evening, found myself on the road leading to Berlin. I wanted to reach West Berlin, get gas, eat something, stay the night, and then get on the road straight to Warsaw in the morning.

The road was empty. I could see the taillights and license plate of a Mercedes in front of me. Night fell. Lights shone somewhere in the distance. Suddenly, that Mercedes turned around sharply, its tires screeched, and it drove past me, disappearing into the darkness. Without accelerating, I reached a well-lit place with barracks and marked borders. I saw guards running out. I stopped. When I lifted my head, I saw automatic weapons pointing at me from both sides of the car. It turned out that I had made a mistake and, in the poor light, had missed the division of the roadway. Instead of going toward West Berlin, I had driven into East Berlin, into the area controlled by Soviet Russia.

With the weapons still pointed at me, I was told to get out of the car and was taken into the barracks. It was gloomy inside, decorated with a debris-covered portrait of Lenin and glaring communist slogans. Someone of higher rank showed up, looked at my passport, and was sure that I was a rightful citizen of the People's Republic of Poland. My car was searched, and then I was allowed to go. I was desperate. I had very little gas in the car, and apart from this outpost, it was completely dark. I didn't have any idea where I could find a gas station and how I would pay for it because I only had dollars. As I stood there by the car not knowing what to do, a militia man riding a motorcycle showed up. He offered to take me to a train station in Unter den Linden where I could exchange dollars, buy gas, and find a hotel to stay the night. I went with him. The train station was dismal and dirty. I found the exchange office; they cheated me incredibly. I changed only what I needed to in order to buy gas and pay for a hotel room. I didn't eat anything. The hotel was unkempt, the sheets weren't fresh, and I didn't sleep. The threat of Soviet terror, the deceit, mess, and destruction of the individual, stood before me and surrounded me. I felt like I was falling deeper and deeper into it, like a prisoner after whom all the doors were closing with a loud bang.

I left the hotel at dawn so as to get on my way. People were already going to work. I was struck by the fact that I didn't see a single smiling face. With bowed heads, seeming somewhat gray and gloomy and not looking at one another, they went to the factory and production offices.

I didn't have that far to go from Berlin. The road was pretty— there were pine trees all around framed by the rising sun, and mushroom caps stuck out here and there in the grass. I was completely alone on the road. I reached the Polish border. The WOP (Polish border patrol) soldiers welcomed me rather politely. They checked my passport and again searched the car, though rather superficially. My Volkswagen 1500 had an engine in the back between the rear wheels, and there was a trunk in both the front and the back. I remember how one of them was astonished and asked, "Where is the engine in this car?"

Then, I started driving through big forests in Poland. The air was clean and filled with the smell of resin. I reached Slupsk, where I illegally bought gas for dollars and exchanged a few for zloty. I stopped at the market and bought a piece of sausage, a loaf of bread and watery lemonade. The bread was good, but the sausage was watery. Still, it was a feast for me after twenty-four hours of going hungry. I was driving further and further. I passed by Poznan and found myself on the road leading to Warsaw. In comparison to Eastern Germany, Poland seemed like a paradise to me.

I began to feel strange. On the one hand, Polish nature—the forests, the fields, the greenery, the birches by the road, the light sky filled with fleece-like clouds—was very familiar to me, and everything stirred my soul. On the other hand, the thought came to me like a sharp thorn that I was again in a cage, that I couldn't make my own decisions anymore, and that the final door had been closed and there was no escape!

I reached Warsaw at dusk feeling incredibly tired. I passed by familiar streets, walls, buildings, and streetcars. I drove by the Krakowskie Przedmiescie, turned onto Miodowa Street, and saw the blocks in which my parents and I had apartments on the second floor. I drove into the familiar courtyard. The trees planted before my departure were now grown, and the resident of the ground floor had made a small flower garden. I went into that same stairwell, where the door straight ahead led into my apartment, and the one to the left into my parents' place. I knocked. In the light falling in from the dining room, I saw the thin, petite silhouette of my mother, and my father leaning out behind her.

"Why did you come back? Why did you do it? You shouldn't have done this!" she yelled. My father was very moved and didn't know what to say.

I unloaded my American treasures. My father was amazed, especially by the sight of the beautiful car, which was extraordinary in the circumstances of those days. My mother was less excited about all the things I had brought back.

"Look how fat you got in America, how awful, you have to go on a diet!"

She didn't have a shadow of a doubt that I had made a mistake. That night, my father came to the same conclusion. But it was too late, and honestly, I would never have left them without the hope of seeing them again in the future.

I felt strange and good to be sleeping on my own convertible bed, in my own sheets, and it was strange to eat breakfast together. I had to report to work. The PAN Neurosurgery Ward was no

longer on the property of the neurosurgery clinic of the Medical
Academy of Warsaw; instead, it had its own floor in the trauma
surgery hospital. I parked my car and went into the ward. Jadza
Srebrzynska, who was the first to see me, yelled out, "Unbelievable,
you came back!"

Witek Sierpinski also welcomed me back warmly. "I told you
he would come back! You didn't believe me, but look, he's standing right here in front of you!"

Others showed up to the news of my return—Tadzio Slowik,
who greeted me with a big smile and firm handshake, Mempel,
and finally Professor Stepien.

Stepien didn't greet me kindly, "Colleague Subczynski, you
have behaved unforgivably! You are an entire week late! This is not
acceptable! Report to my office at three o'clock!"

Well then, I knocked on the dreadful door at the specified time.
"Come in," I heard. Stepien sat behind the desk, and an active party
member and Sierpinski sat in chairs. I stood in front of the desk.
He didn't ask me to sit down.

"Your behavior has been unforgivable! You returned one week
late not even informing anyone about it; this is a disciplinary
matter!"

To my remark that I simply couldn't return any sooner, he
impatiently waved his hand.

"Your behavior demands punishment! Get it out of your head
that you will ever again leave this country! It won't happen! Now
get to work!"

These words fell like stones on my heart. Again, I heard the
sound of prison doors slamming behind me, one after another,
just like when I had gone to see a sick prisoner in the detention
facility hospital.

But Stepien wasn't through with me yet. "I have a task for
you. A Russian woman from the Lomonosow Institute, the most
prestigious neuroscience institute in Russia, has come here, and
someone must take care of her and be her guide. For the next two
weeks of her stay, you will take on this role!"

The next day, I reported to the passport office in the Mostowski palace, gave back my passport, and got my personal identification in return. Again, I had the awful feeling of iron doors slamming behind me.

When I returned to the neurosurgery ward, the woman I was to look after, the Russian woman from the Lomonosow Institute in Moscow, was already waiting for me. She was kind, very plump, and very talkative. I had never learned Russian properly and only knew some from my grandmother who had finished high school in that language. I had read Turgenev's *A Sportsman's Sketches* with her and also Tolstoy's *Childhood, Boyhood, and Youth*. This woman spoke so fluently that in her time she even berated a Russian commander.

But that had been a long time ago, and my ability to express myself in Russian over the later years didn't get any better. This didn't bother the woman after whom I was looking. She was incredibly interested in the fact that I had actually returned from the United States. She was also struck by the fact that I seemed to be in a relatively good mental state.

"Our Wania spent only six months in the U.S.A., and some kind of switch flipped in his head. He doesn't want to talk to anyone and walks around sad and depressed."

Well then, I understood very well why this Wania was in such a state, but I couldn't talk about this matter.

She used Russian perfumes that were suffocating and sweet. We drove through a large part of Warsaw in a taxi. When the ride was over and we got out, the taxi driver opened all the doors, and I can't repeat the repertoire he delivered while doing this.

I have rather good memories of this Russian woman. She was brought up in a system that was completely isolated from the outside world, yet she was interested in everything and tried to fit reality into her way of thinking. When this didn't work, her curiosity got even greater. After a few days, we were communicating rather well. I felt sorry for her despite her youth and career advancement (She had come to the West, to Poland, alone!), because her life reminded me of the life of a bird that had been locked up in a cage.

The time of my looking after her finally came to an end, and the Russian woman left for Moscow, while I returned to the neurosurgery ward.

Professor Gruca, a well-known orthopedic surgeon in Warsaw and Poland, invited me to give a lecture at his clinic. He knew that I had worked on neurogenic disturbances of muscle tone in the paraspinal muscles—a problem manifesting itself as juvenile scoliosis (lateral abnormal curvature of the spine). This condition is treated surgically by orthopedic surgeons who use a variety of methods of straightening the spine and making it more rigid.

Almost everyone liked my lecture, including Professor Gruca, and only one red adjunct came up to me and said, "Have you forgotten how to speak Polish that you have to use American medical terminology? You should cure yourself of this habit!"

He didn't take into account that the terms I had used didn't even exist yet in the Polish language! But I had to be reprimanded for the "capitalist" knowledge that I had brought back from the "rotten West."

I have to digress a bit now and write a few words about Gruca. He was a mountaineer who was incredibly talented, stubborn, sarcastic, and intelligent. He smoked a pipe that he had carved himself in the mountaineer style. I heard that, during a conference for orthopedic surgeons in the United States, he sat next to the president of the American Association of Orthopedic Surgeons at dinner. This president was known for having a really fiery temper and unique demeanor. In his time, he had taken a Japanese delegation out to a farm in the Adirondacks near New York, dressed them in diving suits, and told them to work under water, driven purely by malice. His residents had to spend their honeymoons on his farm.

So, this well-known orthopedic surgeon, whose name I can't remember, and Gruca were sitting next to one another. Gruca started to say something.

"I don't waste time talking to a son of a bitch!" was the response.

To this, Gruca said, "Maybe, but you're one, too!"

They looked at each other. The American boor noticed Gruca's pipe.

"Where did you get that?"

"I carved it."

After that exchange of phrases, they supposedly became the best of friends.

A few days after my lecture there, I was invited to give a lecture in Gdansk together with Tadzio Slowik. It involved something more important, namely the possibility of opening a neurosurgery ward. The trip was not that great. We were tired after a sleepless night in the train, then a whole day of work, a lousy meal (Tadzio was saving money for food for his children), and again an entire night spent getting back to Warsaw.

I went back to work and began seeing patients and operating. The conditions at the Trauma Surgery Hospital were awful. It was cold, there was no fuel for heating, and we lacked the most basic medications. Stepien told me to take care of getting supplies of medication for the ward.

"You're an adjunct, colleague," he said with great irony—you have to take on some of the appropriate responsibilities.

The matter was quite urgent, for we lacked basic antibiotics, bandage materials, and surgical materials, such as gloves, gauze, and surgical drapes. That same day, I went to the hospital pharmacy to meet with the director. I presented her with a list of our most urgently needed supplies. In response, she started crying. Sobbing and speaking brokenly, she said that her entire year's budget was only going to last until April and that she didn't have any money for the next three quarters.

"God, my God, what can I do, what can I offer? I can't sleep at night thinking about the patients who are dying, because they're not getting the proper care."

I comforted her as best I could, but I didn't want to accept defeat. I found out who made up the bureaucracy, including the very top authorities of the Ministry of Health. With the properly prepared document declaring precisely what we needed, I went to the medication supply department and even got into the office of the director of the department. He listened to me, looked at the list, and then showed me the circular, *Personal Regulations of Comrade Premier Cyrankiewicz*, without saying a word. I found myself standing in front of wall that was not going to crumble. It was then that I understood that I wouldn't get anywhere in this system. I would break like a wave against a granite cliff, with the only difference being that, though it may not move forward, the wave always beats and doesn't get ruined, but I would eventually lose my spirit (my soul) and would become just another robot in the service of the regime.

I was depressed. My parents were worried, and my father couldn't forgive himself for not definitively saying earlier that I should not return. As though in a trap, I tried desperately to find a way out. I read somewhere that there was going to be a sports car rally to Monte Carlo with the participation of Polish competitors. I immediately signed up for the automobile club. I got the address of a lawyer in Warsaw from Mr. Laszewski in New York who, together with Wierzbianski, was the owner of the Fregata travel agency; this lawyer had contacts in the Office of State Security and could really do a lot. I went to him; he listened to my story, and then said that it was still too early to be thinking about any such things.

A few weeks after my return, Professor Stepien organized a meeting of Warsaw neurosurgeons from the PAN Neurosurgery Ward and the neurosurgery clinic of the Medical Academy of Warsaw.

We all sat down at a long conference table, and Stepien took the head chair and started the meeting. He had again brought us all together so that we could formally condemn Professor Choróbski and order his move into retirement. The matter of Stepien's getting hired was still churning through the bureaucratic cogs of the Medical Academy machine. Stepien was working toward becoming the full-fledged professor of the Academy as well as the director of the neurosurgery clinic instead of being just a temporary replacement.

His order to condemn Professor Choróbski angered us deeply.

He finished talking. "Please, colleagues, make your declarations, and then we will vote."

A heavy silence fell. He got red. He looked around at the gloomy faces and tightly closed lips.

"I'm listening, now make your statements. This situation cannot continue. You know very well that Choróbski is an untreatable drug addict and isn't good for anything!"

The response to this despicable outburst was grave silence. He couldn't stand it. He turned now to address us personally. "Colleague Rudnicki, of course you know that I am right!"

Rudnicki calmly answered, "My teacher and professor was and is Professor Choróbski. Condemning him or evaluating him is not something that I will do, because it is not my place to do so. Unlike you, I will defend him to the end!"

After this exclamation, others also spoke up.

"You have no right to ask this of us!" yelled Kepski. "We will not do this; it would be the worst form of baseness!"

Stepien, seeing that he hadn't achieved what he wanted and that he had rather made the situation worse, ran out of the room mumbling something under his breath. The neurosurgeons of Warsaw had not condemned Professor Choróbski, and I was pleased that we hadn't given in.

The fall of 1963 came, and it was golden and colorful, lit up by the diagonally falling pale rays of the sun. The trees were quickly losing their leaves and becoming bare, darkening against the backdrop of grey clouds. The rains began, as did November's foul weather.

I was working hard in the neurosurgery ward under Professor Konorski's kind eye and Professor Stepien's all-seeing glance. It had already been proven numerous times that I was being discriminated against by this guy. Well then, I also never tried to please or curry favor from this professor, nor would I speak out against Professor Choróbski, which was in itself a crime in Stepien's mind.

I wasn't the only one having a hard time. This was the period when Moczar, a Belorussian who murdered National Army soldiers, organized a hunt for Jews. Many left Poland and went to Israel. Witek Sierpinski's situation was nothing to envy. Truthfully, he had strong former contacts in the party, and Stepien needed him in order to take over after Choróbski as the head of neurosurgery in the Medical Academy of Warsaw. Still, Sierpinski also understood, as we all did, that the moment Stepien achieved this, he would start working toward destroying him.

Like a flash of lightning on a clear day, we got the news of President Kennedy's assassination by Lee Harvey Oswald. The fact that Oswald was murdered before going to trial by Jack Ruby, a night club owner, proved that there were really strong forces at work in this case. Later in the United States, I had worked with Dr. Humes, a pathologist. He was the one to perform the autopsy of the president's body. He had to take an oath that he would never reveal the secret of the president's injury, and he took this secret to his grave. Much later, the news came out about the connections of the president's father, Joe Kennedy, to the mafia, which actively participated in determining the election. Supposedly, both Kennedy brothers, John and Robert, didn't listen to the advice of the mafia bosses, and both died tragically.

In the beginning of November, the machine for "icicle" surgery that had been promised by Cooper finally arrived—it was essential for stereotactic procedures. This was a great event and somewhat improved my situation. After all, this very valuable gift was the result of a year's worth of hard work on my part!

I thus had basic equipment, but I didn't have the instrument necessary for directing the cannula to the appropriate site in the brain. This matter was significant, because, without this apparatus, I couldn't even think about beginning stereotactic surgeries. I didn't ask Cooper to give me his model, because I was sure that we could make a much more precise one in Poland.

I went to the finance department of the Polish Academy of Science with the appropriate documentation asking for an allotment of funds to make this apparatus. I heard, "We'll fit this into the next five-year budget; the money for this five-year period has already been allotted."

This meant that I wouldn't have a chance of performing surgeries for a good two or three years and that the cryomachine would stand in the corner uselessly. That's what had happened in the neurology clinic. One of the neurologists had brought back a machine for electromyography after his stay in France. This equipment was terrific—it lacked only electrodes that were really inexpensive. Even so, the funding for it had been refused, and the machine stood covered with a sheet and gathering dust.

In despair, I went to Professor Konorski, asking him for help.

"How much money do you need?" he asked.

"I think that two hundred dollars would be enough," I replied.

"I have money that I got in the United States. The Polish Academy of Science doesn't know about it; it is for my own use. We'll use this money to pay for your instrument."

I thanked him with all my heart and immediately went to the department of precision apparatuses of the Polish Academy of Science. I met a group of kind, young, and enthusiastic engineers there. They quickly understood what I needed and began sketching various modifications and suggesting improvements. I thought that I had settled the matter. When it came to discussing the actual production of an apparatus to direct the cannula, however, they got glum. They said that they could not do it, because they were only permitted to produce such an apparatus for export, for which they received hard currency. They suggested that I go to the Factory of Precision Apparatuses in Mokotow and that maybe I'd find some help there.

I found the factory and went to the director's office. He welcomed me warmly, listened to what I had to say, and said, "I didn't see you, don't know you, we never talked, and I don't know about anything. You can go to the third floor to this and that room—this is your own private matter, and I don't know anything about it!"

I listened to these suggestions and found myself in the room of a young engineer who could make a technical drawing of my apparatus. He also brought in a master who would actually make it. All of this took place in secret.

Not too long after, I was let in to the factory at night through the back door. My apparatus was ready; it had a black frame and shiny micrometric screws. It was much more solid and overall better than the one that Cooper used. I was reminded that no one in the factory knew that such an apparatus had been made and that I would have to explain where and how I got it myself. I didn't have any more problems with this, because no one asked me anything. Years later, when I had already left Poland, the main bookkeeper at the Polish Academy of Science supposedly racked his brain and nearly became neurotic, because a valuable apparatus existed for which there was no documentation, not of its purchase or data or even where it came from and who produced it!

To begin operating, I also needed liquid nitrogen so as to freeze the end of the surgical cannula. I found the appropriate factory, drove there in my car, and brought back a heavy bottle of the gas.

I needed an X-ray machine, but that wasn't too hard to get, because we had a portable apparatus that you could wheel in to the operating room. I did have to determine its exact location, the distance from the head, and calculate the difference in measurement that resulted from enlargement.

Finally, the day for the first surgery came. I checked all the details and got to work. My patient was an older man with Parkinson's disease who was tormented by a tremor of the right hand and gradually increasing muscle rigidity. The operation went smoothly; the hand stopped trembling and started working properly.

Stepien said that I had to teach "Colleague" Mempel how to perform stereotactic surgery. Sierpinski also wanted to be taught. I made a deal with him that in exchange for teaching him the surgical technique, he would help me leave for America for the second time.

After the first few surgeries, there was buzz in Warsaw. These were the first surgeries of their kind performed in Poland. Reporters from the newspapers showed up. Stepien harshly prohibited me from speaking with them. The next day after their visit, there were large articles about how Professor Stepien was performing fantastic surgeries with an "icicle!" I don't even have the words!

This lack of publicity didn't bother me at all. I had other goals, and this deceit might even come in handy.

14.

Final Escape

WINTER CAME, AND I had performed thirty or forty stereotactic surgeries. One of the patients who had done
well caught pneumonia in the operating room as a result
of the cold, and because there were no antibiotics, he died. He was
yet another victim of the regime and Soviet occupants!

I wrote a letter to Professor Tarlov and received an official invitation to continue my scientific work under his direction at Flower
and Fifth Avenue Hospitals. My students had already learned a lot,
and it was clear that when they mastered the technique, I would
become unnecessary.

I am indebted to my mother for getting out of that hell.

"Listen, Janusz," she said, "your situation looks bad. Stepien
won't hesitate because he hates you. When you teach them the
surgery, he'll finish you. You have to figure this out!"

I knew that she was right. The next day, I ran into Stepien in
the corridor of the ward.

"Excuse me, Professor." I turned to him. "I have an important
matter that I need to discuss with you today."

"I have more important things to do today than talk with you,
colleague," he barked. "Don't bother me."

I didn't back down. I blocked his path and said, calmly but forcefully, "You don't have anything more important to do today than talk with me. Understand this!"

He nearly jumped with anger. "What is this; look how you're addressing me, giving me orders!"

I listened to his outburst calmly and again repeated emphatically, "You don't have anything more important to do than to talk with me!"

He felt uncertain. He was in the last stage of the game toward becoming a professor in the Medical Academy, and he knew very well what a dirty deed he had committed in giving such false information to the press.

"Fine. Today at three o'clock in my office."

I reported on time. Besides Stepien, Sierpinski was there, as was an active party member.

"What do you want?" he barked.

"As you know, I have begun scientific work in the United States that I was not able to complete during my time working with Dr. Cooper. Professor Tarlov is giving me the opportunity to finish it and to continue tests. On my part, I have undertaken the responsibility of organizing stereotactic surgery in the neurosurgery ward of the Polish Academy of Science, and I have fulfilled this responsibility. About forty patients have already had surgery. I took the responsibility to teach Colleague Mempel and Sierpinski in these procedures. I am convinced that in three months, they will be able to perform the surgery on their own. In exchange for this, for what I did, I ask that you sign this request for a return trip to the United States in three or four months.

He reddened and yelled, "There is no way! You have to do what you are told and that's the end of it. I absolutely refuse!"

I was prepared for this.

"If that is your decision, Professor, then as of now I resign from work at the PAN Neurosurgery Clinic. I would rather work in a small village and help people as much as I can."

His face got almost blue in anger. "You're bluffing, you're bluffing! Colleagues, can't you see that he is trying to play me? What do you say to this?" He turned to the active party member.

Sierpinski shrugged his shoulders and involuntarily noticed, "Why all this fuss? We are learning stereotactic surgery, and I already understand and can do a lot, as can Mempel. If he teaches us and keeps his word, why shouldn't he go? Something useful could still come out of this."

This was like a cold shower on the neck and back of the furious dictator. He muffled his rage and started calculating fiercely. This was the alleged course of his reasoning, "If Subczynski really does what he is threatening to do, the scandal will be known not only in the Polish Academy of Science, not only in the Medical Academy of Warsaw, but in all of Warsaw, in all of Poland! The lies in the press will be brought into the light of day. He had been proud of stereotactic surgery. It's clear that Sierpinski wants Subczynski to go, so they have their deal—and Sierpinski is still necessary to the ultimate confirmation of my professorship at the Medical Academy!"

He also knew that his signature wasn't enough to enable my departure. The regulations of the Polish Academy of Science grounded everyone who came back from another country for at least two years.

"Fine, I'll sign, but it won't do any good. The Academy won't let you go anyway!"

"Thank you very much, Professor," I said and with the signed document; not looking back, I left the office.

The days went by one after another. I operated more and more. I submitted my request to the appropriate department of the Polish Academy of Science. The secretary, a kind woman, looked at it and said, "This application is unsuitable, because you haven't completed the necessary two-year stay in the country since your first departure." I asked her to accept it despite everything so that it could be examined during the first meeting determining plans for international departures.

I knew that Professor Konorski was part of the committee

deciding on these departures. I went to him. I will never forget that moment. He was small, with a balding head barely covered in gray hair, and thick lenses; he sat behind a small desk.

"Oh, it's you," he said when he saw me. "What do you want? I congratulate you on beginning stereotactic surgery; I know it's going well."

I told him about Tarlov's letter, about the fight with Stepien, and about submitting the request to the PAN committee of departures. I didn't conceal anything, just told it like it was.

He was silent for a moment, thinking about it. Finally, he raised his head and looked me straight in the eye.

"You really want to leave?"

This question was packed with significance. I clearly understood that he wasn't asking me about this particular departure but about whether I intended to stay in the United States permanently—if I wanted to escape from the circumstances dominating Poland under Russian occupation.

I read this question in his eyes. Without hesitation, I replied in a quiet voice, "Yes, Professor, I really want to leave."

This time he responded quickly, without hesitating, "Fine, I will help you with this."

It came time for the meeting of the PAN committee of departures. One application after another was examined. The one leading the meeting pulled out my papers and said, "There must be some mistake, he just returned from the States. He shouldn't be allowed to go again now."

Supposedly Konorski stood up and calmly said, "He is one of my people, and he will go."

Silence fell. The one in charge got confused, but no one had the courage to oppose Professor Konorski—he enjoyed that much respect.

The positive decision of the PAN committee of departures didn't finalize the matter. Absolutely every departure, whether or not the person was a party member, went through the PZPR PAN committee of party organization. So, my papers also ended up there. On this level, however, the matter was taken care of by

Sierpinski, who was fulfilling his end of our bargain. He was present when they examined my situation and pushed it through.

And so I got formal permission for a return trip to the United States to continue my scientific work. With this document and all the additional necessary papers, I went to the Mostowski Palace where the passport office was located—it was an agency of the Office of State Security. I went with the application to get a passport. When the worker there determined that I had just returned seven months ago after a two-year stay in the States, he came to the doubtless conclusion that I had to be someone high up in the PRL. I got the passport immediately, and the worker nearly saluted me. From there, I went to the American embassy. There the matter was easily taken care of. I now had the full possibility of leaving and only needed a plane ticket to New York. I went to Orbis and told the worker sitting behind the counter that I wanted to buy a round-trip ticket to New York.

"Fine," she said. "Please, give me your passport."

When I gave it to her, she nearly jumped.

"This is a Polish passport! I cannot sell you a ticket with this passport!"

"Why?" I asked calmly. "I have the right to leave, and all my papers are in order. I'm paying with my own dollars, so what's the matter?"

"I cannot take care of this!" she repeated. "Go to the director and let him decide!"

I went to this dignitary. He looked over my passport and visa. He asked if I was really paying in dollars, inhaled deeply, and said, "You know, I don't see any real reason you shouldn't be able to buy this ticket. But this really is an unusual situation."

I got a ticket, and I was ready to leave. I told my colleagues that I was leaving, but I didn't give them a date.

These were strange times. Everyone feared everyone else; no one could speak freely even in the company of people you had known for years. One of the neurosurgeons was celebrating his name day. I was invited to the event. No one even broached a subject that could be considered "disloyal to the government."

The threat of Russian occupation even squeezed itself into private homes.

A few days before my departure, my closer colleagues visited me. They came alone for private conversations. They said, "Oh, you're lucky that you can go!"

Of course, I had to be careful, and I emphasized the temporality of my second stay in the States, even talked about what I would do when I returned. One of the active party members even showed up at my place.

"Well then, my dear Janusz, you're making a career here. You already have almost completed the requirements for a professorship. Unlimited horizons are opening up for you, and you will be able to choose your position. Just one little thing remains. It's high time for you to declare your allegiance."

Of course, he was talking about signing up for the party. Cold sweat dripped down my back. I thought feverishly about how I should react.

"You know," I said, "I don't think I'm ready for that step yet. And the timing isn't right, as I am about to leave. We'll talk about it more when I return."

Another memorable moment was when one of my closer colleagues, who was a party member but a decent and honest person, came to me and said sincerely, "Janusz, I envy you with all my heart. The doors in front of you are open, through which I can no longer pass. They are irrevocably closed to me. I wish you the best of luck."

He said this sadly, with regret. He knew that he had ruined his professional life. To this day, we send each other cards at the holidays. I think that there is a lot of warmth not only in my heart but also in his that even the regime could not destroy.

My departure was approaching very quickly. My mother's name day—the fifth of April, Irene—went by sadly. I felt sad and uncertain—would we all be able to get out finally, would we ever see each other again? My return to Poland had removed the paragraph 401 clause from my parents which prohibited them from leaving on account of being a "threat to national security," but their chances for emigration were not great. I established contact between my mother and the lawyer who had connections with the UB. I left behind most of my money and the car—it was then worth a lot. All of this created certain possibilities, though nothing could be predicted.

My departure was to be on April 27 at nine a.m. from Okecie airport. I would take a LOT plane to England, and from there, a British Airways flight to New York.

I worked up until the last moment. People already knew about my approaching departure. In the physician's lounge, where we drank coffee, one of the "red" guys, squinting his eyes, suddenly turned to me. "Well, Janusz, don't try to fool us, this time you're leaving for good, right?"

All the eyes in there looked at me tensely after that question had been posed. I knew in a flash that if I started to refute this feverishly, it would seem false. Without thinking, I sputtered, "And what do you think? I'm going to spend my life with a son of a bitch like you? I'm not stupid!"

Everyone burst out laughing.

"He really gave it to him," they laughed.

I felt relieved, but I could feel little beads of sweat on my forehead.

And so I came home on April 26. My mother opened the door. I saw terror in her face.

"Janusz, something very bad is going on. Two young individuals came by and were asking about you—they want to talk to you! When I told them that you were at work, they said that they would come back tonight. Janusz, this is something very bad; they were frightening people!"

Very upset, we barely ate dinner. At nine o'clock, there was a knock at the door. I opened it.

"Janusz?"

"Yes," I replied.

"We wanted to speak with you privately."

I invited them inside, and we sat down. I was completely calm, but I was well aware that I was in danger. These were counterintelligence agents from the GRU, directly under the head office in Moscow. Their Warsaw office was located on Chalubinski Street. The gate was always closed, and the small basement windows were covered with glass bricks, allowing for a negligible amount of light. People, who in one way or another had fallen out of favor with Moscow, were tortured and murdered in those underground rooms.

I was well aware of this and waited to see what would happen.

"We congratulate you on your return departure; it doesn't happen often. You must be someone who stands out at the Polish Academy of Science. We have a proposal for you. We would like for you to work with us, to get us certain information. You will be working as a doctor with the opportunity to move around in various circles, among them Polish circles. We are counting on your cooperation."

I knew that my only defense was to be evasive without giving any negative response.

I started saying that I would have a lot of professional obligations, involving a narrow circle of scientific people. I didn't have any contacts with Polish people there from my previous trip, and I wasn't a specialist at intelligence work, and I understood that it took a certain amount of knowledge and training.

They listened calmly to this obvious nonsense. It was clear that they had been waiting for just such a reply.

"We would not ask a lot of you, as we understand the situation. For example, some road maps of the United States, information about Poles that you meet—that's all."

I understood that they didn't care about getting real information; they cared, rather, about imprisoning me in a web from which there was no escape. I felt as though the ground were literally falling out beneath my feet, because I knew now that there would be no coming back for me. My departure would be final and, most likely, the next morning, I would say goodbye to my parents forever!

I was able to keep calm and even politely and respectfully

remarked that their work must be fascinating. And equally politely, I said farewell to them.

Only after they left did I feel complete relief and repeated the entire conversation to my parents. My mother went pale.

"Leave! You know that you cannot come back! Maybe it's the best thing for you. We will survive."

I didn't sleep most of the night. In the morning, we went early to Okecie airport; my documents were checked. I found myself on the other side of the gate with my suitcase. At this very moment, I can still see my father, with his gray hair and red eyes, and the thin, petite figure of my mother. I see their eyes, full of pain but determination that what should happen would happen. I didn't wave my hand. I couldn't.

With a tight throat, I turned around and went in to the dim interior of the building.

I was flying on a LOT airplane. It stopped in East Berlin on the way to London. After the experiences of the last few days, I felt numb. I looked blindly out the window at the white clouds, and one thought stubbornly rolled around in my mind—there was no coming back! I would have to do everything humanly possible to get my parents out. I didn't think about what awaited me, about obstacles on my path. I carried the American certification of my medical degree with me—from the ECFMG—about which no one yet knew in Poland. I brought my diplomas and grade books that I had coaxed out of the Medical Academy in Poznan and the University of Poznan. These were all the defenses I had. I had a few hundred dollars in my pocket to begin my new life. And I spoke English comfortably.

I was burdened, however, with the worst possible American visa, a so-called "Exchange visa," not authorizing me to compete for rights to stay in the United States permanently, but rather the opposite—it was a terrible obstacle. This visa was marked with a certain number-and-letter code. It wasn't until much later that I found out that code meant that I belonged to a category of dangerous people, most likely agents of the Soviet regime.

With such baggage, I got to Eastern Berlin. The airplane circled around, landed, and rolled up to some large barracks that were not really that close by. To my astonishment, we were all told to get out—that invitation to get out wasn't marked by politeness; it was a harshly given order. We were all hurried to a large, dirty room, placed on some wooden benches, and locked in there!

No one knew what was going on, and no one told us anything about it. After about half an hour, I looked through the window, where I could clearly see our immobile airplane, and noticed militia trucks driving up there from which uniformed individuals were pouring out. They formed into two rows of people from the entrance of the barracks to the door of the airplane. The key scratched in the lock, the door was opened, and we were told to walk in single file through the two rows of people.

I was horrified. I thought that the "authorities" might have decided to send me back, that maybe they came to the conclusion that it was better to lock me up than let me go to the West. A tall, thin person was walking in front of me, who was maybe around fifty years old, with a balding, gray head. His documents were checked—the officer checking them gave orders in German—and two uniformed men grabbed him and led him to the waiting trucks. Never before or after that, in all the years of my medical practice, did I see a person whose face could so quickly go white as a piece of paper! Horror and complete despair were the only things visible on his face.

The other passengers and I were let through without any problem. The door of the plane closed, and we went further on our way. In London, when the plane was circling around the embarkation building, I saw a young technician through the window. He smiled and waved at us in a characteristic Anglo-Saxon wave. It wasn't like in Poland, from top to bottom, but went from left to right, as if he was wiping off a dirty window.

I thought to myself, "I am a free man. And now what?"

The Colors of Life

by Janusz Subczynski

The Story Continues . . .

The adventures of the author did not end at the Heathrow Airport in London. He found himself with a temporary visa to the United States, without any support, without a job. The only advantages he had were his young age, knowledge, and resolve to live a free life with opportunity to fulfill his calling—provide the best care for his patients.

From the condition of psychological suppression in which he had grown, he finds himself in the world of freedom and opportunity. He was out of the Soviet Gulag in the free world—that does not mean that he had a free ride for his future.

He did not forget his heritage and the suffering of his Polish compatriots. He continued fighting for freedom for his native country through the Polish-American anticommunist organization POMOST while at the same time performing the duties of a neurosurgeon.

The final episode has been described in his book *Colors of Life*. In this American part of his life you will witness the struggle the author faced in establishing himself as an American Neurosurgeon, the miracle of final reunification with his parents—escapees from the Soviet paradise—which can only be understood as an action of divine providence.

The Colors of Life is not a story glorifying the author's accomplishments. It is a story of endurance, of moments of happiness and tragedy, of falls and of achievements—a very, very human story.

And, finally, peace.

The Colors of Life
by Janusz Subczynski

KELLER PUBLISHING
590 Fieldstone Dr.
Marco Island, FL 34145

KellerPublishing.com
800-631-1952

About the Author

JANUSZ A. SUBCZYNSKI was born in Poland on the fifth of September, 1928. He completed his primary and secondary education partially in the underground during the Second World War. From 1946 to 1951, he attended medical school in Poznan, and in 1951, he received his diploma of physician (M.D.). Independently, he also completed the study of psychology at the University of Poznan and obtained a Masters in Psychology. In 1957, he became a Specialist of the Polish Board of Neurosurgery.

In 1961, he arrived in the United States to be trained in stereotactic surgery of the brain. In 1963, after establishing this type of surgery in Warsaw, Poland, he returned to the United States. He obtained the title of the Diplomat of American Board of Neurological Surgery. He also became a Fellow of the American College of Surgery.

For over twenty-five years, he worked first as an independent neurosurgeon, then as a chief of the section of neurosurgery at St. John Hospital and Medical Center in Detroit.

After retirement, he wrote three books, published first in Polish. Dr. Subczynski was involved in anticommunist action as a member and then coordinator of the Polish-American organization POMOST.

He is currently retired in the warm climate of Florida, devoting his time to writing and providing political commentary on American/Polish radio.